"If you are looking for a job ... before you go to the newspapers and the help-wanted ads, listen to Bob Adams, publisher of *The Metropolitan New York JobBank*."
-**Tom Brokaw,** *NBC*

"Help on the job hunt ... Anyone who is job-hunting in the New York area can find a lot of useful ideas in a new paperback called *The Metropolitan New York JobBank* ..."
-**Angela Taylor,** *New York Times*

"One of the better publishers of employment almanacs is Adams Media Corporation ... publisher of *The Metropolitan New York JobBank* and similarly named directories of employers in Texas, Boston, Chicago, Northern and Southern California, and Washington DC. A good buy ..."
-*Wall Street Journal's*
National Business Employment Weekly

"For those graduates whose parents are pacing the floor, conspicuously placing circled want ads around the house and typing up resumes, [*The Carolina JobBank*] answers job-search questions."
-*Greensboro News and Record*

"A timely book for Chicago job hunters follows books from the same publisher that were well received in New York and Boston ... [*The Chicago JobBank* is] a fine tool for job hunters ..."
-**Clarence Peterson,** *Chicago Tribune*

"Because our listing is seen by people across the nation, it generates lots of resumes for us. We encourage unsolicited resumes. We'll always be listed [in *The Chicago JobBank*] as long as I'm in this career."
-**Tom Fitzpatrick, Director of Human Resources**
Merchandise Mart Properties, Inc.

"Job-hunting is never fun, but this book can ease the ordeal ... [*The Los Angeles JobBank*] will help allay fears, build confidence, and avoid wheel-spinning."
-**Robert W. Ross,** *Los Angeles Times*

"*The Seattle JobBank* is an essential resource for job hunters."
-**Gil Lopez, Staffing Team Manager**
Battelle Pacific Northwest Laboratories

"*The Phoenix JobBank* is a first-class publication. The information provided is useful and current."

-Lyndon Denton
Director of Human Resources and Materials Management
Apache Nitrogen Products, Inc.

"Job hunters can't afford to waste time. *The Minneapolis-St. Paul JobBank* contains information that used to require hours of research in the library."

-Carmella Zagone
Minneapolis-based Human Resources Administrator

"*The Florida JobBank* is an invaluable job-search reference tool. It provides the most up-to-date information and contact names available for companies in Florida. I should know -- it worked for me!"

-Rhonda Cody, Human Resources Consultant
Aetna Life and Casualty

"I read through the 'Basics of Job Winning' and 'Resumes' sections [in *The Dallas-Fort Worth JobBank*] and found them to be very informative, with some positive tips for the job searcher. I believe the strategies outlined will bring success to any determined candidate."

-Camilla Norder, Professional Recruiter
Presbyterian Hospital of Dallas

"Through *The Dallas-Fort Worth JobBank,* we've been able to attract high-quality candidates for several positions."

-Rob Bertino, Southern States Sales Manager
CompuServe

"Packed with helpful contacts, *The Houston JobBank* empowers its reader to launch an effective, strategic job search in the Houston metropolitan area."

-Andrew Ceperley, Director
College of Communication Career Services
The University of Texas at Austin

"*The San Francisco Bay Area JobBank* ... is a highly useful guide, with plenty of how-to's ranging from resume tips to interview dress codes and research shortcuts."

-A.S. Ross, *San Francisco Examiner*

"[*The Atlanta JobBank* is] one of the best sources for finding a job in Atlanta!"

-Luann Miller, Human Resources Manager
Prudential Preferred Financial Services

What makes the
JobBank series
the nation's premier
line of employment guides?

With vital employment information on thousands of employers across the nation, the JobBank series is the most comprehensive and authoritative set of career directories available today.

Each book in the series provides information on **dozens of different industries** in a given city or area, with the primary employer listings providing contact information, telephone and fax numbers, e-mail addresses, Websites, a summary of the firm's business, internships, and in many cases descriptions of the firm's typical professional job categories.

All of the reference information in the JobBank series is as up-to-date and accurate as possible. Every year, the entire database is thoroughly researched and verified by mail and by telephone. Adams Media Corporation publishes **more local employment guides more often** than any other publisher of career directories.

The JobBank series offers **28 regional titles**, from Minneapolis to Houston, and from Boston to San Francisco as well as **two industry-specific titles**. All of the information is organized geographically, because most people look for jobs in specific areas of the country.

A condensed, but thorough, review of the entire job search process is presented in the chapter **The Basics of Job Winning**, a feature which has received many compliments from career counselors. In addition, each JobBank directory includes a section on **resumes and cover letters** the *New York Times* has acclaimed as "excellent."

The JobBank series gives job hunters the most comprehensive, timely, and accurate career information, organized and indexed to facilitate your job search. An entire career reference library, JobBank books are designed to help you find optimal employment in any market.

Top career publications from Adams Media Corporation

The JobBank Series:
each JobBank book is $17.95

The Atlanta JobBank, 14th Ed.
The Austin/San Antonio JobBank, 3rd
 Ed.
The Boston JobBank, 19th Ed.
The Carolina JobBank, 6th Ed.
The Chicago JobBank, 18th Ed.
The Colorado JobBank, 13th Ed.
The Connecticut JobBank, 2nd Ed.
The Dallas-Fort Worth JobBank, 13th
 Ed.
The Detroit JobBank, 9th Ed.
The Florida JobBank, 15th Ed.
The Houston JobBank, 11th Ed.
The Indiana JobBank, 3rd Ed.
The Las Vegas JobBank, 2nd Ed.
The Los Angeles JobBank, 17th Ed.
The Minneapolis-St. Paul JobBank,
 11th Ed.
The Missouri JobBank, 3rd Ed.
The New Jersey JobBank, 1st Ed.
The Metropolitan New York JobBank,
 18th Ed.
The Ohio JobBank, 10th Ed.
The Greater Philadelphia JobBank,
 14th Ed.
The Phoenix JobBank, 8th Ed.
The Pittsburgh JobBank, 2nd Ed.
The Portland JobBank, 3rd Ed.
The San Francisco Bay Area JobBank,
 16th Ed.
The Seattle JobBank, 12th Ed.
The Tennessee JobBank, 5th Ed.
The Virginia JobBank, 3rd Ed.
The Metropolitan Washington DC
 JobBank, 15th Ed.

The JobBank Guide to Computer &
 High-Tech Companies, 2nd Ed.
 ($17.95)
The JobBank Guide to Health Care
 Companies, 2nd Ed. ($17.95)

The National JobBank, 2003
 (Covers the entire U.S.: $450.00
 hc)

Other Career Titles:
The Adams Cover Letter Almanac ($12.95)
The Adams Internet Job Search Almanac,
 6th Ed. ($12.95)
The Adams Executive Recruiters Almanac,
 2nd Ed. ($17.95)
The Adams Job Interview Almanac
 ($12.95)
The Adams Jobs Almanac, 8th Ed. ($16.95)
The Adams Resume Almanac ($10.95)
Business Etiquette in Brief ($7.95)
Campus Free College Degrees, 8th Ed.
 ($16.95)
Career Tests ($12.95)
Closing Techniques, 2nd Ed. ($8.95)
Cold Calling Techniques, 4th Ed. ($8.95)
College Grad Job Hunter, 4th Ed. ($14.95)
The Complete Resume & Job Search Book
 for College Students, 2nd Ed. ($12.95)
Cover Letters That Knock 'em Dead, 5th
 Ed. ($12.95)
Every Woman's Essential Job Hunting &
 Resume Book ($11.95)
The Everything Cover Letter Book ($12.95)
The Everything Get-A-Job Book ($12.95)
The Everything Hot Careers Book
 ($12.95)
The Everything Job Interview Book
 ($12.95)
The Everything Online Business Book
 ($12.95)
The Everything Online Job Search Book
 ($12.95)
The Everything Resume Book ($12.95)
The Everything Selling Book ($12.95)
First Time Resume ($7.95)
How to Start and Operate a Successful
 Business ($9.95)
Knock 'em Dead, 2003 ($14.95)
Knock 'em Dead Business Presentations
 ($12.95)
Market Yourself and Your Career, 2nd Ed.
 ($12.95)
The New Professional Image ($12.95)
The 150 Most Profitable Home Businesses
 for Women ($9.95)
The Resume Handbook, 3rd Ed. ($7.95)
Resumes That Knock 'em Dead, 5th Ed.
 ($12.95)
The Road to CEO ($20.00 hc)
The 250 Job Interview Questions You'll
 Most Likely Be Asked ($9.95)
Your Executive Image ($10.95)

14th Edition
THE Dallas–
Fort Worth
JobBank

Editor:	Erik L. Herman
Assistant Editor:	Sarah Rocha
Researchers:	Maurice Curran
	Megan Danahy
	Emily Mozzone

Adams Media
AVON, MASSACHUSETTS

Published by Adams Media, an F+W Publications Company
57 Littlefield Street, Avon, MA 02322 U.S.A.
www.adamsmedia.com

ISBN: 1-58062-979-2
ISSN: 1069-5435
Manufactured in the United States of America.

Because addresses and telephone numbers of smaller companies change rapidly, we recommend you call each company and verify the information before mailing to the employers listed in this book. Mass mailings are not recommended.

While the publisher has made every reasonable effort to obtain and verify accurate information, occasional errors are possible due to the magnitude of the data. Should you discover an error, or if a company is missing, please write the editors at the above address so that we may update future editions.

"This publication is designed to provide accurate and authoritative information with regard to the subject matter covered. It is sold with the understanding that the publisher is not engaged in rendering legal, accounting, or other professional advice. If legal advice or other expert assistance is required, the services of a competent professional person should be sought."

--From a *Declaration of Principles* jointly adopted by a Committee of the American Bar Association and a Committee of Publishers and Associations

This book is available on standing order and at quantity discounts for bulk purchases.
For information, call 800/872-5627 (in Massachusetts, 508/427-7100)
or email at jobbank@adamsmedia.com

TABLE OF CONTENTS

- *Automotive Repair Shops*
- *Automotive Stampings*
- *Industrial Vehicles and Moving Equipment*
- *Motor Vehicles and Equipment*
- *Travel Trailers and Campers*

Banking/Savings and Loans/75

Biotechnology, Pharmaceuticals, and Scientific R&D/78
- *Clinical Labs*
- *Lab Equipment Manufacturers*
- *Pharmaceutical Manufacturers and Distributors*

Business Services and Non-Scientific Research/81
- *Adjustment and Collection Services*
- *Cleaning, Maintenance, and Pest Control Services*
- *Credit Reporting Services*
- *Detective, Guard, and Armored Car Services/Security Systems Services*
- *Miscellaneous Equipment Rental and Leasing*
- *Secretarial and Court Reporting Services*

Charities and Social Services/85
- *Job Training and Vocational Rehabilitation Services*

Chemicals/Rubber and Plastics/88
- *Adhesives, Detergents, Inks, Paints, Soaps, Varnishes*
- *Agricultural Chemicals and Fertilizers*
- *Carbon and Graphite Products*
- *Chemical Engineering Firms*
- *Industrial Gases*

Communications: Telecommunications and Broadcasting/94
- *Cable/Pay Television Services*
- *Communications Equipment*
- *Radio and Television Broadcasting Stations*
- *Telephone, Telegraph, and Other Message Communications*

Computer Hardware, Software, and Services/102
- *Computer Components and Hardware Manufacturers*
- *Consultants and Computer Training Companies*
- *Internet and Online Service Providers*
- *Networking and Systems Services*
- *Repair Services/Rental and Leasing*
- *Resellers, Wholesalers, and Distributors*
- *Software Developers/Programming Services*

Educational Services/115
- *Business/Secretarial/Data Processing Schools*
- *Colleges/Universities/Professional Schools*
- *Community Colleges/Technical Schools/Vocational Schools*
- *Elementary and Secondary Schools*
- *Preschool and Child Daycare Services*

Electronic/Industrial Electrical Equipment/124
- *Electronic Machines and Systems*
- *Semiconductor Manufacturers*

Environmental and Waste Management Services/131
- *Environmental Engineering Firms*
- *Sanitary Services*

Fabricated/Primary Metals and Products/132
- *Aluminum and Copper Foundries*
- *Die-Castings*
- *Iron and Steel Foundries/Steel Works, Blast Furnaces, and Rolling Mills*

Financial Services/136
- *Consumer Financing and Credit Agencies*
- *Investment Specialists*

SECTION FOUR: INDEX

Index of Primary Employers by Industry/237

INTRODUCTION

HOW TO USE THIS BOOK

Right now, you hold in your hands one of the most effective job-hunting tools available anywhere. In *The Dallas-Fort Worth JobBank*, you will find valuable information to help you launch or continue a rewarding career. But before you open to the book's employer listings and start calling about current job openings, take a few minutes to learn how best to use the resources presented in *The Dallas-Fort Worth JobBank*.

The Dallas-Fort Worth JobBank will help you to stand out from other jobseekers. While many people looking for a new job rely solely on newspaper help-wanted ads, this book offers you a much more effective job-search method -- direct contact. The direct contact method has been proven twice as effective as scanning the help-wanted ads. Instead of waiting for employers to come looking for you, you'll be far more effective going to them. While many of your competitors will use trial and error methods in trying to set up interviews, you'll learn not only how to get interviews, but what to expect once you've got them.

In the next few pages, we'll take you through each section of the book so you'll be prepared to get a jump-start on your competition.

Basics of Job Winning

Preparation. Strategy. Time management. These are three of the most important elements of a successful job search. *Basics of Job Winning* helps you address these and all the other elements needed to find the right job.

One of your first priorities should be to define your personal career objectives. What qualities make a job desirable to you? Creativity? High pay? Prestige? Use *Basics of Job Winning* to weigh these questions. Then use the rest of the chapter to design a strategy to find a job that matches your criteria.

In *Basics of Job Winning*, you'll learn which job-hunting techniques work, and which don't. We've reviewed the pros and cons of mass mailings, help-wanted ads, and direct contact. We'll show you how to develop and approach contacts in your field; how to research a prospective employer; and how to use that information to get an interview and the job.

Also included in *Basics of Job Winning*: interview dress code and etiquette, the "do's and don'ts" of interviewing, sample interview questions, and more. We also deal with some of the unique problems faced by those jobseekers who are currently employed, those who have lost a job, and college students conducting their first job search.

Resumes and Cover Letters

The approach you take to writing your resume and cover letter can often mean the difference between getting an interview and never being noticed. In this section, we discuss different formats, as well as what to put on (and what to leave off) your resume. We review the benefits and drawbacks of professional resume writers, and the importance of a follow-up letter. Also included in this section are sample resumes and cover letters which you can use as models.

The Employer Listings

Employers are listed alphabetically by industry. When a company does business under a person's name, like "John Smith & Co.," the company is usually listed by the surname's spelling (in this case "S"). Exceptions occur when a company's name is widely recognized, like "JCPenney" or "Howard Johnson Motor Lodge." In those cases, the company's first name is the key ("J" and "H" respectively).

The Shell JobBank covers a very wide range of industries. Each company profile is assigned to one of the industry chapters listed below.

Accounting and Management Consulting	Fabricated/Primary Metals and Products
Advertising, Marketing, and Public Relations	Financial Services
Aerospace	Food and Beverages/Agriculture
Apparel, Fashion, and Textiles	Government
Architecture, Construction, and Engineering	Health Care: Services, Equipment, and Products
Arts, Entertainment, Sports, and Recreation	
Automotive	Hotels and Restaurants
Banking/Savings and Loans	Insurance
Biotechnology, Pharmaceuticals, and Scientific R&D	Legal Services
	Manufacturing: Miscellaneous Consumer
Business Services and Non-Scientific Research	Manufacturing: Miscellaneous Industrial
	Mining/Gas/Petroleum/Energy Related
Charities and Social Services	Paper and Wood Products
Chemicals/Rubber and Plastics	Printing and Publishing
Communications: Telecommunications and Broadcasting	Real Estate
	Retail
Computer Hardware, Software, and Services	Stone, Clay, Glass, and Concrete Products
Educational Services	Transportation/Travel
Electronic/Industrial Electrical Equipment	Utilities: Electric/Gas/Water
Environmental and Waste Management Services	Miscellaneous Wholesaling

Many of the company listings offer detailed company profiles. In addition to company names, addresses, and phone numbers, these listings also include contact names or hiring departments, and descriptions of each company's products and/or services. Many of these listings also feature a variety of additional information including:

Positions advertised - A list of open positions the company was advertising at the time our research was conducted. Note: Keep in mind that *The Dallas-Fort Worth JobBank* is a directory of major employers in the area, not a directory of openings currently available. Positions listed in this book that were advertised at the time research was conducted may no longer be open. Many of the companies listed will be hiring, others will not. However, since most professional job openings are filled without the placement of help-wanted ads, contacting the employers in this book directly is still a more effective method than browsing the Sunday papers.

Special programs - Does the company offer training programs, internships, or apprenticeships? These programs can be important to first time jobseekers and college students looking for practical work experience. Many employer profiles will include information on these programs.

Parent company - If an employer is a subsidiary of a larger company, the name of that parent company will often be listed here. Use this information to supplement your company research before contacting the employer.

Number of employees - The number of workers a company employs.

Company listings may also include information on other U.S. locations and any stock exchanges the firm may be listed on.

A note on all employer listings that appear in *The Dallas-Fort Worth JobBank*: This book is intended as a starting point. It is not intended to replace any effort that you, the jobseeker, should devote to your job hunt. Keep in mind that while a great deal of effort has been put into collecting and verifying the company profiles provided in this book, addresses and contact names change regularly. Inevitably, some contact names listed herein have changed even before you read this. We recommend you contact a company before mailing your resume to ensure nothing has changed.

Index

    The Dallas-Fort Worth JobBank index is listed alphabetically by industry.

THE JOB SEARCH

THE BASICS OF JOB WINNING: A CONDENSED REVIEW

This chapter is divided into four sections. The first section explains the fundamentals that every jobseeker should know, especially first-time jobseekers. The next three sections deal with special situations faced by specific types of jobseekers: those who are currently employed, those who have lost a job, and college students.

THE BASICS:
Things Everyone Needs to Know

Career Planning

The first step to finding your ideal job is to clearly define your objectives. This is better known as career planning (or life planning if you wish to emphasize the importance of combining the two). Career planning has become a field of study in and of itself.

If you are thinking of choosing or switching careers, we particularly emphasize two things. First, choose a career where you will enjoy most of the day-to-day tasks. This sounds obvious, but most of us have at some point found the idea of a glamour industry or prestigious job title attractive without thinking of the key consideration: Would we enjoy performing the *everyday* tasks the position entails?

The second key consideration is that you are not merely choosing a career, but also a lifestyle. Career counselors indicate that one of the most common problems people encounter in jobseeking is that they fail to consider how well-suited they are for a particular position or career. For example, some people, attracted to management consulting by good salaries, early responsibility, and high-level corporate exposure, do not adapt well to the long hours, heavy travel demands, and constant pressure to produce. Be sure to ask yourself how you might adapt to the day-to-day duties and working environment that a specific position entails. Then ask yourself how you might adapt to the demands of that career or industry as a whole.

Choosing Your Strategy

Assuming that you've established your career objectives, the next step of the job search is to develop a strategy. If you don't take the time to develop a plan, you may find yourself going in circles after several weeks of randomly searching for opportunities that always seem just beyond your reach.

The most common jobseeking techniques are:

- following up on help-wanted advertisements (in the newspaper or online)
- using employment services
- relying on personal contacts
- contacting employers directly (the Direct Contact method)

Each of these approaches can lead to better jobs. However, the Direct Contact method boasts twice the success rate of the others. So unless you have specific reasons to employ other strategies, Direct Contact should form the foundation of your job search.

If you choose to use other methods as well, try to expend at least half your energy on Direct Contact. Millions of other jobseekers have already proven that Direct Contact has been twice as effective in obtaining employment, so why not follow in their footsteps?

Setting Your Schedule

Okay, so now that you've targeted a strategy it's time to work out the details of your job search. The most important detail is setting up a schedule. Of course, since job searches aren't something most people do regularly, it may be hard to estimate how long each step will take. Nonetheless, it is important to have a plan so that you can monitor your progress.

When outlining your job search schedule, have a realistic time frame in mind. If you will be job-searching full-time, your search could take at least two months or more. If you can only devote part-time effort, it will probably take at least four months.

You probably know a few people who seem to spend their whole lives searching for a better job in their spare time. Don't be one of them. If you are presently working and don't feel like devoting a lot of energy to jobseeking right now, then wait. Focus on enjoying your present position, performing your best on the job, and storing up energy for when you are really ready to begin your job search.

> **The first step in beginning your job search is to clearly define your objectives.**

Those of you who are currently unemployed should remember that *job-hunting is tough work, both physically and emotionally*. It is also intellectually demanding work that requires you to be at your best. So don't tire yourself out by working on your job campaign around the clock. At the same time, be sure to discipline yourself. The most logical way to manage your time while looking for a job is to keep your regular working hours.

If you are searching full-time and have decided to choose several different strategies, we recommend that you divide up each week, designating some time for each method. By trying several approaches at once, you can evaluate how promising each seems and alter your schedule accordingly. Keep in mind that the *majority of openings are filled without being advertised*. Remember also that positions advertised on the Internet are just as likely to already be filled as those found in the newspaper!

If you are searching part-time and decide to try several different contact methods, we recommend that you try them sequentially. You simply won't have enough time to put a meaningful amount of effort into more than one method at once. Estimate the length of your job search, and then allocate so many weeks or months for each contact method, beginning with Direct Contact. The purpose of setting this schedule is not to rush you to your goal but to help you periodically evaluate your progress.

The Direct Contact Method

Once you have scheduled your time, you are ready to begin your search in earnest. Beginning with the Direct Contact method, the first step is to develop a checklist for categorizing the types of firms for which you'd like to work. You might categorize firms by product line, size, customer type (such as industrial or consumer), growth prospects, or geographical location. Keep in mind, the shorter the list the easier it will be to locate a company that is right for you.

Next you will want to use this *JobBank* book to assemble your list of potential employers. Choose firms where *you* are most likely to be able to find a job. Try matching your skills with those that a specific job demands. Consider where your skills might be in demand, the degree of competition for employment, and the employment outlook at each company.

Separate your prospect list into three groups. The first 25 percent will be your primary target group, the next 25 percent will be your secondary group, and the remaining names will be your reserve group.

After you form your prospect list, begin working on your resume. Refer to the Resumes and Cover Letters section following this chapter for more information.

Once your resume is complete, begin researching your first batch of prospective employers. You will want to determine whether you would be happy working at the firms you are researching and to get a better idea of what their employment needs might be. You also need to obtain enough information to sound highly informed about the company during phone conversations and in mail correspondence. But don't go all out on your research yet! You probably won't be able to arrange interviews with some of these firms, so save your big research effort until you start to arrange interviews. Nevertheless, you should plan to spend several hours researching each firm. Do your research in batches to save time and energy. Start with this book, and find out what you can about each of the firms in your primary target group. For answers to specific questions, contact any pertinent professional associations that may be able to help you learn more about an employer. Read industry publications looking for articles on the firm. (Addresses of associations and names of important publications are listed after each section of employer listings in this book.) Then look up the company on the Internet or try additional resources at your local library. Keep organized, and maintain a folder on each firm.

> **The more you know about a company, the more likely you are to catch an interviewer's eye. (You'll also face fewer surprises once you get the job!)**

Information to look for includes: company size; president, CEO, or owner's name; when the company was established; what each division does; and benefits that are important to you. An abundance of company information can now be found electronically, through the World Wide Web or commercial online services. Researching companies online is a convenient means of obtaining information quickly and easily. If you have access to the Internet, you can search from your home at any time of day.

You may search a particular company's Website for current information that may be otherwise unavailable in print. In fact, many companies that maintain a site update their information daily. In addition, you may also search articles written about the company online. Today, most of the nation's largest newspapers, magazines, trade publications, and regional business periodicals have online versions of their publications. To find additional resources, use a search engine like Yahoo! or Alta Vista and type in the keyword "companies" or "employers."

If you discover something that really disturbs you about the firm (they are about to close their only local office), or if you discover that your chances of getting a job there are practically nil (they have just instituted a hiring freeze), then cross them off your prospect list. If possible, supplement your research efforts by contacting individuals who know the firm well. Ideally you should make an informal contact with someone at that particular firm, but often a direct competitor or a major customer will be able to supply you with just as much information. At the very least, try to obtain whatever printed information the company has available -- not just annual reports, but product brochures, company profiles, or catalogs. This information is often available on the Internet.

Getting the Interview

Now it is time to make Direct Contact with the goal of arranging interviews. If you have read any books on job-searching, you may have noticed that most of these books tell you to avoid the human resources office like the plague. It is said that the human resources office never hires people; they screen candidates. Unfortunately, this is often the case. If you can identify the appropriate manager with the authority to hire you, you should try to contact that person directly.

The obvious means of initiating Direct Contact are:

- Mail (postal or electronic)
- Phone calls

Mail contact is a good choice if you have not been in the job market for a while. You can take your time to prepare a letter, say exactly what you want, and of course include your resume. Remember that employers receive many resumes every day. Don't be surprised if you do not get a response to your inquiry, *and don't spend weeks waiting for responses that may never come.* If you do send a letter, follow it up (or precede it) with a phone call. This will increase your impact, and because of the initial research you did, will underscore both your familiarity with and your interest in the firm. Bear in mind that your goal is to make your name a familiar one with prospective employers, so that when a position becomes available, your resume will be one of the first the hiring manager seeks out.

DEVELOPING YOUR CONTACTS: NETWORKING

Some career counselors feel that the best route to a better job is through somebody you already know or through somebody to whom you can be introduced. These counselors recommend that you build your contact base beyond your current acquaintances by asking each one to introduce you, or refer you, to additional people in your field of interest.

The theory goes like this: You might start with 15 personal contacts, each of whom introduces you to three additional people, for a total of 45 additional contacts. Then each of these people introduces you to three additional people, which adds 135 additional contacts. Theoretically, you will soon know every person in the industry.

Of course, developing your personal contacts does not work quite as smoothly as the theory suggests because some people will not be able to introduce you to anyone. The further you stray from your initial contact base, the weaker your references may be. So, if you do try developing your own contacts, try to begin with as many people that you know personally as you can. Dig into your personal phone book and your holiday greeting card list and locate old classmates from school. Be particularly sure to approach people who perform your personal business such as your lawyer, accountant, banker, doctor, stockbroker, and insurance agent. These people develop a very broad contact base due to the nature of their professions.

If you send a fax, always follow with a hard copy of your resume and cover letter in the mail. Often, through no fault of your own, a fax will come through illegibly and employers do not often have time to let candidates know.

Another alternative is to make a "cover call." Your cover call should be just like your cover letter: concise. Your first statement should interest the employer in you. Then try to subtly mention your familiarity with the firm. Don't be overbearing; keep your introduction to three sentences or less. Be pleasant, self-confident, and relaxed. This will greatly increase the chances of the person at the other end of the line developing the conversation. But don't press. If you are asked to follow up with "something in the mail," this signals the conversation's natural end. Don't try to prolong the conversation once it has ended, and don't ask what they want to receive in the mail. Always send your resume and a highly personalized follow-up letter, reminding the addressee of the phone conversation. *Always* include a cover letter if you are asked to send a resume, and treat your resume and cover letter as a total package. Gear your letter toward the specific position you are applying for and prove why you would be a "good match" for the position.

> **Always include a cover letter if you are asked to send a resume.**

Unless you are in telephone sales, making smooth and relaxed cover calls will probably not come easily. Practice them on your own, and then with your friends or relatives.

DON'T BOTHER WITH MASS MAILINGS OR BARRAGES OF PHONE CALLS

Direct Contact does not mean burying every firm within a hundred miles with mail and phone calls. Mass mailings rarely work in the job hunt. This also applies to those letters that are personalized -- but dehumanized -- on an automatic typewriter or computer. Don't waste your time or money on such a project; you will fool no one but yourself.

The worst part of sending out mass mailings, or making unplanned phone calls to companies you have not researched, is that you are likely to be remembered as someone with little genuine interest in the firm, who lacks sincerity -- somebody that nobody wants to hire.

If you obtain an interview as a result of a telephone conversation, be sure to send a thank-you note reiterating the points you made during the conversation. You will appear more professional and increase your impact. However, unless specifically requested, don't mail your resume once an interview has been arranged. Take it with you to the interview instead.

You should never show up to seek a professional position without an appointment. Even if you are somehow lucky enough to obtain an interview, you will appear so unprofessional that you will not be seriously considered.

HELP WANTED ADVERTISEMENTS

Only a small fraction of professional job openings are advertised. Yet the majority of jobseekers -- and quite a few people not in the job market -- spend a lot of time studying the help wanted ads. As a result, the competition for advertised openings is often very severe.

A moderate-sized employer told us about their experience advertising in the help wanted section of a major Sunday newspaper:

It was a disaster. We had over 500 responses from this relatively small ad in just one week. We have only two phone lines in this office and one was totally knocked out. We'll never advertise for professional help again.

If you insist on following up on help wanted ads, then research a firm before you reply to an ad. Preliminary research might help to separate you from all of the other professionals responding to that ad, many of whom will have only a passing interest in the opportunity. It will also give you insight about a particular firm, to help you determine if it is potentially a good match. That said, your chances of obtaining a job through the want ads are still much smaller than they are with the Direct Contact method.

Preparing for the Interview

As each interview is arranged, begin your in-depth research. You should arrive at an interview knowing the company upside-down and inside-out. You need to know the company's products, types of customers, subsidiaries, parent company, principal locations, rank in the industry, sales and profit trends, type of ownership, size, current plans, and much more. By this time you have probably narrowed your job search to one industry. Even if you haven't, you should still be familiar with common industry terms, the trends in the firm's industry, the firm's principal competitors and their relative performance, and the direction in which the industry leaders are headed.

Dig into every resource you can! Surf the Internet. Read the company literature, the trade press, the business press, and if the company is public, call your stockbroker (if you have one) and ask for additional information. If possible, speak to someone at the firm before the interview, or if not, speak to someone at a competing firm. The more time you spend, the better. Even if you feel extremely pressed for time, you should set aside several hours for pre-interview research.

> **You should arrive at an interview knowing the company upside-down and inside-out.**

If you have been out of the job market for some time, don't be surprised if you find yourself tense during your first few interviews. It will probably happen every time you re-enter the market, not just when you seek your first job after getting out of school.

Tension is natural during an interview, but knowing you have done a thorough research job should put you more at ease. Make a list of questions that you think might be asked in each interview. Think out your answers carefully and practice them with a friend. Tape record your responses to the problem questions. (See also in this chapter: Informational Interviews.) If you feel particularly unsure of your interviewing skills, arrange your first interviews at firms you are not as interested in. (But remember it is common courtesy to seem enthusiastic about the possibility of working for any firm at which you interview.) Practice again on your own after these first few interviews. Go over the difficult questions that you were asked.

Take some time to really think about how you will convey your work history. Present "bad experiences" as "learning experiences." Instead of saying "I hated my position as a salesperson because I had to bother people on the phone," say "I realized that cold-calling was not my strong suit. Though I love working with people, I decided my talents would be best used in a more face-to-face atmosphere." Always find some sort of lesson from previous jobs, as they all have one.

Interview Attire

How important is the proper dress for a job interview? Buying a complete wardrobe, donning new shoes, and having your hair styled every morning are not enough to guarantee you a career position as an investment banker. But on the other hand, if you can't find a clean, conservative suit or won't take the time to wash your hair, then you are just wasting your time by interviewing at all.

Personal grooming is as important as finding appropriate clothes for a job interview. Careful grooming indicates both a sense of thoroughness and self-confidence. This is not the time to make a statement -- take out the extra earrings and avoid any garish hair colors not found in nature. Women should not wear excessive makeup, and both men and women should refrain from wearing any perfume or cologne (it only takes a small spritz to leave an allergic interviewer with a fit of sneezing and a bad impression of your meeting). Men should be freshly shaven, even if the interview is late in the day, and men with long hair should have it pulled back and neat.

Men applying for any professional position should wear a suit, preferably in a conservative color such as navy or charcoal gray. It is easy to get away with wearing the same dark suit to consecutive interviews at the same company; just be sure to wear a different shirt and tie for each interview.

Women should also wear a business suit. Professionalism still dictates a suit with a skirt, rather than slacks, as proper interview garb for women. This is usually true even at companies where pants are acceptable attire for female employees. As much as you may disagree with this guideline, the more prudent time to fight this standard is after you land the job.

The final selection of candidates for a job opening won't be determined by dress, of course. However, inappropriate dress can quickly eliminate a first-round candidate. So while you shouldn't spend a fortune on a new wardrobe, you should be sure that your clothes are adequate. The key is to dress at least as formally or slightly more formally and more conservatively than the position would suggest.

What to Bring

Be complete. Everyone needs a watch, a pen, and a notepad. Finally, a briefcase or a leather-bound folder (containing extra, unfolded, copies of your resume) will help complete the look of professionalism.

Sometimes the interviewer will be running behind schedule. Don't be upset, be sympathetic. There is often pressure to interview a lot of candidates and to quickly fill a demanding position. So be sure to come to your interview with good reading material to keep yourself occupied and relaxed.

The Interview

The very beginning of the interview is the most important part because it determines the tone for the rest of it. Those first few moments are especially crucial. Do you smile when you meet? Do you establish enough eye contact, but not too much? Do you walk into the office with a self-assured and confident stride? Do you shake hands firmly? Do you make small talk easily without being garrulous? It is

---

BE PREPARED:
Some Common Interview Questions

Tell me about yourself.

Why did you leave your last job?

What excites you in your current job?

Where would you like to be in five years?

How much overtime are you willing to work?

What would your previous/present employer tell me about you?

Tell me about a difficult situation that you
faced at your previous/present job.

What are your greatest strengths?

What are your weaknesses?

Describe a work situation where you took initiative
and went beyond your normal responsibilities.

Why should we hire you?

---

human nature to judge people by that first impression, so make sure it is a good one. But most of all, try to be yourself.

Often the interviewer will begin, after the small talk, by telling you about the company, the division, the department, or perhaps, the position. Because of your detailed research, the information about the company should be repetitive for you, and the interviewer would probably like nothing better than to avoid this regurgitation of the company biography. So if you can do so tactfully, indicate to the interviewer that you are very familiar with the firm. If he or she seems intent on providing you with background information, despite your hints, then acquiesce.

But be sure to remain attentive. If you can manage to generate a brief discussion of the company or the industry at this point, without being forceful, great. It will help to further build rapport, underscore your interest, and increase your impact.

> ## The interviewer's job is to find a reason to turn you down; your job is to not provide that reason.
>
> -John L. LaFevre, author,
> *How You Really Get Hired*
>
> Reprinted from the 1989/90 *CPC Annual*, with permission of the National Association of Colleges and Employers (formerly College Placement Council, Inc.), copyright holder.

Soon (if it didn't begin that way) the interviewer will begin the questions, many of which you will have already practiced. This period of the interview usually falls into one of two categories (or somewhere in between): either a structured interview, where the interviewer has a prescribed set of questions to ask; or an unstructured interview, where the interviewer will ask only leading questions to get you to talk about yourself, your experiences, and your goals. Try to sense as quickly as possible in which direction the interviewer wishes to proceed. This will make the interviewer feel more relaxed and in control of the situation.

Remember to keep attuned to the interviewer and make the length of your answers appropriate to the situation. If you are really unsure as to how detailed a response the interviewer is seeking, then ask.

As the interview progresses, the interviewer will probably mention some of the most important responsibilities of the position. If applicable, draw parallels between your experience and the demands of the position as detailed by the interviewer. Describe your past experience in the same manner that you do on your resume: emphasizing results and achievements and not merely describing activities. But don't exaggerate. Be on the level about your abilities.

The first interview is often the toughest, where many candidates are screened out. If you are interviewing for a very competitive position, you will have to make an impression that will last. Focus on a few of your greatest strengths that are relevant to the position. Develop these points carefully, state them again in different words, and then try to summarize them briefly at the end of the interview.

Often the interviewer will pause toward the end and ask if you have any questions. Particularly in a structured interview, this might be the one chance to really show your knowledge of and interest in the firm. Have a list prepared of specific questions that are of real interest to you. Let your questions subtly show your research and your knowledge of the firm's activities. It is wise to have an extensive list of questions, as several of them may be answered during the interview.

Do not turn your opportunity to ask questions into an interrogation. Avoid reading directly from your list of questions, and ask questions that you are fairly certain the interviewer can answer (remember how you feel when you cannot answer a question during an interview).

Even if you are unable to determine the salary range beforehand, do not ask about it during the first interview. You can always ask later. Above all, don't ask about fringe benefits until you have been offered a position. (Then be sure to get all the details.)

Try not to be negative about anything during the interview, particularly any past employer or any previous job. Be cheerful. Everyone likes to work with someone who seems to be happy. Even if you detest your current/former job or manager, do not make disparaging comments. The interviewer may construe this as a sign of a potential attitude problem and not consider you a strong candidate.

Don't let a tough question throw you off base. If you don't know the answer to a question, simply say so -- do not apologize. Just smile. Nobody can answer every question -- particularly some of the questions that are asked in job interviews.

Before your first interview, you may be able to determine how many rounds of interviews there usually are for positions at your level. (Of course it may differ quite a bit even within the different levels of one firm.) Usually you can count on attending at least two or three interviews, although some firms are known to give a minimum of six interviews for all professional positions. While you should be more relaxed as you return for subsequent interviews, the pressure will be on. The more prepared you are, the better.

Depending on what information you are able to obtain, you might want to vary your strategy quite a bit from interview to interview. For instance, if the first interview is a screening interview, then be sure a few of your strengths really stand out. On the other hand, if later interviews are primarily with people who are in a position to veto your hiring, but not to push it forward, then you should primarily focus on building rapport as opposed to reiterating and developing your key strengths.

If it looks as though your skills and background do not match the position the interviewer was hoping to fill, ask him or her if there is another division or subsidiary that perhaps could profit from your talents.

After the Interview

Write a follow-up letter immediately after the interview, while it is still fresh in the interviewer's mind (see the sample follow-up letter format found in the Resumes and Cover Letters chapter). Not only is this a thank-you, but it also gives you the chance to provide the interviewer with any details you may have forgotten (as long as they can be tactfully added in). If you haven't heard back from the interviewer within a week of sending your thank-you letter, call to stress your continued interest in the firm and the position. If you lost any points during the interview for any reason, this letter can help you regain footing. Be polite and make sure to stress your continued interest and competency to fill the position. Just don't forget to proofread it thoroughly. If you are unsure of the spelling of the interviewer's name, call the receptionist and ask.

THE BALANCING ACT:
Looking for a New Job While Currently Employed

For those of you who are still employed, job-searching will be particularly tiring because it must be done in addition to your normal work responsibilities. So don't overwork yourself to the point where you show up to interviews looking exhausted or start to slip behind at your current job. On the other hand, don't be tempted to quit your present job! The long hours are worth it. Searching for a job while you have one puts you in a position of strength.

Making Contact

If you must be at your office during the business day, then you have additional problems to deal with. How can you work interviews into the business day? And if you work in an open office, how can you even call to set up interviews? Obviously, you should keep up the effort and the appearances on your present job. So maximize your use of the lunch hour, early mornings, and late afternoons for calling. If you keep trying, you'll be surprised how often you will be able to reach the executive you are trying to contact during your out-of-office hours. You can catch people as early as 8 a.m. and as late as 6 p.m. on frequent occasions.

Scheduling Interviews

Your inability to interview at any time other than lunch just might work to your advantage. If you can, try to set up as many interviews as possible for your lunch hour. This will go a long way to creating a relaxed atmosphere. But be sure the interviews don't stray too far from the agenda on hand.

Lunchtime interviews are much easier to obtain if you have substantial career experience. People with less experience will often find no alternative to taking time off for interviews. If you have to take time off, you have to take time off. But try to do this as little as possible. Try to take the whole day off in order to avoid being blatantly obvious about your job search, and try to schedule two to three interviews for the same day. (It is very difficult to maintain an optimum level of energy at more than three interviews in one day.) Explain to the interviewer why you might have to juggle your interview schedule; he/she should honor the respect you're showing your current employer by minimizing your days off and will probably appreciate the fact that another prospective employer is interested in you.

> **Try calling as early as 8 a.m. and as late as 6 p.m. You'll be surprised how often you will be able to reach the executive you want during these times of the day.**

References

What do you tell an interviewer who asks for references from your current employer? Just say that while you are happy to have your former employers contacted, you are trying to keep your job search confidential and would rather that your current employer not be contacted until you have been given a firm offer.

IF YOU'RE FIRED OR LAID OFF:
Picking Yourself Up and Dusting Yourself Off

If you've been fired or laid off, you are not the first and will not be the last to go through this traumatic experience. In today's changing economy, thousands of professionals lose their jobs every year. Even if you were terminated with just cause, do not lose heart. Remember, being fired is not a reflection on you as a person. It is usually a reflection of your company's staffing needs and its perception of your recent job performance and attitude. And if you were not performing up to par or enjoying your work, then you will probably be better off at another company anyway.

> **Be prepared for the question "Why were you fired?" during job interviews.**

A thorough job search could take months, so be sure to negotiate a reasonable severance package, if possible, and determine to what benefits, such as health insurance, you are still legally entitled. Also, register for unemployment compensation immediately. Don't be surprised to find other professionals collecting unemployment compensation -- it is for everyone who has lost their job.

Don't start your job search with a flurry of unplanned activity. Start by choosing a strategy and working out a plan. Now is not the time for major changes in your life. If possible, remain in the same career and in the same geographical location, at least until you have been working again for a while. On the other hand, if the only industry for which you are trained is leaving, or is severely depressed in your area, then you should give prompt consideration to moving or switching careers.

Avoid mentioning you were fired when arranging interviews, but be prepared for the question "Why were you fired?" during an interview. If you were laid off as a result of downsizing, briefly explain, being sure to reinforce that your job loss was not due to performance. If you were in fact fired, be honest, but try to detail the reason as favorably as possible and portray what you have learned from your mistakes. If you are confident one of your past managers will give you a good reference, tell the interviewer to contact that person. Do not to speak negatively of your past employer and try not to sound particularly worried about your status of being temporarily unemployed.

Finally, don't spend too much time reflecting on why you were let go or how you might have avoided it. Think positively, look to the future, and be sure to follow a careful plan during your job search.

THE COLLEGE STUDENT:
Conducting Your First Job Search

While you will be able to apply many of the basics covered earlier in this chapter to your job search, there are some situations unique to the college student's job search.

THE GPA QUESTION

You are interviewing for the job of your dreams. Everything is going well: You've established a good rapport, the interviewer seems impressed with your qualifications, and you're almost positive the job is yours. Then you're asked about your GPA, which is pitifully low. Do you tell the truth and watch your dream job fly out the window?

Never lie about your GPA (they may request your transcript, and no company will hire a liar). You can, however, explain if there is a reason you don't feel your grades reflect your abilities, and mention any other impressive statistics. For example, if you have a high GPA in your major, or in the last few semesters (as opposed to your cumulative college career), you can use that fact to your advantage.

Perhaps the biggest problem college students face is lack of experience. Many schools have internship programs designed to give students exposure to the field of their choice, as well as the opportunity to make valuable contacts. Check out your school's career services department to see what internships are available. If your school does not have a formal internship program, or if there are no available internships that appeal to you, try contacting local businesses and offering your services. Often, businesses will be more than willing to have an extra pair of hands (especially if those hands are unpaid!) for a day or two each week. Or try contacting school alumni to see if you can "shadow" them for a few days, and see what their daily duties are like.

Informational Interviews

Although many jobseekers do not do this, it can be extremely helpful to arrange an informational interview with a college alumnus or someone else who works in your desired industry. You interview them about their job, their company, and their industry with questions you have prepared in advance. This can be done over the phone but is usually done in person. This will provide you with a contact in the industry who may give you more valuable information -- or perhaps even a job opportunity -- in the future. Always follow up with a thank you letter that includes your contact information.

The goal is to try to begin building experience and establishing
contacts as early as possible in your college career.

What do you do if, for whatever reason, you weren't able to get experience directly related to your desired career? First, look at your previous jobs and see if there's anything you can highlight. Did you supervise or train other employees? Did you reorganize the accounting system, or boost productivity in some way? Accomplishments like these demonstrate leadership, responsibility, and innovation -- qualities that most companies look for in employees. And don't forget volunteer activities and school clubs, which can also showcase these traits.

On-Campus Recruiting

Companies will often send recruiters to interview on-site at various colleges. This gives students a chance to interview with companies that may not have interviewed them otherwise. This is particularly true if a company schedules "open" interviews, in which the only screening process is who is first in line at the sign-ups. Of course, since many more applicants gain interviews in this format, this also means that many more people are rejected. The on-campus interview is generally a screening interview, to see if it is worth the company's time to invite you in for a second interview. So do everything possible to make yourself stand out from the crowd.

The first step, of course, is to check out any and all information your school's career center has on the company. If the information seems out of date, check out the company on the Internet or call the company's headquarters and ask for any printed information.

Many companies will host an informational meeting for interviewees, often the evening before interviews are scheduled to take place. DO NOT MISS THIS MEETING. The recruiter will almost certainly ask if you attended. Make an effort to stay after the meeting and talk with the company's representatives. Not only does this give you an opportunity to find out more information about both the company and the position, it also makes you stand out in the recruiter's mind. If there's a particular company that you had your heart set on, but you weren't able to get an interview with them, attend the information session anyway. You may be able to persuade the recruiter to squeeze you into the schedule. (Or you may discover that the company really isn't the right fit for you after all.)

Try to check out the interview site beforehand. Some colleges may conduct "mock" interviews that take place in one of the standard interview rooms. Or you may be able to convince a career counselor (or even a custodian) to let you sneak a peek during off-hours. Either way, having an idea of the room's setup will help you to mentally prepare.

Arrive at least 15 minutes early to the interview. The recruiter may be ahead of schedule, and might meet you early. But don't be surprised if previous interviews have run over, resulting in your 30-minute slot being reduced to 20 minutes (or less). Don't complain or appear anxious; just use the time you do have as efficiently as possible to showcase the reasons *you* are the ideal candidate. Staying calm and composed in these situations will work to your advantage.

LAST WORDS

A parting word of advice. Again and again during your job search you will face rejection. You will be rejected when you apply for interviews. You will be rejected after interviews. For every job offer you finally receive, you probably will have been rejected many times. Don't let rejections slow you down. Keep reminding yourself that the sooner you go out, start your job search, and get those rejections flowing in, the closer you will be to obtaining the job you want.

RESUMES AND COVER LETTERS

When filling a position, an employer will often have 100-plus applicants, but time to interview only a handful of the most promising ones. As a result, he or she will reject most applicants after only briefly skimming their resumes.

Unless you have phoned and talked to the employer -- which you should do whenever you can -- you will be chosen or rejected for an interview entirely on the basis of your resume and cover letter. *Your cover letter must catch the employer's attention, and your resume must hold it.* (But remember -- a resume is no substitute for a job search campaign. *You* must seek a job. Your resume is only one tool, albeit a critical one.)

RESUME FORMAT:
Mechanics of a First Impression

The Basics

Employers dislike long resumes, so unless you have an unusually strong background with many years of experience and a diversity of outstanding achievements, keep your resume length to one page. If you must squeeze in more information than would otherwise fit, try using a smaller typeface or changing the margins. Watch also for "widows" at the end of paragraphs. You can often free up some space if you can shorten the information enough to get rid of those single words taking up an entire line. Another tactic that works with some word processing programs is to decrease the font size of your paragraph returns and changing the spacing between lines.

Print your resume on standard 8 1/2" x 11" paper. Since recruiters often get resumes in batches of hundreds, a smaller-sized resume may be lost in the pile. Oversized resumes are likely to get crumpled at the edges, and won't fit easily in their files.

First impressions matter, so make sure the recruiter's first impression of your resume is a good one. Never hand-write your resume (or cover letter)! Print your resume on quality paper that has weight and texture, in a conservative color such as white, ivory, or pale gray. Good resume paper is easy to find at many stores that sell stationery or office products. It is even available at some drug stores. Use *matching* paper and envelopes for both your resume and cover letter. One hiring manager at a major magazine throws out all resumes that arrive on paper that differs in color from the envelope!

Do not buy paper with images of clouds and rainbows in the background or anything that looks like casual stationery that you would send to your favorite aunt. Do not spray perfume or cologne on your resume. Do not include your picture with your resume unless you have a specific and appropriate reason to do so.

Another tip: Do a test print of your resume (and cover letter), to make sure the watermark is on the same side as the text so that you can read it. Also make sure it is right-side up. As trivial as this may sound, some recruiters check for this! One recruiter at a law firm in New Hampshire sheepishly admitted this is the first thing he checks. *"I open each envelope and check the watermarks on the resume and cover letter. Those candidates that have it wrong go into a different pile."*

Getting it on Paper

Modern photocomposition typesetting gives you the clearest, sharpest image, a wide variety of type styles, and effects such as italics, bold-facing, and book-like justified margins. It is also too expensive for many jobseekers. The quality of today's laser printers means that a computer-generated resume can look just as impressive as one that has been professionally typeset.

A computer with a word processing or desktop publishing program is the most common way to generate your resume. This allows you the flexibility to make changes almost instantly and to store different drafts on disk. Word processing and desktop publishing programs also offer many different fonts to choose from, each taking up different amounts of space. (It is generally best to stay between 9-point and 12-point font size.) Many other options are also available, such as bold-facing or italicizing for emphasis and the ability to change and manipulate spacing. It is generally recommended to leave the right-hand margin unjustified as this keeps the spacing between the text even and therefore easier to read. It is not wrong to justify both margins of text, but if possible try it both ways before you decide.

For a resume on paper, the end result will be largely determined by the quality of the printer you use. Laser printers will generally provide the best quality. Do not use a dot matrix printer.

Many companies now use scanning equipment to screen the resumes they receive, and certain paper, fonts, and other features are more compatible with this technology. White paper is preferable, as well as a standard font such as Courier or Helvetica. You should use at least a 10-point font, and avoid bolding, italics, underlining, borders, boxes, or graphics.

Household typewriters and office typewriters with nylon or other cloth ribbons are *not* good enough for typing your resume. If you don't have access to a quality word processing program, hire a professional with the resources to prepare your resume for you. Keep in mind that businesses such as Kinko's (open 24 hours) provide access to computers with quality printers.

Don't make your copies on an office photocopier. Only the human resources office may see the resume you mail. Everyone else may see only a copy of it, and copies of copies quickly become unreadable. Furthermore, sending photocopies of your resume or cover letter is completely unprofessional. Either print out each copy individually, or take your resume to a professional copy shop, which will generally offer professionally-maintained, extra-high-quality photocopiers and charge fairly reasonable prices. You want your resume to represent you with the look of polished quality.

Proof with Care

Whether you typed it or paid to have it produced professionally, mistakes on resumes are not only embarrassing, but will usually remove you from consideration (particularly if something obvious such as your name is misspelled). No matter how much you paid someone else to type, write, or typeset your resume, *you* lose if there is a mistake. So proofread it as carefully as possible. Get a friend to help you. Read your draft aloud as your friend checks the proof copy. Then have your friend read aloud while you check. Next, read it letter by letter to check spelling and punctuation.

If you are having it typed or typeset by a resume service or a printer, and you don't have time to proof it, pay for it and take it home. Proof it there and bring it back later to get it corrected and printed.

If you wrote your resume with a word processing program, use the built-in spell checker to double-check for spelling errors. Keep in mind that a spell checker will not find errors such as "to" for "two" or "wok" for "work." Many spell check programs do not recognize missing or misused punctuation, nor are they set to check the spelling of capitalized words. It's important that you still proofread your resume to check for grammatical mistakes and other problems, even after it has been spellchecked. If you find mistakes, do not make edits in pen or pencil or use white-out to fix them on the final copy!

Electronic Resumes

As companies rely increasingly on emerging technologies to find qualified candidates for job openings, you may opt to create an electronic resume in order to remain competitive in today's job market. Why is this important? Companies today sometimes request that resumes be submitted by e-mail, and many hiring managers regularly check online resume databases for candidates to fill unadvertised job openings. Other companies enlist the services of electronic employment database services, which charge jobseekers a nominal fee to have their resumes posted to the database to be viewed by potential employers. Still other companies use their own automated applicant tracking systems, in which case your resume is fed through a scanner that sends the image to a computer that "reads" your resume, looking for keywords, and files it accordingly in its database.

Whether you're posting your resume online, e-mailing it directly to an employer, sending it to an electronic employment database, or sending it to a company you suspect uses an automated applicant tracking system, you must create some form of electronic resume to take advantage of the technology. Don't panic! An electronic resume is simply a modified version of your conventional resume. An electronic resume is one that is sparsely formatted, but filled with keywords and important facts.

In order to post your resume to the Internet -- either to an online resume database or through direct e-mail to an employer -- you will need to change the way your resume is formatted. Instead of a Word, WordPerfect, or other word processing document, save your resume as a plain text, DOS, or ASCII file. These three terms are basically interchangeable, and describe text at its simplest, most basic level, without the formatting such as boldface or italics that most jobseekers use to make their resumes look more interesting. If you use e-mail, you'll notice that all of your messages are written and received in this format. First, you should remove all formatting from your resume including boldface, italics, underlining, bullets, differing font sizes, and graphics. Then, convert and save your resume as a plain text file. Most word processing programs have a "save as" feature that allows you to save files in different formats. Here, you should choose "text only" or "plain text."

Another option is to create a resume in HTML (hypertext markup language), the text formatting language used to publish information on the World Wide Web. However, the real usefulness of HTML resumes is still being explored. Most of the major online databases do not accept HTML resumes, and the vast majority of companies only accept plain text resumes through their e-mail.

Finally, if you simply wish to send your resume to an electronic employment database or a company that uses an automated applicant tracking system, there is no need to convert your resume to a plain text file. The only change you need to make is to organize the information in your resume by keywords. Employers are likely to do keyword searches for information, such as degree held or knowledge of particular types of software. Therefore, using the right keywords or key phrases in your resume is critical to its ultimate success. Keywords are usually nouns or short phrases that the computer searches for which refer to experience, training, skills, and abilities. For example, let's say an employer searches an employment database for a sales representative with the following criteria:

BS/BA
exceeded quota
cold calls
high energy
willing to travel

Even if you have the right qualifications, neglecting to use these keywords would result in the computer passing over your resume. Although there is no way to know for sure which keywords employers are most likely to search for, you can make educated guesses by checking the help-wanted ads or online job postings for your type of job. You should also arrange keywords in a keyword summary, a paragraph listing your qualifications that immediately follows your name and address (see sample letter in this chapter). In addition, choose a nondecorative font with clear, distinct characters, such as Helvetica or Times. It is more difficult for a scanner to accurately pick up the more unusual fonts. Boldface and all capital letters are best used only for major section headings, such as "Experience" and "Education." It is also best to avoid using italics or underlining, since this can cause the letters to bleed into one another.

For more specific information on creating and sending electronic resumes, see *The Adams Internet Job Search Almanac.*

Types of Resumes

The most common resume formats are the functional resume, the chronological resume, and the combination resume. (Examples can be found at the end of this chapter.) A functional resume focuses on skills and de-emphasizes job titles, employers, etc. A functional resume is best if you have been out of the work force for a long time or are changing careers. It is also good if you want to highlight specific skills and strengths, especially if all of your work experience has been at one company. This format can also be a good choice if you are just out of school or have no experience in your desired field.

Choose a chronological format if you are currently working or were working recently, and if your most recent experiences relate to your desired field. Use reverse chronological order and include dates. To a recruiter your last job and your latest schooling are the most important, so put the last first and list the rest going back in time.

A combination resume is perhaps the most common. This resume simply combines elements of the functional and chronological resume formats. This is used by many jobseekers with a solid track record who find elements of both types useful.

Organization

Your name, phone number, e-mail address (if you have one), and a complete mailing address should be at the top of your resume. Try to make your name stand out by using a slightly larger font size or all capital letters. Be sure to spell out everything. Never abbreviate St. for Street or Rd. for Road. If you are a college student, you should also put your home address and phone number at the top.

Change your message on your answering machine if necessary -- RUSH blaring in the background or your sorority sisters screaming may not come across well to all recruiters. If you think you may be moving within six months then include a second address and phone number of a trusted friend or relative who can reach you no matter where you are.

Remember that employers will keep your resume on file and
may contact you months later if a position opens that fits your qualifications.
All too often, candidates are unreachable because they have moved and had not
previously provided enough contact options on their resume.

Next, list your experience, then your education. If you are a recent graduate, list your education first, unless your experience is more important than your education. (For example, if you have just graduated from a teaching school, have some business experience, and are applying for a job in business, you would list your business experience first.)

Keep everything easy to find. Put the dates of your employment and education on the left of the page. Put the names of the companies you worked for and the schools you attended a few spaces to the right of the dates. Put the city and state, or the city and country, where you studied or worked to the right of the page.

The important thing is simply to break up the text in some logical way that makes your resume visually attractive and easy to scan, so experiment to see which layout works best for your resume. However you set it up, *stay consistent.* Inconsistencies in fonts, spacing, or tenses will make your resume look sloppy. Also, be sure to use tabs to keep your information vertically lined up, rather than the less precise space bar.

RESUME CONTENT:
Say it with Style
Sell Yourself

You are selling your skills and accomplishments in your resume, so it is important to inventory yourself and know yourself. If you have achieved something, say so. Put it in the best possible light, but avoid subjective statements, such as "I am a hard worker" or "I get along well with my coworkers." Just stick to the facts.

While you shouldn't hold back or be modest, don't exaggerate your achievements to the point of misrepresentation. Be honest. Many companies will immediately drop an applicant from consideration (or fire a current employee) upon discovering inaccurate or untrue information on a resume or other application material.

Write down the important (and pertinent) things you have done, but do it in as few words as possible. Your resume will be scanned, not read, and short, concise phrases are much more effective than long-winded sentences. Avoid the use of "I" when emphasizing your accomplishments. Instead, use brief phrases beginning with action verbs.

While some technical terms will be unavoidable, you should try to avoid excessive "technicalese." Keep in mind that the first person to see your resume may be a human resources person who won't necessarily know all the jargon -- and how can they be impressed by something they don't understand?

Keep it Brief

Also, try to hold your paragraphs to six lines or less. If you have more than six lines of information about one job or school, put it in two or more paragraphs. A short resume will be examined more carefully. Remember: Your resume usually has between eight and 45 seconds to catch an employer's eye. So make every second count.

Job Objective

A functional resume may require a job objective to give it focus. One or two sentences describing the job you are seeking can clarify in what capacity your skills will be best put to use. Be sure that your stated objective is in line with the position you're applying for.

Examples:

> An entry-level editorial assistant position in the publishing industry.
> A senior management position with a telecommunications firm.

Don't include a job objective on a chronological resume unless your previous work experiences are <u>completely</u> unrelated to the position for which you're applying. The presence of an overly specific job objective might eliminate you from consideration for other positions that a recruiter feels are a better match for your qualifications. But even if you don't put an objective on paper, having a career goal in mind as you write can help give your resume a solid sense of direction.

USE ACTION VERBS

How you write your resume is just as important as *what* you write. In describing previous work experiences, the strongest resumes use short phrases beginning with action verbs. Below are a few you may want to use. (This list is not all-inclusive.)

achieved	developed	integrated	purchased
administered	devised	interpreted	reduced
advised	directed	interviewed	regulated
arranged	distributed	launched	represented
assisted	established	managed	resolved
attained	evaluated	marketed	restored
budgeted	examined	mediated	restructured
built	executed	monitored	revised
calculated	expanded	negotiated	scheduled
collaborated	expedited	obtained	selected
collected	facilitated	operated	served
compiled	formulated	ordered	sold
completed	founded	organized	solved
computed	generated	participated	streamlined
conducted	headed	performed	studied
consolidated	identified	planned	supervised
constructed	implemented	prepared	supplied
consulted	improved	presented	supported
controlled	increased	processed	tested
coordinated	initiated	produced	trained
created	installed	proposed	updated
determined	instructed	published	wrote

Some jobseekers may choose to include both "Relevant Experience" and "Additional Experience" sections. This can be useful, as it allows the jobseeker to place more emphasis on certain experiences and to de-emphasize others.

Emphasize continued experience in a particular job area or continued interest in a particular industry. De-emphasize irrelevant positions. It is okay to include one opening line providing a general description of each company you've worked at. Delete positions that you held for less than four months (unless you are a very recent college grad or still in school). Stress your <u>results</u> and your achievements, elaborating on how you contributed in your previous jobs. Did you increase sales, reduce costs, improve a product, implement a new program? Were you promoted? Use specific numbers (i.e., quantities, percentages, dollar amounts) whenever possible.

Education

Keep it brief if you have more than two years of career experience. Elaborate more if you have less experience. If you are a recent college graduate, you may choose to include any high school activities that are directly relevant to your career. If you've been out of school for a while you don't need to list your education prior to college.

Mention degrees received and any honors or special awards. Note individual courses or projects you participated in that might be relevant for employers. For example, if you are an English major applying for a position as a business writer, be sure to mention any business or economics courses. Previous experience such as Editor-in-Chief of the school newspaper would be relevant as well.

If you are uploading your resume to an online job hunting site such as CareerCity.com, action verbs are still important, but the key words or key nouns that a computer would search for become more important. For example, if you're seeking an accounting position, key nouns that a computer would search for such as "Lotus 1-2-3" or "CPA" or "payroll" become very important.

Highlight Impressive Skills

Be sure to mention any computer skills you may have. You may wish to include a section entitled "Additional Skills" or "Computer Skills," in which you list any software programs you know. An additional skills section is also an ideal place to mention fluency in a foreign language.

Personal Data

This section is optional, but if you choose to include it, keep it brief. A one-word mention of hobbies such as fishing, chess, baseball, cooking, etc., can give the person who will interview you a good way to open up the conversation.

Team sports experience is looked at favorably. It doesn't hurt to include activities that are somewhat unusual (fencing, Akido, '70s music) or that somehow relate to the position or the company to which you're applying. For instance, it would be worth noting if you are a member of a professional organization in your industry of interest. Never include information about your age, alias, date of birth, health, physical characteristics, marital status, religious affiliation, or political/moral beliefs.

References

The most that is needed is the sentence "References available upon request" at the bottom of your resume. If you choose to leave it out, that's fine. This line is not really necessary. It is understood that references will most likely be asked for and provided by you later on in the interviewing process. Do not actually send references with your resume and cover letter unless specifically requested.

HIRING A RESUME WRITER:
Is it the Right Choice for You?

If you write reasonably well, it is to your advantage to write your own resume. Writing your resume forces you to review your experiences and figure out how to explain your accomplishments in clear, brief phrases. This will help you when you explain your work to interviewers. It is also easier to tailor your resume to each position you're applying for when you have put it together yourself.

If you write your resume, everything will be in your own words; it will sound like you. It will say what you want it to say. If you are a good writer, know yourself well, and have a good idea of which parts of your background employers are looking for, you should be able to write your own resume better than someone else. If you decide to write your resume yourself, have as many people as possible review and proofread it. Welcome objective opinions and other perspectives.

When to Get Help

If you have difficulty writing in "resume style" (which is quite unlike normal written language), if you are unsure which parts of your background to emphasize, or if you think your resume would make your case better if it did not follow one of the standard forms outlined either here or in a book on resumes, then you should consider having it professionally written.

Even some professional resume writers we know have had their resumes written with the help of fellow professionals. They sought the help of someone who could be objective about their background, as well as provide an experienced sounding board to help focus their thoughts.

If You Hire a Pro

The best way to choose a writer is by reputation: the recommendation of a friend, a personnel director, your school placement officer, or someone else knowledgeable in the field.

Important questions:
- "How long have you been writing resumes?"
- "If I'm not satisfied with what you write, will you go over it with me and change it?"
- "Do you charge by the hour or a flat rate?"

There is no sure relation between price and quality, except that you are unlikely to get a good writer for less than $50 for an uncomplicated resume and you shouldn't have to pay more than $300 unless your experience is very extensive or complicated. There will be additional charges for printing. Assume nothing no matter how much you pay. It is your career at stake if there are mistakes on your resume!

Few resume services will give you a firm price over the phone, simply because some resumes are too complicated and take too long to do for a predetermined price. Some services will quote you a price that applies to almost all of their customers. Once you decide to use a specific writer, you should insist on a firm price quote *before* engaging their services. Also, find out how expensive minor changes will be.

COVER LETTERS:
Quick, Clear, and Concise

Always mail a cover letter with your resume. In a cover letter you can show an interest in the company that you can't show in a resume. You can also point out one or two of your skills or accomplishments the company can put to good use.

Make it Personal

The more personal you can get, the better, so long as you keep it professional. If someone known to the person you are writing has recommended that you contact the company, get permission to include his/her name in the letter. If you can get the name of a person to send the letter to, address it directly to that person (after first calling the company to verify the spelling of the person's name, correct title, and mailing address). Be sure to put the person's name and title on both the letter and the envelope. This will ensure that your letter will get through to the proper person, even if a new person now occupies this position. It will not always be possible to get the name of a person. Always strive to get at least a title.

Be sure to mention something about why you have an interest in the company - - *so many candidates apply for jobs with no apparent knowledge of what the company does!* This conveys the message that they just want any job.

Type cover letters in full. Don't try the cheap and easy ways, like using a computer mail merge program or photocopying the body of your letter and typing in the inside address and salutation. You will give the impression that you are mailing to a host of companies and have no particular interest in any one.

Print your cover letter on the same color and same high-quality paper as your resume.

Cover letter basic format

Paragraph 1: State what the position is that you are seeking. It is not always necessary to state how you found out about the position -- often you will apply without knowing that a position is open.

Paragraph 2: Include what you know about the company and why you are interested in working there. Mention any prior contact with the company or someone known to the hiring person if relevant. Briefly state your qualifications and what you can offer. (Do not talk about what you cannot do).

Paragraph 3: Close with your phone number and where/when you can be reached. Make a request for an interview. State when you will follow up by phone (or mail or e-mail if the ad requests no phone calls). Do not wait long -- generally five working days. If you say you're going to follow up, then actually do it! This phone call can get your resume noticed when it might otherwise sit in a stack of 225 other resumes.

Cover letter do's and don'ts

- *Do* keep your cover letter brief and to the point.
- *Do* be sure it is error-free.
- *Do* accentuate what you can offer the company, not what you hope to gain.
- *Do* be sure your phone number and address is on your cover letter just in case it gets separated from your resume (this happens!).
- *Do* check the watermark by holding the paper up to a light -- be sure it is facing forward so it is readable -- on the same side as the text, and right-side up.
- *Do* sign your cover letter (or type your name if you are sending it electronically). Blue or black ink are both fine. Do not use red ink.
- *Don't* just repeat information verbatim from your resume.
- *Don't* overuse the personal pronoun "I."
- *Don't* send a generic cover letter -- show your personal knowledge of and interest in that particular company.

THANK YOU LETTERS:
Another Way to Stand Out

As mentioned earlier, *always* send a thank you letter after an interview (see the sample later in this section). So few candidates do this and it is yet another way for you to stand out. Be sure to mention something specific from the interview and restate your interest in the company and the position.

It is generally acceptable to handwrite your thank you letter on a generic thank you card (but *never* a postcard). Make sure handwritten notes are neat and legible. However, if you are in doubt, typing your letter is always the safe bet. If you met with several people it is fine to send them each an individual thank you letter. Call the company if you need to check on the correct spelling of their names.

Remember to:
- Keep it short.
- Proofread it carefully.
- Send it *promptly*.

FUNCTIONAL RESUME

C.J. RAVENCLAW
129 Pennsylvania Avenue
Washington DC 20500
202/555-6652
e-mail: ravenclaw@dcpress.net

Objective
A position as a graphic designer commensurate with my acquired skills and expertise.

Summary
Extensive experience in plate making, separations, color matching, background definition, printing, mechanicals, color corrections, and personnel supervision. A highly motivated manager and effective communicator. Proven ability to:

- **Create Commercial Graphics**
- **Produce Embossed Drawings**
- **Color Separate**
- **Control Quality**
- **Resolve Printing Problems**
- **Analyze Customer Satisfaction**

Qualifications
Printing:
Knowledgeable in black and white as well as color printing. Excellent judgment in determining acceptability of color reproduction through comparison with original. Proficient at producing four- or five-color corrections on all media, as well as restyling previously reproduced four-color artwork.

Customer Relations:
Routinely work closely with customers to ensure specifications are met. Capable of striking a balance between technical printing capabilities and need for customer satisfaction through entire production process.

Specialties:
Practiced at creating silk screen overlays for a multitude of processes including velo bind, GBC bind, and perfect bind. Creative design and timely preparation of posters, flyers, and personalized stationery.

Personnel Supervision:
Skillful at fostering atmosphere that encourages highly talented artists to balance high-level creativity with maximum production. Consistently beat production deadlines. Instruct new employees, apprentices, and students in both artistry and technical operations.

Experience
Graphic Arts Professor, Ohio State University, Columbus OH (1992-1996).
Manager, Design Graphics, Washington DC (1997-present).

Education
Massachusetts Conservatory of Art, Ph.D. 1990
University of Massachusetts, B.A. 1988

CHRONOLOGICAL RESUME

HARRY SEABORN
557 Shoreline Drive
Seattle, WA 98404
(206) 555-6584
e-mail: hseaborn@centco.com

EXPERIENCE

THE CENTER COMPANY   Seattle, WA
Systems Programmer   1996-present
- Develop and maintain customer accounting and order tracking database using a Visual Basic front end and SQL server.
- Plan and implement migration of company wide transition from mainframe-based dumb terminals to a true client server environment using Windows NT Workstation and Server.
- Oversee general local and wide area network administration including the development of a variety of intranet modules to improve internal company communication and planning across divisions.

INFO TECH, INC.   Seattle, WA
Technical Manager   1994-1996
- Designed and managed the implementation of a network providing the legal community with a direct line to Supreme Court cases across the Internet using SQL Server and a variety of Internet tools.
- Developed a system to make the entire library catalog available on line using PERL scripts and SQL.
- Used Visual Basic and Microsoft Access to create a registration system for university registrar.

EDUCATION

SALEM STATE UNIVERSITY   Salem, OR
    M.S. in Computer Science.   1993
    B.S. in Computer Science.   1991

COMPUTER SKILLS

- Programming Languages: Visual Basic, Java, C++, SQL, PERL
- Software: SQL Server, Internet Information Server, Oracle
- Operating Systems: Windows NT, UNIX, Linux

FUNCTIONAL RESUME

Donna Hermione Moss
703 Wizard's Way
Chicago, IL 60601
(312) 555-8841
e-mail: donna@cowfire.com

OBJECTIVE:
To contribute over five years of experience in promotion, communications, and administration to an entry-level position in advertising.

SUMMARY OF QUALIFICATIONS:
- Performed advertising duties for small business.
- Experience in business writing and communications skills.
- General knowledge of office management.
- Demonstrated ability to work well with others, in both supervisory and support staff roles.
- Type 75 words per minute.

SELECTED ACHIEVEMENTS AND RESULTS:
Promotion:
Composing, editing, and proofreading correspondence and public relations materials for own catering service. Large-scale mailings.

Communication:
Instruction; curriculum and lesson planning; student evaluation; parent-teacher conferences; development of educational materials. Training and supervising clerks.

Computer Skills:
Proficient in MS Word, Lotus 1-2-3, Excel, and Filemaker Pro.

Administration:
Record-keeping and file maintenance. Data processing and computer operations, accounts receivable, accounts payable, inventory control, and customer relations. Scheduling, office management, and telephone reception.

PROFESSIONAL HISTORY:
Teacher; Self-Employed (owner of catering service); Floor Manager; Administrative Assistant; Accounting Clerk.

EDUCATION:
Beloit College, Beloit, WI, BA in Education, 1991

CHRONOLOGICAL RESUME

PERCY ZIEGLER
16 Josiah Court
Marlborough CT 06447
203/555-9641 (h)
203/555-8176, x14 (w)

EDUCATION
Keene State College, Keene NH
Bachelor of Arts in Elementary Education, 1998
- Graduated *magna cum laude*
- English minor
- Kappa Delta Pi member, inducted 1996

EXPERIENCE
September 1998-
Present

Elmer T. Thienes Elementary School, Marlborough CT
Part-time Kindergarten Teacher
- Instruct kindergartners in reading, spelling, language arts, and music.
- Participate in the selection of textbooks and learning aids.
- Organize and supervise class field trips and coordinate in-class presentations.

Summers
1995-1997

Keene YMCA, Youth Division, Keene NH
Child-care Counselor
- Oversaw summer program for low-income youth.
- Budgeted and coordinated special events and field trips, working with Program Director to initiate variations in the program.
- Served as Youth Advocate in cooperation with social worker to address the social needs and problems of participants.

Spring 1997

Wheelock Elementary School, Keene NH
Student Teacher
- Taught third-grade class in all elementary subjects.
- Designed and implemented a two-week unit on Native Americans.
- Assisted in revision of third-grade curriculum.

Fall 1996

Child Development Center, Keene NH
Daycare Worker
- Supervised preschool children on the playground and during art activities.
- Created a "Wishbone Corner," where children could quietly look at books or take a voluntary "time-out."

ADDITIONAL INTERESTS
Martial arts, Pokemon, politics, reading, skiing, writing.

ELECTRONIC RESUME

GRIFFIN DORE
69 Dursley Drive
Cambridge, MA 02138
(617) 555-5555

KEYWORD SUMMARY

Senior financial manager with over ten years experience in Accounting and Systems Management, Budgeting, Forecasting, Cost Containment, Financial Reporting, and International Accounting. MBA in Management. Proficient in Lotus, Excel, Solomon, and Windows.

EXPERIENCE

COLWELL CORPORATION, Wellesley, MA
Director of Accounting and Budgets, 1990 to present
   Direct staff of twenty in General Ledger, Accounts Payable, Accounts Receivable, and International Accounting.
   Facilitate month-end closing process with parent company and auditors.
   Implemented team-oriented cross-training program within accounting group, resulting in timely month-end closings and increased productivity of key accounting staff.
   Developed and implemented a strategy for Sales and Use Tax Compliance in all fifty states.
   Prepare monthly financial statements and analyses.

FRANKLIN AND DELANEY COMPANY, Melrose, MA
Senior Accountant, 1987-1990
   Managed Accounts Payable, General Ledger, transaction processing, and financial reporting. Supervised staff of five.

Staff Accountant, 1985-1987
   Managed Accounts Payable, including vouchering, cash disbursements, and bank reconciliation.
   Wrote and issued policies.
   Maintained supporting schedules used during year-end audits.
   Trained new employees.

EDUCATION

MBA in Management, Northeastern University, Boston, MA, 1989
BS in Accounting, Boston College, Boston, MA, 1985

ASSOCIATIONS

National Association of Accountants

GENERAL MODEL
FOR A COVER LETTER

Your mailing address
Date

Contact's name
Contact's title
Company
Company's mailing address

Dear Mr./Ms. _____:

Immediately explain why your background makes you the best candidate for the position that you are applying for. Describe what prompted you to write (want ad, article you read about the company, networking contact, etc.). Keep the first paragraph short and hard-hitting.

Detail what you could contribute to this company. Show how your qualifications will benefit this firm. Describe your interest in the corporation. Subtly emphasizing your knowledge about this firm and your familiarity with the industry will set you apart from other candidates. Remember to keep this letter short; few recruiters will read a cover letter longer than half a page.

If possible, your closing paragraph should request specific action on the part of the reader. Include your phone number and the hours when you can be reached. Mention that if you do not hear from the reader by a specific date, you will follow up with a phone call. Lastly, thank the reader for their time, consideration, etc.

Sincerely,

(signature)

Your full name (typed)

Enclosure (use this if there are other materials, such as your resume, that are included in the same envelope)

SAMPLE COVER LETTER

16 Josiah Court
Marlborough CT 06447
January 16, 2000

Ms. Leona Malfoy
Assistant Principal
Laningham Elementary School
43 Mayflower Drive
Keene NH 03431

Dear Ms. Malfoy:

Toby Potter recently informed me of a possible opening for a third grade teacher at Laningham Elementary School. With my experience instructing third-graders, both in schools and in summer programs, I feel I would be an ideal candidate for the position. Please accept this letter and the enclosed resume as my application.

Laningham's educational philosophy that every child can learn and succeed interests me, since it mirrors my own. My current position at Elmer T. Thienes Elementary has reinforced this philosophy, heightening my awareness of the different styles and paces of learning and increasing my sensitivity toward special needs children. Furthermore, as a direct result of my student teaching experience at Wheelock Elementary School, I am comfortable, confident, and knowledgeable working with third-graders.

I look forward to discussing the position and my qualifications for it in more detail. I can be reached at 203/555-9641 evenings or 203/555-8176, x14 weekdays. If I do not hear from you before Tuesday of next week, I will call to see if we can schedule a time to meet. Thank you for your time and consideration.

Sincerely,

Percy Ziegler

Percy Ziegler

Enclosure

GENERAL MODEL FOR A
THANK YOU/FOLLOW-UP LETTER

Your mailing address
Date

Contact's name
Contact's title
Company
Company's mailing address

Dear Mr./Ms._____:

Remind the interviewer of the reason (i.e., a specific opening, an informational interview, etc.) you were interviewed, as well as the date. Thank him/her for the interview, and try to personalize your thanks by mentioning some specific aspect of the interview.

Confirm your interest in the organization (and in the opening, if you were interviewing for a particular position). Use specifics to re-emphasize that you have researched the firm in detail and have considered how you would fit into the company and the position. This is a good time to say anything you wish you had said in the initial meeting. Be sure to keep this letter brief; a half page is plenty.

If appropriate, close with a suggestion for further action, such as a desire to have an additional interview, if possible. Mention your phone number and the hours you can be reached. Alternatively, you may prefer to mention that you will follow up with a phone call in several days. Once again, thank the person for meeting with you, and state that you would be happy to provide any additional information about your qualifications.

Sincerely,

(signature)

Your full name (typed)

PRIMARY EMPLOYERS

ACCOUNTING AND MANAGEMENT CONSULTING

You can expect to find the following types of companies in this chapter:
*Consulting and Research Firms • Industrial Accounting Firms •
Management Services • Public Accounting Firms •
Tax Preparation Companies*

CHESHIER AND FULLER, L.L.P.
14175 Proton Road, Dallas TX 75244-3604. 972/387-4300. **Toll-free phone:** 800/834-8586. **Fax:** 972/960-2810. **Contact:** Firm Administrator. **World Wide Web address:** http://www.cheshier-fuller.com. **Description:** Offers accounting, tax, audit, management advisory, business valuation, and litigation support services. Founded in 1956. **Positions advertised include:** Staff Auditor. **Special programs:** Training; Summer Jobs. **Office hours:** Monday - Friday, 8:30 a.m. - 5:30 p.m. **Corporate headquarters location:** This location. **Listed on:** Privately held.

DELOITTE & TOUCHE
5550 LBJ Freeway, Suite 700, Dallas TX 75240. 972/776-6000. **Contact:** Human Resources. **World Wide Web address:** http://www. us.deloitte.com. **Description:** An international firm of certified public accountants providing professional accounting, auditing, tax, and management consulting services to widely diversified clients. The company has a specialized program consisting of national industry groups and functional groups that cross industry lines. Groups are involved in various disciplines including accounting, auditing, taxation management advisory services, small and growing businesses, mergers and acquisitions, and computer applications. **Corporate headquarters location:** Wilton CT. **Number of employees nationwide:** 30,000.

DELOITTE & TOUCHE
2200 Ross Avenue, Suite 1600, Dallas TX 75201. 214/777-7000. **Contact:** Steve Gass, Human Resources Director. **World Wide Web address:** http://www.us.deloitte.com. **Description:** An international firm of certified public accountants providing professional accounting, auditing, tax, and management consulting services to widely diversified clients. The company has a specialized program consisting of national industry groups and functional groups that cross industry lines. Groups are involved in various disciplines including accounting, auditing, taxation management advisory

services, small and growing businesses, mergers and acquisitions, and computer applications. **Special programs:** Internships. **Corporate headquarters location:** Wilton CT. **Operations at this facility include:** Regional Headquarters. **Number of employees nationwide:** 30,000.

ECKERT, INGRUM, TINKLER, OLIPHANT, & FEATHERSTON, L.L.P.
P.O. Box 5821, San Angelo TX 76902-5821. 915/944-3571. **Fax:** 915/942-1093. **Contact:** Hiring Partner. **Description:** An accounting firm involved in bookkeeping, taxes, and auditing of various institutions including schools, governments, and banks. **NOTE:** Entry-level positions are offered. **Corporate headquarters location:** This location.

ERNST & YOUNG LLP
2121 San Jacinto, Suite 1500, Dallas TX 75201. 214/969-8000. **Fax:** 214/969-8587. **Contact:** Director of Human Resources. **World Wide Web address:** http://www.ey.com. **Description:** A certified public accounting firm that also provides management consulting services. Services include data processing, financial modeling, financial feasibility studies, production planning and inventory management, management sciences, health care planning, human resources, cost accounting, and budgeting systems. **Corporate headquarters location:** New York NY. **Other U.S. locations:** Nationwide. **Listed on:** Privately held.

GRANT THORNTON LLP
1717 Main Street, Suite 500, Dallas TX 75201. 214/855-7300. **Fax:** 214/561-2370. **Contact:** Personnel. **World Wide Web address:** http://www.grantthornton.com. **Description:** An international certified public accounting organization offering consulting and accounting services as well as strategic and tactical planning assistance to a diverse clientele. **NOTE:** Entry-level positions are offered. **Special programs:** Internships; Training. **Corporate headquarters location:** Chicago IL. **Other U.S. locations:** Nationwide. **Operations at this facility include:** Administration; Regional Headquarters; Sales; Service. **Listed on:** Privately held. **Annual sales/revenues:** More than $300 million. **Number of employees nationwide:** 2,700. **Number of employees worldwide:** 21,700.

H&R BLOCK
3701 West NW Highway, Suite 210, Dallas TX 75220. 214/358-4560. **Contact:** Personnel. **World Wide Web address:** http://www.hrblock.com. **Description:** Primarily engaged in consumer tax preparation, operating more than 9,500 U.S. offices and preparing more than 10 million tax returns each year. H&R Block has established offices in over 750 Sears stores in both the United States and Canada. The company is also engaged in a number of other tax-related activities including group tax programs, executive tax service, tax training schools, and real estate tax awareness seminars. **Corporate headquarters location:** Kansas City MO. **Listed on:** New York Stock Exchange. **Stock exchange symbol:** HRB. **Number of employees nationwide:** 80,000.

MERCER MANAGEMENT CONSULTING
3500 Chase Tower, 2200 Ross Avenue, Dallas TX 75201. 214/758-1880. **Contact:** Human Resources. **World Wide Web address:** http://www.mercermc.com. **Description:** Provides strategy and management consulting services.

PRICEWATERHOUSECOOPERS
2001 Ross Avenue, Suite 1800, Dallas TX 75201. 214/999-1400. **Contact:** Vicki Bennett, Human Resources Coordinator. **World Wide Web address:** http://www.pricewaterhousecoopers.com. **Description:** One of the largest certified public accounting firms in the world. PricewaterhouseCoopers provides public accounting, business advisory, management consulting, and taxation services. **Corporate headquarters location:** New York NY. **Other U.S. locations:** Nationwide.

ADVERTISING, MARKETING, AND PUBLIC RELATIONS

You can expect to find the following types of companies in this chapter:
*Advertising Agencies • Direct Mail Marketers •
Market Research Firms • Public Relations Firms*

ACKERMAN McQUEEN, INC.

545 East John Carpenter Freeway, Suite 600, Irving TX 75062-3932. 972/444-9000. **Fax:** 972/869-4363. **Contact:** Human Resources. **World Wide Web address:** http://www.am.com. **Description:** A full-service advertising agency. Founded in 1939. **NOTE:** Entry-level positions are offered. **Positions advertised include:** Administrative Assistant; Advertising Executive; Computer Support Technician; Desktop Publishing Specialist; Graphic Designer; Technical Writer/Editor. **Special programs:** Internships. **Internship information:** Unpaid internships are offered each fall, spring, and summer semester for college credit. **Corporate headquarters location:** Oklahoma City OK. **Other U.S. locations:** CO; OK.

AEGIS COMMUNICATIONS GROUP

8001 Bent Branch Drive, Suite 150, Irving TX 75063. 972/830-1800. **Fax:** 972/868-0267. **Contact:** Human Resources Department. **World Wide Web address:** http://www.aegiscomgroup.com. **Description:** A teleservices provider that offers integrated marketing services to large corporations. Services include customer acquisition, customer care, and marketing research. **Positions advertised include:** Senior Instructional Designer. **Corporate headquarters location:** This location. **Listed on:** NASDAQ. **Stock exchange symbol:** AGIS.

BURK ADVERTISING & MARKETING, INC.

2906 McKinney Avenue, Suite 100, Dallas TX 75204. 214/953-0494. **Contact:** Human Resources. **World Wide Web address:** http://www.wambam.com. **Description:** An advertising and marketing agency offering a variety of print and multimedia services.

DDB NEEDHAM

1999 Bryan Street, Suite 2300, Dallas TX 75201. 214/259-4200. **Contact:** Human Resources Department. **World Wide Web address:** http://www.ddb.com. **Description:** A full-service, international advertising agency. **Corporate headquarters location:** New York NY.

DECISION ANALYST, INC.

604 Avenue H East, Arlington TX 76011. 817/640-6166. **Fax:** 817/640-6567. **Contact:** Human Resources. **World Wide Web address:** http://www.decisionanalyst.com. **Description:** A market research and consulting firm offering product testing, tracking research, and Internet surveys. **Positions advertised include:** Research Analyst. **Corporate headquarters location:** This location.

THE DOZIER COMPANY

2021 Farrington, Dallas TX 75207. 214/744-2800. **Fax:** 214/744-1240. **Contact:** Human Resources. **World Wide Web address:** http://www.thedoziercompany.com. **Description:** A full-service advertising and public relations agency. Founded in 1987. **Special programs:** Internships. **Corporate headquarters location:** This location.

BERNARD HODES ADVERTISING

7502 Greenville Avenue, Suite 630, Dallas TX 75231. 214/361-9986. **Contact:** Branch Manager. **World Wide Web address:** http://www.hodes.com. **Description:** An advertising agency specializing in recruitment and employee communications. **Corporate headquarters location:** New York NY. **Other U.S. locations:** Nationwide.

THE M/A/R/C GROUP

7850 North Beltline Road, Irving TX 75063. 972/506-3400. **Contact:** Human Resources. **World Wide Web address:** http://www.marcgroup.com. **Description:** The M/A/R/C Group is a holding company for M/A/R/C Research and Targetbase. M/A/R/C Research (also at this location) specializes in providing strategic customer research for marketing purposes. Targetbase (also at this location) is a customer relationship management firm. **Other U.S. locations:** CA; GA; IL; NC.

PUBLICIS USA

14185 North Dallas Parkway, Dallas TX 75254. 972/628-7500. **Contact:** Personnel Director. **World Wide Web address:** http://www.publicis-usa.com. **Description:** An advertising agency. Founded in 1952.

THE RICHARDS GROUP

8750 North Central Expressway, Suite 1200, Dallas TX 75231-6437. 214/891-5700. **Contact:** Human Resources. **World Wide Web address:** http://www.richards.com. **Description:** A full-service advertising agency offering direct marketing, promotional marketing, naming, graphic design, and interactive communications services. **Listed on:** Privately held.

J. WALTER THOMPSON
350 North Saint Paul, Suite 2500, Dallas TX 75201. 214/754-9316. **Contact:** Human Resources. **World Wide Web address:** http://www. jwtworld.com. **Description:** One of the largest advertising agencies in the nation. **Positions advertised include:** Retail Automotive Account Representative. **Corporate headquarters location:** New York NY.

WITHERSPOON ADVERTISING & PUBLIC RELATIONS
P.O. Box 2137, Fort Worth TX 76113. 817/335-1373. **Contact:** Mike Wilie, Executive Vice President. **World Wide Web address:** http:// www.witherspoon.com. **Description:** A national advertising and public relations agency. **Corporate headquarters location:** This location. **Operations at this facility include:** Service.

AEROSPACE

You can expect to find the following types of companies in this chapter:
Aerospace Products and Services • Aircraft Equipment and Parts

ASSOCIATED AIRCRAFT SUPPLY CO., INC.
6020 Cedar Springs Road, P.O. Box 35788, Dallas TX 75235. 214/331-4381. **Fax:** 214/339-9840. **Contact:** Tommy DeRossett, Human Resources. **World Wide Web address:** http://www. associated-aircraft.com. **Description:** A distributor of aircraft parts and machinery. Products include switches, relays, and circuit breakers. **Corporate headquarters location:** This location.

BELL HELICOPTER TEXTRON
P.O. Box 482, Fort Worth TX 76101. 817/280-2011. **Contact:** Employment Department. **World Wide Web address:** http://www. bellhelicopter.textron.com. **Description:** Bell Helicopter Textron manufactures a variety of commercial and civilian helicopters and also conducts extensive research and development activities. **Positions advertised include:** Chief Liaison; Engineering Specialist; Principal Engineer; Lofter; Manufacturing Operations Administrative Specialist. **Corporate headquarters location:** This location. **Parent company:** Textron Inc.

BOEING-IRVING
331 Astoria Road West, Irving TX 75038. 972/659-2600. **Contact:** Human Resources Department. **World Wide Web address:** http:// www.boeing.com. **Description:** Manufactures electrical components for aircraft. **Corporate headquarters location:** Seattle WA. **Parent company:** The Boeing Company. **Listed on:** New York Stock Exchange. **Stock Exchange symbol:** BA.

FOXTRONICS INC.
3448 West Mockingbird Lane, Dallas TX 75235. 214/358-2490. **Contact:** Human Resources. **World Wide Web address:** http://www. foxtronics.com. **Description:** Engaged in the sale and service of aircraft batteries.

GULFSTREAM AEROSPACE CORPORATION
P.O. Box 7145, Dallas TX 75209. 214/902-7500. **Fax:** 214/902-4964. **Contact:** Dee Oliver, Personnel Director. **World Wide Web address:** http://www.gulfstream.com. **Description:** Refurbishes and

performs completion work on corporate aircraft. **Parent company:** General Dynamics.

HELI-DYNE SYSTEMS, INC.
P.O. Box 966, Hurst TX 76053. 817/282-9804. **Contact:** Human Resources. **World Wide Web address:** http://www.heli-dyne.com. **Description:** A helicopter completion company with a specialty in special mission, air medical, executive transport, and multimission aircraft. The company is an affiliate of Corporate Jets, Inc.

INTERNATIONAL AVIATION COMPOSITES (IAC)
P.O. Box 376, Haslet TX 76052-0376. 817/491-6755. **Contact:** Human Resources. **World Wide Web address:** http://www.iac-ltd. com. **Description:** Repairs main and tail rotor blades on helicopters. **Corporate headquarters location:** This location. **Operations at this facility include:** Administration; Manufacturing; Research and Development; Sales; Service. **Listed on:** Privately held.

LOCKHEED MARTIN TACTICAL AIRCRAFT SYSTEMS
P.O. Box 748, Fort Worth TX 76101-0748. 817/777-2000. **Recorded jobline:** 817/777-1000. **Contact:** Human Resources. **World Wide Web address:** http://www.lmtas.com. **Description:** Engaged in the development and production of tactical aircraft. **NOTE:** Jobseekers are encouraged to submit their resume via the Website: http://www. lockheedmartin.com. **Positions advertised include:** Aircraft Assembler; Administrative Assistant; Aeronautical Engineer; Systems Engineer. **Other U.S. locations:** Nationwide. **Parent company:** Lockheed Martin Corporation operates in five major areas: Space Systems develops space technology systems such as rocket systems, Space Shuttle support technology, and other products; Missile Systems produces fleet ballistic missiles for military applications; Advanced Systems operates as the research and development organization exploring military, commercial, and scientific needs; Information Processing develops comprehensive database systems to process the specific needs of other company divisions; and the Austin Division is responsible for designing and producing military tactical support systems. **Operations at this facility include:** Administration; Manufacturing; Research and Development. **Listed on:** New York Stock Exchange. **Stock exchange symbol:** LM. **Number of employees nationwide:** 125,000.

LOCKHEED MARTIN VOUGHT SYSTEMS

P.O. Box 650003, Mail Stop LHR-PE, Dallas TX 75265-0003. 972/603-1000. **Contact:** Human Resources. **World Wide Web address:** http://www.lmco.com. **Description:** Manufactures advanced tactical missiles, rockets, and space systems. **Positions advertised include:** Metrologist; Network Engineer; Subcontract Administrator. **Corporate headquarters location:** This location. **Parent company:** Lockheed Martin Corporation operates in five major areas: Space Systems develops space technology systems such as rocket systems, Space Shuttle support technology, and other products; Missile Systems produces fleet ballistic missiles for military applications; Advanced Systems operates as the research and development organization exploring military, commercial, and scientific needs; Information Processing develops comprehensive database systems to process the specific needs of other company divisions; and the Austin Division is responsible for designing and producing military tactical support systems. **Operations at this facility include:** Administration; Divisional Headquarters; Manufacturing; Research and Development. **Listed on:** New York Stock Exchange. **Number of employees nationwide:** 180,000.

LUMINATOR

1200 East Plano Parkway, Plano TX 75074. 972/424-6511. **Contact:** Denise Boyd, Human Resources. **World Wide Web address:** http://www.luminatorusa.com. **Description:** Manufactures aircraft parts, bus products, and rail products. Luminator aircraft products include batteries, lamps, searchlights, interiors, and crew stations. Bus products include flip-out signs and voice systems. Rail products include various types of lighting, flip dot sign systems, electronic maps, voice systems, and air diffusers. **Corporate headquarters location:** This location. **Parent company:** Mark IV Industries.

MARATHON POWER TECHNOLOGIES COMPANY

P.O. Box 8233, Waco TX 76714-8233. 254/776-0650. **Fax:** 254/776-1309. **Contact:** Jeff Oliver, Personnel Manager. **World Wide Web address:** http://www.mptc.com. **Description:** Manufactures nickel-cadmium aircraft batteries and electronic assemblies. **Corporate headquarters location:** This location.

PRATT & WHITNEY

1177 North Great Southwest Parkway, Grand Prairie TX 75050. 972/647-7800. **Fax:** 972/343-1301. **Contact:** Human Resources Manager. **World Wide Web address:** http://www.pratt-whitney.com.

Description: Repairs aircraft engine components, blades, vanes, and casings. **NOTE:** Entry-level positions and second and third shifts are offered. **Special programs:** Internships; Co-ops. **Parent company:** United Technologies Corporation. **Number of employees worldwide:** 30,000.

PRECISION AVIATION
5240 South Collins Street, Suite 100, Arlington TX 76018. 817/465-0908. **Contact:** Human Resources. **World Wide Web address:** http://www.bobflies.com. **Description:** An aircraft maintenance company that works primarily on small passenger planes.

SKYLINE INDUSTRIES, INC.
P.O. Box 821, Fort Worth TX 76101. 817/551-1967. **Contact:** Human Resources. **World Wide Web address:** http://www.skyline-usa.com. **Description:** A manufacturer of aircraft parts including armored pilot seats, floor armor, seat covers, ground handling equipment, and aerospace fasteners. **Corporate headquarters location:** This location.

UNISHIPPERS ASSOCIATION
800 West Airport Freeway, Suite 611, Lock Box 6065, Irving TX 75062. 972/445-0088. **Contact:** Personnel. **World Wide Web address:** http://www.unishippers.com. **Description:** An authorized reseller of airplanes for airfreight companies.

APPAREL, FASHION, AND TEXTILES

You can expect to find the following types of companies in this chapter:
Broadwoven Fabric Mills • Knitting Mills • Curtains and Draperies •
Footwear • Nonwoven Fabrics • Textile Goods and Finishing •
Yarn and Thread Mills

BORDER APPAREL INC.
1817 Myrtle Avenue, El Paso TX 79901. 915/542-4548. **Contact:** Hector Cervantes, Plant Manager. **World Wide Web address:** http:// www.blaundry.com. **Description:** Manufactures jeans. **Corporate headquarters location:** El Paso TX.

L.D. BRINKMAN/HOLLYTEX
1655 Waters Ridge Drive, Louisville TX 75057. 972/353-3500. **Contact:** Human Resources. **World Wide Web address:** http://www. ldbrinkman.com. **Description:** A wholesaler of carpet and related flooring products.

BROWNWOOD MANUFACTURING COMPANY
1600 Custer Road, Brownwood TX 76801-6496. 915/646-9505. **Contact:** Human Resources. **Description:** A manufacturer of military raincoats, Navy uniforms, and Cripple Creek brand jackets. **Corporate headquarters location:** This location.

HAGGAR CLOTHING COMPANY
6113 Lemmon Avenue, Dallas TX 75209. 214/956-4235. **Fax:** 214/ 956-4419. **Contact:** Human Resources. **World Wide Web address:** http://www.haggar.com. **Description:** A leading designer, manufacturer, importer, and marketer of men's dress and casual clothing. **Positions advertised include:** Associate Accountant; Programmer/Analyst; Senior Assistant Pattern Maker; Staff Accountant. **Corporate headquarters location:** This location. **Parent company:** Haggar Corporation. **Operations at this facility include:** Administration; Research and Development; Service. **Listed on:** NASDAQ. **Stock exchange symbol:** HGGR.

HATCO
601 Marion Drive, Garland TX 75042. 972/494-0511. **Contact:** Personnel Manager. **World Wide Web address:** http://www. resistolhat.com. **Description:** Manufactures a variety of men's weather-resistant hats and headgear. **Corporate headquarters location:** This location.

JUSTIN BOOT COMPANY

610 West Dagget Street, Fort Worth TX 76104. 817/332-4385. **Contact:** Personnel Director. **World Wide Web address:** http://www. justinboots.com. **Description:** Manufactures cowboy boots, leather belts, handbags, and billfolds. **Parent company:** Berkshire Hathaway.

TONY LAMA COMPANY

1137 Tony Lama Street, El Paso TX 79915. 915/778-8311. **Fax:** 915/778-5237. **Contact:** Human Resources. **World Wide Web address:** http://www.tonylama.com. **Description:** A manufacturer of men's and women's cowboy boots. **Corporate headquarters location:** Fort Worth TX. **Parent company:** Berkshire Hathaway.

LUCCHESE BOOT COMPANY

40 Walter Jones Boulevard, El Paso TX 79906. 915/778-3066. **Contact:** Hilda Matthews, Human Resources Manager. **World Wide Web address:** http://www.lucchese.com. **Description:** A manufacturer, retailer, and marketer of men's and women's cowboy boots.

PILLOWTEX CORPORATION

4111 Mint Way, Dallas TX 75237. 214/333-3225x114. **Fax:** 214/333-0512. **Contact:** Personnel Director. **E-mail address:** human_ resources@pillowtex.com. **World Wide Web address:** http://www. pillowtex.com. **Description:** A manufacturer of bed pillows, comforters, and mattress pads. **Note:** All human resources correspondences should be directed to One Lake Circle Drive, Kannapolis NC 28081. **Corporate headquarters location:** This location. **Other U.S. locations:** Monroe NC; Lando SC. **Operations at this facility include:** Administration.

PINDLER & PINDLER INC.

1617 Hi Line Drive, Suite 250, Dallas TX 75207. 214/939-9116. **Contact:** Human Resources. **World Wide Web address:** http://www. pindler.com. **Description:** Designs and distributes upholstery and drapery fabrics.

SAVANE INTERNATIONAL CORPORATION

P.O. Box 13800, 4171 North Mesa Building D, El Paso TX 79902. 915/496-7000. **Contact:** Human Resources. **World Wide Web address:** http://www.savane.com. **Description:** A manufacturer of men's wear. **Parent company:** Tropical Sportswear International Corporation. **Listed on:** NASDAQ. **Stock exchange symbol:** TSIC.

STITCHES INC.
1144 Vista De Oro Drive, El Paso TX 79935. 915/593-2990. **Contact:** Human Resources. **Description:** A textile sewing and cutting contractor. **Corporate headquarters location:** This location.

TANDY BRANDS ACCESSORIES
690 East Lamar Boulevard, Suite 200, Arlington TX 76011. 817/548-0090. **Contact:** Human Resources. **World Wide Web address:** http://www.tandybrands.com. **Description:** Designs, manufactures, and markets belts, ties, suspenders, and other leather products. **Listed on:** NASDAQ. **Stock exchange symbol:** TBAC.

WALLS INDUSTRIES, INC.
P.O. Box 98, Cleburne TX 76033. 817/645-4366. **Contact:** Human Resources. **World Wide Web address:** http://www.wallsoutdoors. com. **Description:** Manufactures outerwear for men, women, and children. **Corporate headquarters location:** This location.

WALLS INDUSTRIES, INC.
P.O. Box 196, Sweetwater TX 79556-0196. 915/235-5456. **Fax:** 915/235-8512. **Contact:** Personnel. **World Wide Web address:** http://www.wallsoutdoors.com. **Description:** Manufactures outerwear for men, women, and children. **Corporate headquarters location:** Cleburne TX.

WILLIAMSON-DICKIE MANUFACTURING COMPANY
P.O. Box 1779, Fort Worth TX 76101. 817/336-7201. **Contact:** Marett Cobb, Director of Human Resources. **World Wide Web address:** http://www.dickies.com. **Description:** Manufactures apparel for men and boys including casual slacks and work pants. **Positions advertised include:** Industrial Engineer; Quality Assurance Manager. **Corporate headquarters location:** This location.

HOWARD B. WOLF INC.
3710 Rawlins, Suite 970, Dallas TX 75219. 214/252-0124. **Fax:** 214/219-7410. **Contact:** Human Resources. **Description:** An apparel company specializing in the manufacture of women's fashions. **Operations at this facility include:** Administration; Manufacturing; Research and Development; Sales.

ARCHITECTURE, CONSTRUCTION, AND ENGINEERING

You can expect to find the following types of companies in this chapter:
Architectural and Engineering Services • Civil and Mechanical Engineering Firms • Construction Products, Manufacturers, and Wholesalers • General Contractors/ Specialized Trade Contractors

APAC TEXAS, INC.
P.O. Box 224048, Dallas TX 75222-4048. 214/741-3531. **Fax:** 214/742-3540. **Contact:** Human Resources. **World Wide Web address:** http://www.apac.com. **Description:** A general contracting company specializing in concrete and asphalt paving work. **Other U.S. locations:** Beaumont TX.

AUSTIN COMMERCIAL INC.
P.O. Box 2879, Dallas TX 75221. 214/443-5700. **Contact:** Human Resources Department. **E-mail address:** jbox@austin-ind.com. **World Wide Web address:** http://www.austin-ind.com. **Description:** A commercial construction company providing general contracting, construction management, and preconstruction services including cost estimating and scheduling. **Positions advertised include:** Administrative Assistant; Project Manager; Project Engineer; Project Accountant; Maintenance Reliability Engineer. **Parent company:** Austin Industries.

BUELL DOOR COMPANY
5200 East Grand Avenue, Dallas TX 75223. 214/827-9260. **Toll-free phone:** 800/556-0155. **Fax:** 214/826-9163. **Contact:** Human Resources. **World Wide Web address:** http://www.buelldoor.com. **Description:** A manufacturer of architectural doors and hardware.

CAVALIER HOMES, INC.
P.O. Box 5003, Wichita Falls TX 76307. 940/723-5523. **Physical address:** 719 Scott Street, Suite 600, Wichita Falls TX 76301. **Contact:** Human Resources. **World Wide Web address:** http://www.cavhomesinc.com. **Description:** Overall, Cavalier Homes, Inc. designs and manufactures a wide range of homes and markets them through approximately 500 independent dealers nationwide. **Corporate headquarters location:** Addison AL. **Operations at this facility include:** This location houses administrative offices. **Subsidiaries include:** Cavalier Acceptance Corporation provides installment sale financing to qualifying retail customers of these

exclusive dealers. **Listed on:** New York Stock Exchange. **Stock Exchange symbol:** CAV.

CENTEX CONSTRUCTION COMPANY, INC.
3100 McKinnon, 7th Floor, Dallas TX 75201. 214/468-4700. **Contact:** Human Resources. **E-mail address:** human.resources@ checmail.com. **World Wide Web address:** http://www.centex-construction.com. **Description:** A commercial general contractor that provides preconstruction, construction, management, and general contracting services. **Positions advertised include:** Branch Support Specialist; Loan Officer. **Corporate headquarters location:** This location. **Other U.S. locations:** Fairfax VA. **Subsidiaries include:** Centex Landis (New Orleans LA). **Parent company:** Centex Corporation. **Listed on:** New York Stock Exchange. **Stock exchange symbol:** CTX.

ELCOR CORPORATION
14643 Dallas Parkway, Suite 1000, Dallas TX 75254. 972/851-0500. **Contact:** Human Resources. **World Wide Web address:** http://www.elcor.com. **Description:** Manufactures roofing products including fiberglass asphalt shingles. **Corporate headquarters location:** This location. **Subsidiaries include:** Elk Corporation of Texas. **Listed on:** New York Stock Exchange. **Stock exchange symbol:** ELK.

FM GLOBAL
5800 Granite Parkway, Suite 600, Plano TX 75024. 972/377-4808. **Fax:** 972/731-1800. **Contact:** Human Resources. **World Wide Web address:** http://www.fmglobal.com. **Description:** A loss control services organization. FM Global helps owner company policyholders to protect their properties and occupancies from damage caused by fire, wind, flood, and explosion; boiler, pressure vessel, and machinery accidents; and many other insured hazards. **Corporate headquarters location:** Johnston RI. **Other U.S. locations:** Nationwide. **International locations:** Worldwide.

GAF MATERIALS CORPORATION
2600 Singleton Boulevard, Dallas TX 75212. 214/637-1060. **Contact:** Human Resources. **World Wide Web address:** http://www.gaf.com. **Description:** A multiproduct manufacturer with sales in both consumer and industrial markets. The company's product line includes building, roofing, and insulation materials for the construction trades; specialty chemicals and plastics; and reprographic products. **Corporate headquarters location:** Wayne NJ.

Other U.S. locations: Nationwide. **Operations at this facility include:** Manufacturing; Sales. **Listed on:** Privately held.

GENERAL ALUMINUM CORPORATION

P.O. Box 819022, Dallas TX 75381. 972/242-5271. **Contact:** Human Resources. **Description:** Manufactures aluminum doors and windows, partition screens, sliding glass doors, and related products.

HDR, INC.

1711 Preston Road, Suite 300, Dallas TX 75248. 972/960-4000. **Fax:** 972/960-4185. **Contact:** Human Resources. **World Wide Web address:** http://www.hdrinc.com. **Description:** Offers architectural and engineering design services, in addition to construction consulting and interior design services. The company's three main business sectors are health care, justice, and science and industry. Founded in 1917. **Corporate headquarters location:** Omaha NE. **Other U.S. locations:** Alexandria VA. **Operations at this facility include:** Administration; Marketing; Regional Headquarters; Service. **Listed on:** Privately held.

HNTB CORPORATION

5910 West Plano Parkway, Suite 200, Plano TX 75093. 972/661-5626. **Fax:** 972/661-5614. **Contact:** Human Resources. **World Wide Web address:** http://www.hntb.com. **Description:** Offers architectural, engineering, and planning services to public agencies and private industry. **NOTE:** Entry-level positions are offered. Interested jobseekers should check the company's employment page on the World Wide Web and fax a resume. **Positions advertised include:** Senior Public Involvement Representative; Graphic Design Supervisor; Intelligent Transportation Systems Specialist. **Special programs:** Training. **Corporate headquarters location:** Kansas City MO. **Other U.S. locations:** Nationwide. **Subsidiaries include:** Alcyone Group, Inc.; Infrastructure Management Group; Thomas K. Dyer, Inc. **Operations at this facility include:** Sales. **Listed on:** Privately held.

D.R. HORTON, INC.

1901 Ascension Boulevard, Suite 210, Arlington TX 76006. 817/856-8200. **Fax:** 817/856-8238. **Contact:** Human Resources Department. **World Wide Web address:** http://www.drhorton.com. **Description:** D.R. Horton, Inc. and its operating subsidiaries are engaged primarily in the construction and sale of single-family homes designed principally for the entry-level and move-up market segments. **Positions advertised include:** Internal Auditor. **Listed on:** New York Stock Exchange. **Stock exchange symbol:** DHI. **Number of employees nationwide:** 4,300.

HOWE-BAKER ENGINEERS, INC.
P.O. Box 956, Tyler TX 75710. 903/597-0311. **Physical address:** 3102 East Fifth Street, Tyler TX 75701. **Contact:** Human Resources. **World Wide Web address:** http://www.howebaker.com. **Description:** Provides mechanical, civil, and electrical engineering services. **Positions advertised include:** Process Engineer; Project Engineer; Mechanical Engineer; Civil Engineer; Electrical Engineer.

LAUREN ENGINEERS & CONSTRUCTORS
P.O. Box 1761, Abilene TX 79604. 915/670-9660. **Contact:** Human Resources. **World Wide Web address:** http://www.laurenec.com. **Description:** Designs and builds power plants, refineries, and related large-scale projects. **Corporate headquarters location:** This location.

LENNOX INTERNATIONAL, INC.
P.O. Box 799900, Dallas TX 75379-9900. 972/497-5000. **Physical address:** 2140 Lake Park Boulevard, Richardson TX 75080. **Fax:** 972/497-5476. **Contact:** Human Resources. **World Wide Web address:** http://www.lennoxinternational.com. **Description:** Manufactures heating and air conditioning equipment. **Special programs:** Internships. **Corporate headquarters location:** This location. **Subsidiaries include:** Armstrong Air Conditioning Inc.; Heatcraft Inc.; Lennox Global Ltd.; Lennox Industries, Inc. **Operations at this facility include:** Administration. **Listed on:** New York Stock Exchange. **Stock exchange symbol:** LII. **Number of employees worldwide:** 21,000.

MORGAN
P.O. Box 660280, Dallas TX 75266-0280. 972/840-1200. **Physical address:** 2800 McCree Road, Garland TX 75041. **Fax:** 972/864-7316. **Contact:** Leslie McLoed, Personnel Coordinator. **E-mail address:** employ@morganusa.com. **World Wide Web address:** http://www.morganusa.com. **Description:** Manufactures, transports, and retails relocatable buildings, spas, recreational vehicles, swimming pools, and decks to consumers, businesses, government buyers, and institutional buyers. **Corporate headquarters location:** This location. **Other U.S. locations:** AL; AR; CO; GA; LA; MO; MS; NM; OK; TN. **Operations at this facility include:** Administration. **Listed on:** Privately held.

MORRISON SUPPLY COMPANY

311 East Vickery Boulevard, Fort Worth TX 76104. 817/336-0451. **Contact:** Charles Allen, Personnel Manager. **World Wide Web address:** http://www.morsco.com. **Description:** A wholesaler of plumbing and heating equipment, tools, and supplies. **Corporate headquarters location:** This location.

O'HAIR SHUTTERS

P.O. Box 2764, Lubbock TX 79408. 806/765-5791. **Contact:** Hiring Manager. **World Wide Web address:** http://www.ohair.com. **Description:** Manufactures outdoor shutters for homes. **Corporate headquarters location:** This location.

OVERHEAD DOOR CORPORATION

1900 Crown Drive, Farmer's Branch TX 75234. 972/233-6611. **Contact:** Human Resources. **World Wide Web address:** http://www. overheaddoor.com. **Description:** Manufactures aluminum, steel, fiberglass, and wooden overhead doors, rolling steel fire doors, grilles, and metal insulated entrance doors. Products are distributed through a network of more than 400 authorized distributors in the United States and Canada. The company also manufactures truck and trailer doors. **Corporate headquarters location:** This location. **Other area locations:** Carrollton TX; Corpus Christi TX; Fort Worth TX; Houston TX; Mount Pleasant TX; Richardson TX. **Parent company:** Sanwa Shutter Corporation.

QUALITY CABINETS

515 Big Stone Gap Road, Duncanville TX 75137. 972/298-6101. **Contact:** Human Resources. **World Wide Web address:** http://www. qualitycabinets.com. **Description:** Manufactures cabinets. **Corporate headquarters location:** This location. **Parent company:** Texwood Industries.

TD INDUSTRIES, INC.

P.O. Box 819060, Dallas TX 75381-9060. 972/888-9505. **Physical address:** 13850 Diplomat Drive, Dallas TX 75234. **Fax:** 972/888-9507. **Contact:** Human Resources. **E-mail address:** tddallasjobs@tdindustries.com. **World Wide Web address:** http://www.tdindustries.com. **Description:** A national construction and service company that designs, installs, and repairs HVAC, plumbing, high-purity process piping, and energy management systems in commercial and industrial markets. Founded in 1946. **NOTE:** Entry-level positions are offered. **Positions advertised include:** HVAC

Technician; Evening Dispatcher; Fire and Life Safety Technician; Building Technician. **Corporate headquarters location:** This location. **Other U.S. locations:** Houston TX; San Antonio TX. **Listed on:** Privately held.

THE VISTAWALL GROUP

P.O. Box 629, 803 Airport Road, Terrell TX 75160. 972/551-6100. **Fax:** 972/551-6210. **Contact:** Human Resources. **E-mail address:** careers@vistawall.com. **World Wide Web address:** http://www. vistawall.com. **Description:** The Vistawall Group, through its subsidiaries, designs, manufactures, and distributes entrances, storefront and low-rise framing systems, skylight systems, and engineered curtain wall systems. **Positions advertised include:** Sales Representative; Engineered Products Manager. **Corporate headquarters location:** This location. **Subsidiaries include:** Moduline Window Systems; Naturalite Skylight Systems; Skywall Translucent Systems; Vistawall Architectural Products. **Parent company:** Butler Manufacturing Company.

WASHINGTON GROUP INTERNATIONAL

5220 Spring Valley Road, Suite 204, Dallas TX 75254. 972/385-1635. **Contact:** Personnel Director. **World Wide Web address:** http://www.wgint.com. **Description:** Provides a variety of technical construction services including design, engineering, and consulting with a customer base consisting mainly of petroleum refining, petrochemical, and chemical plants. **Positions advertised include:** Accountant.

H.B. ZACHRY COMPANY

P.O. Box 531558, Grand Prairie TX 75053-1558. 972/262-8898. **Contact:** Human Resources. **World Wide Web address:** http://www. zachry.com. **Description:** H.B. Zachry is an industrial construction management company operating through the following divisions: Process; Power; Heavy; Maintenance & Service; Commercial; International; and Pipeline. The company builds power plants, highways, and pipelines in the southern United States, as well as in foreign countries. H.B. Zachry Company does not handle residential construction contracts. Founded in 1923. **Corporate headquarters location:** San Antonio TX. **Operations at this facility include:** This location is a district field office. **Listed on:** Privately held.

H.B. ZACHRY COMPANY

P.O. Box 7309, Longview TX 75607-7309. 903/947-3243. **Fax:** 903/947-2695. **Contact:** Human Resources. **World Wide Web address:** http://www.zachry.com. **Description:** An industrial construction management company operating through the following divisions: Process; Power; Heavy; Maintenance & Service; Commercial; International; and Pipeline. The company builds power plants, highways, and pipelines in the southern United States, as well as in foreign countries. H.B. Zachry Company does not handle residential construction contracts. Founded in 1923. **Corporate headquarters location:** San Antonio TX. **Listed on:** Privately held.

ARTS, ENTERTAINMENT, SPORTS, AND RECREATION

You can expect to find the following types of companies in this chapter:
Botanical and Zoological Gardens • Entertainment Groups • Motion Picture and Video Tape Production and Distribution • Museums and Art Galleries • Physical Fitness Facilities • Professional Sports Clubs • Public Golf Courses • Racing and Track Operations • Sporting and Recreational Camps • Theatrical Producers

24HOUR FITNESS
4600 West Park Boulevard, Plano TX 75075. 972/612-6960. **Contact:** Manager. **World Wide Web address:** http://www.24hourfitness.com. **Description:** A sports and fitness facility.

ALLIED VAUGHN
6305 North O'Connor Road, Suite 111, Building 4, Irving TX 75039. 972/869-0100. **Fax:** 972/869-2117. **Contact:** Human Resources. **World Wide Web address:** http://www.allied-digital.com. **Description:** One of the nation's leading independent multimedia manufacturing companies, offering CD-audio and CD-ROM mastering and replication; videocassette and audiocassette duplication; laser video disc recording; off-line and online video editing; motion picture film processing; film-to-tape and tape-to-film transfers; and complete finishing, packaging, warehousing, and fulfillment services. **Listed on:** Privately held.

DALLAS COWBOYS
One Cowboys Parkway, Irving TX 75063. 972/556-9900. **Contact:** Human Resources. **Description:** Administrative offices for the National Football League team. **Corporate headquarters location:** This location.

DALLAS MUSEUM OF ART
1717 North Harwood Street, Dallas TX 75201. 214/922-1215. **Contact:** Scott Gensemer, Director of Personnel. **World Wide Web address:** http://www.dm-art.org. **Description:** Offers a wide range of exhibits in all art media. **NOTE:** All candidates for open positions should have Master's or Ph.D. degrees. **Positions advertised include:** Curator of American Art; Museum Store General Manager; Senior Curator; Production Artist.

DALLAS MUSEUM OF NATURAL HISTORY

P.O. Box 150349, Dallas TX 75315-0349. 214/421-3466. **Contact:** Human Resources. **E-mail address:** employment@dmnhnet.org. **World Wide Web address:** http://www.dallasdino.org. **Description:** Operates a natural history museum offering a full range of exhibits and presentations. **Positions advertised include:** Accounting Manager; Volunteer Coordinator; Marketing Assistant.

EL PASO ASSOCIATION FOR THE PERFORMING ARTS

P.O. Box 31340, El Paso TX 79931. 915/565-6900. **Contact:** Human Resources. **World Wide Web address:** http://www.viva-ep.org. **Description:** Hosts various Shakespeare productions in conjunction with the McKelligon Canyon Amphitheater (also at this location).

NESTFAMILY.COM, INC.

1461 South Beltline Road, Suite 500, Coppell TX 75019. 972/402-7100. **Contact:** Human Resources. **World Wide Web address:** http://www.nestfamily.com. **Description:** Develops educational games, CD-ROMs, music, and videotapes for children. Founded in 1988.

PRIMEDIA WORKPLACE LEARNING

4101 International Parkway, Carrollton TX 75007. 972/309-4000. **Fax:** 972/309-4986. **Contact:** Human Resources. **E-mail address:** jobs@pwpl.com. **World Wide Web address:** http://www.pwpl.com. **Description:** Produces and distributes educational videos to academic, corporate, and industrial clients.

TEXAS STADIUM

2401 East Airport Freeway, Irving TX 75062. 972/438-7676. **Contact:** Human Resources Department. **Description:** A sporting arena. Texas Stadium is the home field of the Dallas Cowboys professional football team.

WESTERN PLAYLAND INC.

6900 Delta Drive, El Paso TX 79905. 915/772-3953. **Contact:** Human Resources. **World Wide Web address:** http://www.western playland.com. **Description:** An amusement park.

AUTOMOTIVE

You can expect to find the following types of companies in this chapter:
Automotive Repair Shops • Automotive Stampings • Industrial Vehicles and Moving Equipment • Motor Vehicles and Equipment • Travel Trailers and Campers

DAIMLERCHRYSLER CORPORATION
P.O. Box 110370, Carrollton TX 75011. 972/418-4600. **Contact:** Human Resources. **World Wide Web address:** http://www1. daimlerchrysler.com. **Description:** Manufactures cars, trucks, minivans, and sport-utility vehicles for customers in more than 100 countries. **Listed on:** New York Stock Exchange. **Stock exchange symbol:** DCX.

HILITE INDUSTRIES, INC.
1671 South Broadway, Carrollton TX 75006. 972/242-2116. **Contact:** Human Resources. **World Wide Web address:** http://www. hilite-ind.com. **Description:** Designs, manufactures, and sells automotive components including brake proportioning valves, electromagnetic clutches and machined components, springs, stampings, and assemblies.

PETERBILT MOTORS COMPANY
P.O. Box 550, Denton TX 76202. 940/566-7100. **Contact:** Human Resources Manager. **World Wide Web address:** http://www. peterbilt.com. **Description:** Designs and markets custom heavy-duty trucks. Founded in 1939. **Positions advertised include:** Mechanical Design Engineer. **Operations at this facility include:** Divisional Headquarters.

SCS/FRIGETTE CORPORATION
P.O. Box 40550, Fort Worth TX 76140. 817/293-5313. **Contact:** Human Resources. **World Wide Web address:** http://www. scsfrigette.com. **Description:** A manufacturer of automobile air conditioning and heating systems, cruise controls, security systems, and accessories. **Corporate headquarters location:** This location. **Operations at this facility include:** Administration; Manufacturing; Research and Development; Sales; Service. **Listed on:** Privately held.

BANKING/SAVINGS AND LOANS

You can expect to find the following types of companies in this chapter:
Banks • Bank Holding Companies and Associations •
Lending Firms/Financial Services Institutions

AMARILLO NATIONAL BANK

P.O. Box 1, Amarillo TX 79105. 806/378-8000. **Fax:** 806/378-8066. **Contact:** Human Resources. **World Wide Web address:** http://www. anb.com. **Description:** A full-service bank with 12 locations. Services include intra-bank funds transfers, mortgages, and online banking.

BANK OF AMERICA

303 West Wall Street, Midland TX 79701. 915/685-2000. **Contact:** Human Resources. **World Wide Web address:** http://www. bankofamerica.com. **Description:** Bank of America is a full-service banking and financial institution. The company operates through four business segments: Global Corporate and Investment Banking, Principal Investing and Asset Management, Commercial Banking, and Consumer Banking. **Corporate headquarters location:** Charlotte NC. **Operations at this facility include:** This location is a bank. **Listed on:** New York Stock Exchange. **Stock exchange symbol:** BAC.

BANK ONE TEXAS

500 Throckmorton Street, Fort Worth TX 76102. 817/884-4000. **Contact:** Human Resources. **World Wide Web address:** http:// www.bankone.com. **Description:** A full-service, commercial bank. **Positions advertise include:** Banking Center Manager. **Corporate headquarters location:** Chicago IL. **Other U.S. locations:** Nationwide. **Parent company:** Bank One Corporation. **Listed on:** New York Stock Exchange **Stock exchange symbol:** BAC.

CHASE BANK OF TEXAS

2200 Ross Avenue, Suite 720, Dallas TX 75201. 214/965-2925. **Contact:** Human Resources. **World Wide Web address:** http:// www.chase.com. **Description:** Operates through a network of 40 member banks in Texas. Operations include energy, commercial, real estate, and international banking. **Corporate headquarters location:** Houston TX. **Other U.S. locations:** Denver CO; New York NY. **International locations:** Worldwide.

FIRST NATIONAL BANK OF ABILENE
P.O. Box 701, Abilene TX 79604. 915/627-7000. **Contact:** Pam Mann, Director of Human Resources. **World Wide Web address:** http://www.fnbabilene.com. **Description:** A full-service bank that offers online banking, loan, and investment services. **Positions advertised include:** Item Processing Specialist; Bookkeeper; Mortgage Loan Officer.

U.S. FEDERAL RESERVE BANK OF DALLAS
P.O. Box 655906, Dallas TX 75265-5906. 214/922-6000. **Physical address:** 2200 North Pearl Street, Dallas TX 75201. **Recorded jobline:** 214/922-6166. **Contact:** Employment. **World Wide Web address:** http://www.dallasfed.org. **Description:** One of 12 regional Federal Reserve banks that, along with the Federal Reserve Board of Governors in Washington DC and the Federal Open Market Committee, comprise the Federal Reserve System. As the nation's central bank, the Federal Reserve is charged with three major responsibilities: monetary policy, banking supervision and regulation, and processing payments. **Special programs:** Internships. **Other U.S. locations:** Nationwide.

WELLS FARGO BANK
P.O. Box 1241, Lubbock TX 79408-1241. 806/765-8861. **Contact:** Human Resources. **World Wide Web address:** http://www. wellsfargo.com. **Description:** A diversified financial institution with over $234 billion in assets. Wells Fargo serves over 17 million customers through 5,300 independent locations worldwide. The company also maintains several stand-alone ATMs and branches within other retail outlets. Services include community banking, credit and debit cards, home equity and mortgage loans, online banking, student loans, and insurance. Wells Fargo also offers a complete line of commercial and institutional financial services. Founded in 1852. **Positions advertised include:** Banker; Teller. **NOTE:** Jobseekers are encouraged to submit resumes via the Website: http://www.wfjobs.com. **Corporate headquarters location:** San Francisco CA. **Other U.S. locations:** Nationwide. **International locations:** Worldwide. **Listed on:** New York Stock Exchange. **Stock exchange symbol:** WFC. **Number of employees worldwide:** 123,000.

WELLS FARGO BANK
P.O. Box 1891, San Angelo TX 76902. 915/657-8600. **Contact:** Human Resources. **World Wide Web address:** http://www.

wellsfargo.com. **Description:** A diversified financial institution with over $234 billion in assets. Wells Fargo serves over 17 million customers through 5,300 independent locations worldwide. The company also maintains several stand-alone ATMs and branches within other retail outlets. Services include community banking, credit and debit cards, home equity and mortgage loans, online banking, student loans, and insurance. Wells Fargo also offers a complete line of commercial and institutional financial services. Founded in 1852. **Positions advertised include:** Banker; Teller. **NOTE:** Jobseekers are encouraged to submit resumes via the Website: http://www.wfjobs.com. **Corporate headquarters location:** San Francisco CA. **Other U.S. locations:** Nationwide. **International locations:** Worldwide. **Listed on:** New York Stock Exchange. **Stock exchange symbol:** WFC. **Number of employees worldwide:** 123,000.

BIOTECHNOLOGY, PHARMACEUTICALS, AND SCIENTIFIC R&D

You can expect to find the following types of companies in this chapter:
Clinical Labs • Lab Equipment Manufacturers
Pharmaceutical Manufacturers and Distributors

ABBOTT DIAGNOSTICS
1921 Hurd Street, Irving TX 75038. 972/518-6000. **Contact:** Human Resources. **World Wide Web address:** http://www.abbott.com. **Description:** Designs, develops, and manufactures automated laboratory instruments, primarily used in the fields of clinical chemistry, microbiology, and therapeutic drug monitoring. **Positions advertised include:** Pharmaceuticals Sales Representative; District Secretary; Account Manager; Project Manager. **Corporate headquarters location:** Abbott Park IL. **Parent company:** Abbott Laboratories is an international manufacturer of a wide range of health care products including pharmaceuticals, hospital products, diagnostic products, chemical products, and nutritional products. **Listed on:** New York Stock Exchange. **Stock exchange symbol:** ABT.

ALLERGAN, INC.
P.O. Box 2675, Waco TX 76702-2675. 254/666-3331. **Contact:** Human Resources. **World Wide Web address:** http://www.allergan. com. **Description:** Develops, manufactures, and distributes prescription and nonprescription pharmaceutical products in the specialty fields of ophthalmology and dermatology.

ALLIANCE CLINICAL LABORATORIES
4747 Irving Boulevard, Suite 245, Dallas TX 75247. 214/630-5227. **Contact:** Human Resources. **Description:** A full-service medical laboratory that provides comprehensive clinical laboratory services, such as tests and blood work, for long-term care facilities and for people in home health care. **Parent company:** Horizon/CMS Healthcare Corporation acquires and operates long-term care facilities throughout the United States; provides health care services, such as nursing care, rehabilitation, and other therapies; provides institutional pharmacy services; provides specialty care to Alzheimer's patients; and offers subacute care.

CARRINGTON LABORATORIES
2001 Walnut Hill Lane, Irving TX 75038. 972/518-1300. **Contact:** Human Resources. **World Wide Web address:** http://www.

carringtonlabs.com. **Description:** Develops, manufactures, and markets a number of wound care products, pharmaceutical products, and veterinary products, all of which are based on complex carbohydrates derived from aloe vera. Products include Carrasyn Hydrogel Wound Dressing; CarraSorb H Calcium Alginate Wound Dressing; CarraFilm Transparent Film Dressing; CarraSorb M Freeze-Dried Gel; DiaB, a line of wound care products for diabetics; and RadiaCare, a line of products to treat radiation dermatitis. **Corporate headquarters location:** This location. **Subsidiaries include:** Caraloe, Inc. manufactures and markets nutritional aloe drinks.

LABORATORY CORPORATION OF AMERICA (LABCORP)

7777 Forest Lane, Building C, Suite 350, Dallas TX 75230. 972/566-3353. **Toll-free phone:** 800/788-9892. **Fax:** 972/991-0381. **Recorded jobline:** 800/645-5680. **Contact:** Human Resources. **E-mail address:** employment@labcorp.com. **World Wide Web address:** http://www.labcorp.com. **Description:** One of the nation's leading clinical laboratory companies, providing services primarily to physicians, hospitals, clinics, nursing homes, and other clinical labs nationwide. LabCorp performs tests on blood, urine, and other body fluids and tissue, aiding the diagnosis of disease. **Positions advertised include:** Phlebotomist. **Corporate headquarters location:** Burlington NC. **Other U.S. locations:** Nationwide. **Listed on:** New York Stock Exchange. **Stock exchange symbol:** LH. **Number of employees nationwide:** 19,600.

PHARMERICA

4171 North Mesa, Suite 210A, El Paso TX 79902. 915/545-1955. **Contact:** Human Resources. **World Wide Web address:** http://www.pharmerica.com. **Description:** A supplier of pharmaceuticals and related products to long-term care facilities, hospitals, and assisted living communities. PharMerica also provides nurse consultant services, infusion therapy and training, medical records consulting, and educational programs. **Corporate headquarters location:** Tampa FL.

QUEST DIAGNOSTICS INCORPORATED

3450 West Wheatland Road, Suite 206, Dallas TX 75237-3471. 972/298-0799. **Contact:** Personnel. **World Wide Web address:** http://www.questdiagnostics.com. **Description:** One of the largest clinical laboratories in North America, providing a broad range of clinical laboratory services to health care clients that include physicians, hospitals, clinics, dialysis centers, pharmaceutical companies, and corporations. The company offers and performs tests on blood, urine, and other bodily fluids and tissues to provide information on health and well-being. **Listed on:** New York Stock Exchange. **Stock exchange symbol:** DGX.

TEXAS VETERINARY MEDICAL DIAGNOSTIC LABORATORY
P.O. Box 3200, Amarillo TX 79116-3200. 806/353-7478. **Physical address:** 6610 Amarillo Boulevard West, Amarillo TX 79106. **Toll-free phone:** 888/646-5624. **Fax:** 806/359-0636. **Contact:** Human Resources. **World Wide Web address:** http://wwwtvmdl.tamu.edu. **Description:** A diagnostic laboratory that performs medical testing on animals to assist veterinarians with diagnosis and prognosis. Test fields include chemistry, hematology, urology, toxicology, serology, histology, bacteriology, and necropsies. **Office hours:** Monday - Friday, 8:00 a.m. - 5:00 p.m.; Saturday, 8:00 a.m. - 12:00 p.m. **Other U.S. locations:** College Station TX.

VERTEX RSI
A TRIPOINT GLOBAL COMPANY
2600 North Longview Street, Kilgore TX 75662. 903/984-0555. **Fax:** 903/984-7769. **Contact:** Melissa Harris, Manager of Personnel. **World Wide Web address:** http://www.tripointglobal.com. **Description:** Designs and manufactures satellite Earth station antennas that use domestic, international, and military radio frequencies. The company also offers a complete line of standard antenna products. **NOTE:** Entry-level positions are offered. **Operations at this facility include:** Administration; Manufacturing; Research and Development; Sales; Service.

BUSINESS SERVICES AND NON-SCIENTIFIC RESEARCH

You can expect to find the following types of companies in this chapter:
Adjustment and Collection Services • Cleaning, Maintenance, and Pest Control Services • Credit Reporting • Detective, Guard, and Armored Car Services • Miscellaneous Equipment Rental and Leasing • Secretarial and Court Reporting Services

ACS, INC.

2828 North Haskell, Dallas TX 75204. 214/841-6111. **Contact:** Human Resources. **World Wide Web address:** http://www.acs-inc.com. **Description:** A full-service provider of data processing services, computer outsourcing, facilities management, electronic transaction processing, and telecommunications services. The firm owns several data centers across the United States and a telecommunications network that encompasses leading-edge technologies. The company uses many different computer platforms including IBM, Amdahl, Hewlett-Packard, Tandem, and UNIX-based systems. **Positions advertised include:** Call Center Representative; Project Manager; Prepper; Staff Accountant; Senior Recovery Services Analyst; Financial Analyst; Media Operator; Vendor Maintenance Administrator; International Benefits Analyst; Worker's Compensation Specialist; Inserter Operator.

ACE AMERICA'S CASH EXPRESS INC.

1231 Greenway Drive, Suite 800, Irving TX 75038. 972/550-5000. **Fax:** 972/582-1410. **Contact:** Personnel. **World Wide Web address:** http://www.acecashexpress.com. **Description:** One of the largest check cashing companies in the United States, offering check cashing services for government and payroll checks. **Other U.S. locations:** Nationwide. **Listed on:** NASDAQ. **Stock exchange symbol:** AACE.

AUTOMATIC DATA PROCESSING (ADP)

2735 North Stemmons Freeway, Dallas TX 75207. 214/630-9311. **Toll-free phone:** 800/829-2237. **Fax:** 214/905-2828. **Contact:** Eric Gierschick, Director of Human Resources. **World Wide Web address:** http://www.adp.com. **Description:** Provides computerized transaction processing, record keeping, data communications, and information services. ADP helps more than 500,000 clients improve their business performance by providing services such as payroll, payroll tax, and human resource information management;

brokerage industry market data, back office, and proxy services; industry-specific services to auto and truck dealers; and computerized auto repair and replacement estimating for auto insurance companies and body repair shops. The company's four largest businesses are Employer Services, Brokerage Services, Dealer Services, and Claims Services. **Positions advertised include:** Major Accounts Sales Representative; Sandy Trainer; Implementation Manager; Client Technical Analyst; Software Engineer; Associate Computer Operator; Account Executive; Call Center Operator. **Other U.S. locations:** Nationwide. **Listed on:** New York Stock Exchange. **Stock exchange symbol:** ADP.

BMS ENTERPRISES INC.
308 Arthur Street, Fort Worth TX 76107. 817/810-9200. **Contact:** Human Resources. **Description:** A high-tech restoration and cleaning firm with affiliate companies involved in providing environmental services. BMS Enterprises Inc. has specific technical expertise with electronics and wet document recovery. The company provides disaster restoration services following fire and water catastrophes. BMS Enterprises Inc. is also involved in providing HVAC services to improve indoor air quality. **Corporate headquarters location:** This location. **Operations at this facility include:** Administration; Research and Development; Sales; Service. **Listed on:** Privately held.

THE DWYER GROUP
P.O. Box 3146, 1010 North University Parks Drive, Waco TX 76707. 254/745-2444. **Contact:** Human Resources. **World Wide Web address:** http://www.dwyergroup.com. **Description:** An international provider of specialty services through a group of service-based franchisers. **Subsidiaries include:** Rainbow International Carpet Dyeing & Cleaning Company has more than 480 franchises in the United States, 30 franchises in Canada, and more than 120 franchise operations in 16 other foreign countries. Rainbow specializes in indoor restoration and cleaning services including upholstery and drapery cleaning, carpet dyeing and cleaning, ceiling cleaning, deodorization, and comprehensive fire and water damage restoration and cleanup. Mr. Rooter Corporation is a complete residential and commercial plumbing service company, with a total of 240 franchises in the United States and five foreign countries. General Business Services, Inc. (GBS) and E.K. Williams & Company provide small business owners with business counseling, tax planning, tax research, tax return preparation, record-keeping systems, computer services, and financial management

planning. GBS has a total of 320 franchises in the United States and Canada. E.K. Williams has more than 185 franchises located throughout the United States. Aire Serv Heating & Air Conditioning, Inc. is a franchiser of heating, ventilation, and air conditioning maintenance and repair services. The primary client base for its franchisees includes residential and light commercial applications. Aire Serv has nearly 40 U.S. franchises. Mr. Electric, an electrical contracting service franchise has one U.S. franchise. **Listed on:** NASDAQ. **Stock exchange symbol:** DWYR.

NATIONAL LINEN SERVICE
620 Yorktown Road, Dallas TX 75208. 214/741-1751. **Contact:** Human Resources Manager. **World Wide Web address:** http://www. national-linen.com. **Description:** A service that launders and delivers various kinds of linens including tablecloths and napkins to hotels and restaurants.

PINKERTON SECURITY & INVESTIGATION SERVICES
4150 International Plaza, Suite 100, Fort Worth TX 76109. 817/731-7590. **Contact:** Human Resources. **World Wide Web address:** http:// www.pinkertons.com. **Description:** Offers a full range of specialized protective services including premier property and high-rise services, health care and hospital services, special event services, ATM services, and patrol services. The company serves thousands of companies worldwide with investigation, threat assessment, and executive protection services. **Corporate headquarters location:** Westlake Village CA. **Operations at this facility include:** This location is engaged in industrial and private security, investigation, and security consulting. **Parent company:** Securitas.

PINKERTON SECURITY & INVESTIGATION SERVICES
1155 Westmoreland, Suite 201, El Paso TX 79925. 915/772-7030. **Contact:** Human Resources. **World Wide Web address:** http://www. pinkertons.com. **Description:** Offers a full range of specialized protective services including premier property and high-rise services, health care and hospital services, special event services, ATM services, and patrol services. The company serves thousands of companies worldwide with investigation, threat assessment, and executive protection services. **Corporate headquarters location:** Westlake Village CA. **Parent company:** Securitas.

PINKERTON SECURITY & INVESTIGATION SERVICES
9441 LBJ Freeway, Suite 25, Dallas TX 75243. 972/238-5994.
Contact: Human Resources. **World Wide Web address:** http://www.
pinkertons.com. **Description:** Offers a full range of specialized
protective services including premier property and high-rise services,
health care and hospital services, special event services, ATM
services, and patrol services. The company serves thousands of
companies worldwide with investigation, threat assessment, and
executive protection services. **Corporate headquarters location:**
Westlake Village CA. **Operations at this facility include:** This
location is engaged in industrial and private security, investigation,
and security consulting. **Parent company:** Securitas.

QUANTUM RESEARCH INTERNATIONAL
7505B Lockheed Drive, El Paso TX 79925. 915/772-2700. **Contact:**
Personnel Manager. **World Wide Web address:** http://www.
quantum-intl.com. **Description:** Engaged in weapons research and
general engineering for the army. **Corporate headquarters location:**
Huntsville AL.

RIA
2395 Midway Road, Carrollton TX 75006. 972/250-7000. **Fax:**
972/250-7763. **Contact:** Personnel Manager. **World Wide Web
address:** http://www.riahome.com. **Description:** One of the world's
largest providers of solutions for tax research, compliance, and
information. **Parent company:** Thomson Tax and Accounting.

WARRANTECH CORPORATION
150 Westpark Way, Suite 200, Euless TX 76040. 817/283-7267.
Contact: Human Resources. **World Wide Web address:** http://www.
warrantech.com. **Description:** Provides extended service contracts
and limited warranties to retailers, distributors, and manufacturers of
automobiles, recreational vehicles, automotive components, home
appliances, home entertainment products, computers and
peripherals, and office and communications equipment. **Corporate
headquarters location:** This location. **Other U.S. locations:** Stamford
CT.

CHARITIES AND SOCIAL SERVICES

You can expect to find the following types of organizations in this chapter:

Social and Human Service Agencies • Job Training and Vocational Rehabilitation Services • Nonprofit Organizations

AMERICAN HEART ASSOCIATION (AHA)

7272 Greenville Avenue, Dallas TX 75231. 214/373-6300. **Fax:** 214/706-1191. **Contact:** Human Resources Department. **World Wide Web address:** http://www.americanheart.org. **Description:** One of the oldest and largest national, nonprofit, voluntary health associations dedicated to reducing disability and death from cardiovascular diseases and stroke. AHA-funded research has yielded such discoveries as CPR, bypass surgery, pacemakers, artificial heart valves, microsurgery, life-extending drugs, and new surgical techniques to repair heart defects. The AHA's interactive public education programs emphasize quitting smoking; controlling high blood pressure; eating a low-fat; low-cholesterol diet; and being physically active. The AHA also teaches the warning signs of heart attack and stroke and what to do if they occur. The association trains about 5 million Americans per year in emergency care procedures. Founded in 1924. **Special programs:** Internships. **Corporate headquarters location:** This location. **Other U.S. locations:** Nationwide.

BETTY HARDWICK CENTER

2616 South Clack, Abilene TX 79606. 915/690-5100. **Fax:** 915/690-5136. **Contact:** Human Resources. **World Wide Web address:** http://www.bhcmhmr.org. **Description:** An outpatient counseling facility for mentally challenged people. **Positions advertised include:** HCS Trainer; Case Coordinator; C&A Rehabilitation Skills Trainer; MRLA Service Coordinator; Substance Abuse Counselor.

BOY SCOUTS OF AMERICA

1325 West Walnut Hill Lane, P.O. Box 152079, Irving TX 75015-2079. 972/580-2000. **Contact:** Professional Selection and Placement. **World Wide Web address:** http://www.scouting.org. **Description:** The national scouting organization for young men. Boy Scouts of America has more than 300 local councils nationwide. **Special programs:** Internships. **Corporate headquarters location:** This location. **Other U.S. locations:** Nationwide. **Listed on:** Privately held.

CHILD CARE ASSOCIATES
P.O. Box 7935, Fort Worth TX 76111. 817/838-0055. **Contact:** Human Resources. **World Wide Web address:** http://www.childcare associates.org. **Description:** A nonprofit daycare association. The organization's primary function is assisting low-income families in finding affordable daycare.

E.O.A.C.
500 Franklin Avenue, Waco TX 76701. 254/753-0331. **Contact:** Employment. **Description:** Offers Head Start programs for three- and four-year-olds; charter school for children ages five years through third grade; Youth in Action, an alcohol and drug prevention program for teenagers; assistance with rent and utilities payments; and a variety of services for the homeless. **Operations at this facility include:** This is the central office of E.O.A.C.

THE GLADNEY CENTER
2300 Hemphill Street, Fort Worth TX 76110. 817/922-6000. **Contact:** Human Resources. **World Wide Web address:** http://www. gladney.org. **Description:** A nonprofit adoption agency providing services to young women who seek adoptive parents for their infant; individuals seeking to build their families through adoptions; and adoptees. Founded in 1887.

GOODWILL INDUSTRIES
2800 North Hampton Road, Dallas TX 75212. 214/638-2800. **Contact:** Human Resources. **World Wide Web address:** http://www. goodwill.org. **Description:** A nonprofit provider of employment training for the disabled and the poor, operating 1,800 thrift stores nationwide. **Other U.S. locations:** Nationwide.

HARMONY FAMILY SERVICES
P.O. Box 6579, Abilene TX 79608. 915/677-4663. **Contact:** Human Resources. **World Wide Web address:** http://www.hfsi.org. **Description:** A social services agency that offers many programs including a residential treatment center for runaway and homeless youths.

PANHANDLE COMMUNITY SERVICES
P.O. Box 763, Clarendon TX 79226. 806/874-2573. **Contact:** Human Resources. **Description:** Offers housing, energy, transportation, and food banks for homeless and low-income families.

TOWN NORTH YMCA

4332 Northaven Road, Dallas TX 75229. 214/357-8431. **Contact:** Human Resources. **World Wide Web address:** http://www.ymca.org. **Description:** One of the nation's largest and most comprehensive nonprofit service organizations. The YMCA provides health and fitness, social and personal development, sports and recreation, education and career development, and camps and conferences to children, teens, adults, seniors, families, disabled individuals, refugees and foreign nationals, YMCA residents, and community residents through a broad range of specific programs. **Other U.S. locations:** Nationwide.

UNITED WAY OF METROPOLITAN DALLAS

901 Ross Avenue, Dallas TX 75202. 214/978-0000. **Contact:** Human Resources. **World Wide Web address:** http://www.united waydallas.com. **Description:** A nonprofit organization that helps to meet the health and human-care needs of Dallas area residents. Overall, the United Way includes approximately 1,900 organizations. **Special programs:** Internships. **Office hours:** Monday - Friday, 8:15 a.m. - 5:00 p.m. **Corporate headquarters location:** Alexandria VA.

YMCA OF METROPOLITAN FORT WORTH

512 Lamar Street, Fort Worth TX 76102. 817/332-3281. **Contact:** Human Resources. **World Wide Web address:** http://www.ymca. com. **Description:** One of the nation's largest and most comprehensive service organizations. The YMCA provides health and fitness, social and personal development, sports and recreation, education and career development, and camps and conferences to children, youths, adults, the elderly, families, the disabled, refugees and foreign nationals, YMCA residents, and community residents, through a broad range of specific programs. **Other U.S. locations:** Nationwide.

CHEMICALS/RUBBER AND PLASTICS

You can expect to find the following types of companies in this chapter:
Adhesives, Detergents, Inks, Paints, Soaps, Varnishes • Agricultural
Chemicals and Fertilizers • Carbon and Graphite Products •
Chemical Engineering Firms• Industrial Gases

AMERICAN EXCELSIOR COMPANY
900 Avenue H East, Arlington TX 76005. 817/640-2161. **Fax:**
817/649-5714. **Contact:** Bob Vesey, Branch Manager. **World Wide
Web address:** http://www.amerexcel.com. **Description:** A packaging
company engaged in the production of environmentally sound,
water-soluble packaging materials, foam protective shipping pads,
fabricated polyurethane foam, shaped packaging, and other related
packaging products. **Operations at this facility include:**
Administration; Manufacturing; Sales. **Number of employees
nationwide:** 650.

CAPROCK MANUFACTURING, INC.
2303 120th Street, Lubbock TX 79423. 806/745-6454. **Contact:**
Human Resources. **World Wide Web address:** http://www.caprock-
mfg.com. **Description:** A plastic injection molding company that
manufactures plastic parts for cellular phones including phone
windows and battery cases. **NOTE:** Second and third shifts are
offered. **Corporate headquarters location:** This location. **Listed on:**
Privately held. **Number of employees at this location:** 160.

CARROLL COMPANY
2900 West Kingsley Road, Garland TX 75041. 972/278-1304. **Toll-
free phone:** 800/527-5722. **Fax:** 972/840-0678. **Recorded jobline:**
972/278-1304x600. **Contact:** Human Resources Manager. **World
Wide Web address:** http://www.carrollco.com. **Description:** A
manufacturer of institutional cleaning products. Founded in 1921.
NOTE: Entry-level positions and second and third shifts are offered.
Corporate headquarters location: This location. **Other U.S.
locations:** CA; OH. **Operations at this facility include:**
Administration; Manufacturing; Regional Headquarters; Research
and Development; Sales. **Listed on:** Privately held.

CHEMICAL LIME COMPANY
3700 Hulen Street, Fort Worth TX 76107. 817/732-8164. **Contact:**
Ken Cage, Director of Human Resources. **World Wide Web address:**
http://www.chemicallime.com. **Description:** A manufacturer and

distributor of chemical lime products. The company's principal products are high calcium limestone, dolomite limestone, dolomite glass flux, high-calcium quicklime, dolomitic quicklime, calcium-hydrated lime, and dolomitic-hydrated lime under the trade name Type S Hydrated Lime for use in the construction industry. **Corporate headquarters location:** This location.

CYRO INDUSTRIES
101 East Park Boulevard, Suite 1039, Plano TX 75074. 972/424-6830. **Contact:** Human Resources. **E-mail address:** human-resources@cyro.com. **World Wide Web address:** http://www.cyro.com. **Description:** Cyro Industries is a manufacturer of acrylite plastic sheets. **Operations at this facility include:** This location is a sales office.

CYTEC FIBERITE INC.
4300 Jackson Street, Greenville TX 75402. 903/454-2004. **Contact:** Human Resources. **World Wide Web address:** http://www.cytec.com. **Description:** Cytec Fiberite manufactures advanced composite and adhesives for aerospace, industrial, recreational, and other applications. **Corporate headquarters location:** West Paterson NJ. **Operations at this facility include:** This location manufactures graphite composite materials. **Listed on:** New York Stock Exchange. **Stock exchange symbol:** CYT.

HUNTSMAN POLYMERS CORPORATION
P.O. Box 3986, Odessa TX 79760. 915/640-7200. **Toll-free phone:** 800/333-7210. **Fax:** 915/640-8400. **Contact:** Human Resources. **World Wide Web address:** http://www.huntsman.com. **Description:** Manufactures plastic materials (including plastic films), thermoplastic resins, and other synthetic resins, polyethylene, and polypropylene. The company's products are used to make a wide variety of products ranging from dashboards to diapers and medical supplies. **Office hours:** Monday - Friday, 7:30 a.m. - 4:30 p.m. **Number of employees worldwide:** 14,000.

INDUSTRIAL MOLDING CORPORATION
616 East Slaton Road, Lubbock TX 79404. 806/474-1000. **Contact:** Keri Mathews, Human Resources Manager. **World Wide Web address:** http://www.indmolding.com. **Description:** Manufactures injection molded plastics. **Corporate headquarters location:** This location.

JAMAK FABRICATION, INC.

1401 North Bowie Drive, Weatherford TX 76086. 817/594-8771. **Fax:** 817/594-8324. **Contact:** Human Resources. **World Wide Web address:** http://www.jamak.com. **Description:** Manufacturers of synthetic silicone rubber products. Founded in 1971. **Parent company:** JMK International. **Number of employees at this location:** 300. **Number of employees worldwide:** 700.

JONES BLAIR COMPANY

P.O. Box 35286, Dallas TX 75235. 214/353-1661. **Contact:** Human Resources. **World Wide Web address:** http://www.jones-blair.com. **Description:** A manufacturer of paints, resins, elastomers, and powder coatings. **Corporate headquarters location:** This location. **Other U.S. locations:** Chattanooga TN. **Operations at this facility include:** Administration; Manufacturing; Research and Development; Sales; Service. **Listed on:** Privately held.

KELLY-SPRINGFIELD TIRE COMPANY

P.O. Box 4670, Tyler TX 75712-4670. 903/535-1500. **Contact:** Human Resources. **World Wide Web address:** http://www.kelly-springfield.com. **Description:** Manufactures tires and inner tubes. **Corporate headquarters location:** Cumberland MD. **Other U.S. locations:** Freeport IL; Fayetteville NC. **Parent company:** Goodyear Tire & Rubber Company. **Listed on:** New York Stock Exchange. **Stock exchange symbol:** GT.

LUBRICATION ENGINEERS INC.

P.O. Box 7128, Fort Worth TX 76111. 817/834-6321. **Physical address:** 3851 Airport Freeway, Fort Worth TX 76111. **Contact:** Karen May, Personnel Director. **World Wide Web address:** http://www.le-inc.com. **Description:** Produces a variety of industrial lubricants including lubrication oils, greases, transmission fluids, synthetic fuels, and oil supplements. **Positions advertised include:** Sales Representative. **Corporate headquarters location:** This location.

MOHAWK LABORATORIES

2730 Carl Road, Irving TX 75062. 972/438-0551. **Contact:** Human Resources Department. **Description:** Operates two laboratories that manufacture specialty cleaning and polishing chemicals.

OCCIDENTAL CHEMICAL CORPORATION

P.O. Box 809050, Dallas TX 75380-9050. 972/404-3800. **Contact:** James F. Reder, Recruiter. **World Wide Web address:** http://www. oxychem.com. **Description:** Manufactures commodity and specialty chemicals. The company has approximately 25 manufacturing facilities nationwide. **Corporate headquarters location:** This location. **Other U.S. locations:** Nationwide. **Parent company:** Occidental Petroleum Corporation. **Listed on:** New York Stock Exchange. **Stock exchange symbol:** OXY. **Number of employees nationwide:** 8,200.

POLY-AMERICA INC.

2000 West Marshall Drive, Grand Prairie TX 75051. 972/647-4374. **Fax:** 972/337-7410. **Recorded jobline:** 972/337-7107. **Contact:** Human Resources Department. **World Wide Web address:** http:// www.poly-america.com. **Description:** A leading producer of polyethylene construction film and trash bags and a leading supplier of geomembrane liners. **Positions advertised include:** Administrative Assistant; Sales Representative; Receptionist; Sales Assistant; Machine Operator; Warehouse Staff. **Corporate headquarters location:** This location. **Other U.S. locations:** Cottage Grove MN; Las Vegas NV; Columbia SC; Mt. Belvieu TX. **Number of employees at this location:** 1,000. **Number of employees nationwide:** 1,500.

POLYONE CORPORATION

9001 South Freeway, Fort Worth TX 76140. 817/293-1555. **Contact:** Ms. Mardell Everett, Personnel Manager. **World Wide Web address:** http://www.polyone.com. **Description:** Manufactures and develops thermoplastic compounds, specialty resins, engineered films, color and additive systems, specialty polymers, rubber compounding, and vinyl compounds. **Corporate headquarters location:** Cleveland OH. **Other U.S. locations:** Nationwide. **International locations:** Worldwide. **Listed on:** New York Stock Exchange. **Stock exchange symbol:** POL.

REGAL INTERNATIONAL INC.

P.O. Box 1237, Corsicana TX 75151. 903/872-3091. **Fax:** 903/872-1070. **Contact:** Human Resources. **World Wide Web address:** http:// www.regalrubber.com. **Description:** A diversified manufacturer of rubber products for oil field, offshore marine, industrial, and custom applications. **Positions advertised include:** Tool and Die Mold Maker; Class A Machinist; Electrical Maintenance Technician. **Corporate headquarters location:** This location.

RIBELIN SALES INC.
P.O. Box 461673, Garland TX 75046-1673. 972/272-1594. **Contact:** Human Resources. **World Wide Web address:** http://www.ribelin. com. **Description:** Ribelin Sales Inc. is a wholesale distributor of raw materials for the paint and coating industry. Founded in 1936.

THE SHERWIN-WILLIAMS COMPANY
P.O. Box 38469, Dallas TX 75238-0469. 214/553-2950. **Physical address:** 10440 East NW Highway, Dallas TX 75238. **Fax:** 214/553-3903. **Contact:** Division Recruiting Manager. **World Wide Web address:** http://www.sherwin.com. **Description:** Manufactures, sells, and distributes coatings and related products. Coatings are produced for original equipment manufacturers in various industries, as well as for the automotive aftermarket, the industrial maintenance market, and the traffic paint market. Sherwin-Williams labeled architectural and industrial coatings are sold through company-owned specialty paint and wallcovering stores. The Sherwin-Williams Company also manufactures paint under the Acme, Dutch Boy, Kem-Tone, Lucas, Martin-Senour, Minwax, Pratt & Lambert, Rogers, and Thompson brand names, as well as private labels, and markets its products to independent dealers, mass merchandisers, and home improvement centers. **Positions advertised include:** Computer Help Desk Attendant; IT Specialist; MIS Specialist. **Corporate headquarters location:** Cleveland OH. **Other U.S. locations:** Nationwide. **Listed on:** New York Stock Exchange. **Stock exchange symbol:** SHW. **Number of employees nationwide:** 25,000.

STYROCHEM INTERNATIONAL
3607 North Sylvania, Fort Worth TX 76111. 817/759-4400. **Contact:** Estella Hernandez, Human Resources Manager. **World Wide Web address:** http://www.styrochem.com. **Description:** StyroChem International manufactures raw plastic beads.

TEXAS EASTMAN
P.O. Box 7444, Longview TX 75607. 903/237-5000. **Contact:** Human Resources. **World Wide Web address:** http://www.eastman. com. **Description:** Manufactures more than 40 chemical and plastic products. The company primarily uses propane and ethane to create its products. **Positions advertised include:** Consolidations and External Reporting Accountant; Technical Marketing Representative; Technical Services Representative. **Parent company:** Eastman Chemicals. **Listed on:** New York Stock Exchange. **Stock exchange symbol:** EMN.

TEXAS REFINERY CORPORATION
P.O. Box 711, Fort Worth TX 76101. 817/332-1161. **Contact:** Jim Peel, Personnel Director. **World Wide Web address:** http://www. texasrefinery.com. **Description:** Manufactures specialty lubricant products and building maintenance products such as roof coatings. **Positions advertised include:** Sales Representative.

TORO IRRIGATION
9455 Railroad Drive, El Paso TX 79924-6702. 915/757-2586. **Contact:** Human Resources. **Description:** Manufactures and assembles plastic molding injections for the irrigation industry. **Corporate headquarters location:** Laguna CA.

COMMUNICATIONS: TELECOMMUNICATIONS AND BROADCASTING

You can expect to find the following types of companies in this chapter:
Cable/Pay Television Services • Communications Equipment•
Radio and Television Broadcasting Systems • Telephone, Telegraph, and
other Message Communications

ALCATEL USA INC.
3400 West Plano Parkway, Suite 210, Plano TX 75075-5813. 972/519-3000. **FAX:** 800/561-4847. **Contact:** Human Resources. **World Wide Web address:** http://www.usa.alcatel.com. **Description:** Manufactures telecommunications equipment including fiber-optic transmission systems and optical networks. **Corporate headquarters location:** This location. **Listed on:** New York Stock Exchange. **Stock exchange symbol:** ALA.

ANDREW CORPORATION
2701 Mayhill Road, Denton TX 76208. 940/891-0965. **Fax:** 940/381-3158. **Contact:** Tim Dee, Personnel Manager. **World Wide Web address:** http://www.andrew.com. **Description:** A manufacturer of telecommunications equipment including Earth station satellite, cellular, and microwave antennas, towers, shelters, cables, and associated equipment. **Special programs:** Internships. **Corporate headquarters location:** Orland Park IL. **Other U.S. locations:** GA; IL; KS. **Operations at this facility include:** Administration; Divisional Headquarters; Manufacturing; Regional Headquarters; Research and Development; Sales; Service. **Listed on:** NASDAQ. **Stock exchange symbol:** ANDW. **Number of employees nationwide:** More than 5,000.

A.H. BELO CORPORATION
THE DALLAS MORNING NEWS
P.O. Box 655237, Dallas TX 75265. 214/977-6600. **Contact:** Employment Manager. **World Wide Web address:** http://www.belo. com. **Description:** A.H. Belo Corporation owns and operates newspapers and network-affiliated television stations in seven U.S. metropolitan areas. The Dallas Morning News (also at this location) has a circulation of 550,000 during the week and 800,000 on Sunday. A.H. Belo traces its roots to The Galveston Daily News, which was first published in 1842. **Positions advertised include:** Expositions Sales Manager; Human Resources Manager; Auditor;

Corporate Accountant. **Subsidiaries include:** DFW Printing Company, Inc.; DFW Suburban Newspapers, Inc.

BICKEL & BREWER
1717 Main Street, Suite 4800, Dallas TX 75201. 214/653-4000. **Contact:** Human Resources. **World Wide Web address:** http://www. bickelbrewer.com. **Description:** A law firm specializing in corporate litigation including bankruptcy.

CONTINENTAL ELECTRONICS CORPORATION
4212 South Buckner Boulevard, Dallas TX 75227-0879. 214/381-7161. **Contact:** Human Resources. **E-mail address:** hradmin@ contelec.com. **World Wide Web address:** http://www.contelec.com. **Description:** A manufacturer and distributor of radio and television transmitters and machinery. **Positions advertised include:** Electrical Engineer. **Corporate headquarters location:** This location. **Parent company:** Tech-Sym Corporation. **Operations at this facility include:** Administration; Divisional Headquarters; Manufacturing; Research and Development; Sales.

CORNING CABLE SYSTEMS
9275 Denton Highway, Keller TX 76248. 817/431-1521. **Contact:** Human Resources. **World Wide Web address:** http://www. corningcablesystems.com. **Description:** Manufactures fiber-optic telecommunications equipment.

DECIBEL PRODUCTS INC.
P.O. Box 569610, Dallas TX 75356. 214/634-8502. **Fax:** 214/819-4262. **Contact:** Human Resources. **World Wide Web address:** http:// www.decibelproducts.com. **Description:** A manufacturer and distributor of telecommunications products including cables, connectors, and sway brace kits. **Corporate headquarters location:** Beachwood OH. **Parent company:** Allen Telecom Systems. **Operations at this facility include:** Manufacturing.

ERICSSON INC.
6300 Legacy Drive, Plano TX 75024. 972/583-0000. **Contact:** Human Resources. **World Wide Web address:** http://www. ericsson.com. **Description:** Designs and manufactures advanced telecommunications equipment for wired and mobile communications in public and private networks. **Corporate headquarters location:** Sweden. **Other U.S. locations:** New York

NY; Lynchburg VA. **Operations at this facility include:** Research and Development. **Listed on:** NASDAQ. **Stock exchange symbol:** ERICY.

FUJITSU CONSULTING

900 One Galleria Tower, 13355 Noel Road, Suite 800, Dallas TX 75240. 972/503-3700. **Toll-free phone:** 800/259-0012. **Fax:** 972/408-3177. **Contact:** Personnel. **World Wide Web address:** http://www.consulting.fujitsu.com. **Description:** Provides computer consulting services including outsourcing and systems integration.

GENERAL CABLE COMPANY

800 East Second Street, Bonham TX 75418. 903/583-2181. **Contact:** Human Resources. **World Wide Web address:** http://www.general cable.com. **Description:** The company's business units include the Electrical Group, the Telecommunications and Electronics Group, the Consumer Products Group, and the Manufacturing Group. The Electrical Group operates under the business units General Cable/Guardian, which manufactures and distributes a full line of copper building wire, tray cable, power cable, and other cable products; Carol Cable Electrical, which manufactures industrial, power, mining, and control cable, THHN building wire, entertainment cable, rubber portable cord, and cordsets insulated with plastic and thermosetting compounds; and Capital Wire and Cable, which manufactures insulated wire and cable using both aluminum and copper conductors. The Telecommunications and Electronics Group operates under the business units Outside Products, which markets wire and cable designed for use in the outside plant network; Premise Products, which manufactures wire products that support the central office and commercial premise markets; and Electronics, which manufactures computer and control cables, IBM cabling products, ethernet, coaxial, twin axial, and fire alarm cables. The Consumer Products Group operates under the business units Carol Cable, which manufactures extension cords, portable lights, and home office power supplies; General/Capital Wire Retail, which sells building wire to the retail market; and the OEM Engineered Cordsets Division, which manufactures cord and cordsets for data processing equipment, tools, floor care products, and other appliances. **Corporate headquarters location:** Highland Heights KY. **Operations at this facility include:** This location produces commercial cable for telephone companies. **Listed on:** New York Stock Exchange. **Stock exchange symbol:** BGC.

KFDA-TV
NEWS CHANNEL 10
P.O. Box 10, Amarillo TX 79105. 806/383-1010. **Contact:** Human Resources. **World Wide Web address:** http://www.newschannel 10.com. **Description:** A CBS-affiliated television broadcasting station.

KLBK-TV
7403 South University Avenue, Lubbock TX 79423. 806/745-2345. **Contact:** Human Resources. **World Wide Web address:** http://www. klbk.com. **Description:** A CBS-affiliated television broadcasting station.

KRLD/TEXAS STATE NETWORKS
1080 Ballpark Way, Arlington TX 76011. 817/543-5400. **Contact:** Human Resources. **World Wide Web address:** http://www.krld.com. **Description:** An AM, all news format radio station.

KVII-TV
One Broadcast Center, Amarillo TX 79101. 806/373-1787. **Contact:** Human Resources. **E-mail address:** pronews7@kvii.com. **World Wide Web address:** http://www.kvii.com. **Description:** An ABC-affiliated television broadcasting station.

KVIL-AM/FM 103.7
4131 North Central Expressway, Suite 1200, Dallas TX 75204. 214/691-1037. **Fax:** 214/891-7966. **Contact:** Human Resources. **World Wide Web address:** http://www.kvil.com. **Description:** An adult contemporary radio station broadcasting on AM and FM. **Parent company:** Infinity Broadcasting Corporation of Texas.

KXXV-TV
P.O. Box 2522, Waco TX 76702. 254/754-2525. **Contact:** Human Resources. **World Wide Web address:** http://www.kxxv.com. **Description:** An ABC-affiliated television station.

LUCENT TECHNOLOGIES INC.
3000 Skyline Drive, Mesquite TX 75149. 972/284-2000. **Contact:** Human Resources Department. **World Wide Web address:** http://www.lucent.com. **Description:** Lucent Technologies Inc. manufactures communications products including switching, transmission, fiber-optic cable, wireless systems, and operations systems, to supply the needs of telephone companies and other

communications services providers. **Corporate headquarters location:** Murray Hill NJ. **Operations at this facility include:** This location manufactures electronic power components for the communications industry. **Listed on:** New York Stock Exchange. **Stock exchange symbol:** LU.

MARCONI COMMUNICATIONS

8616 Freeport Parkway, Irving TX 75063. 817/267-3141. **Contact:** Employee Relations Manager. **World Wide Web address:** http:// www.marconicomms.com. **Description:** Provides services and equipment for the Internet, enterprise networks, and telecommunications systems. **Corporate headquarters location:** Pittsburgh PA. **Parent company:** Marconi plc (London, England). **Listed on:** NASDAQ. **Stock exchange symbol:** MONI.

MOTOROLA, INC.

5555 North Beach Street, Fort Worth TX 76137. 817/245-6000. **Contact:** Human Resources. **World Wide Web address:** http://www. mot.com. **Description:** Motorola manufactures communications equipment and electronic products including car radios, cellular phones, semiconductors, computer systems, cellular infrastructure equipment, pagers, cordless phones, and LAN systems. **Special programs:** Internships. **Corporate headquarters location:** Schaumburg IL. **Other U.S. locations:** Nationwide. **International locations:** Worldwide. **Operations at this facility include:** This location manufactures pagers. **Listed on:** New York Stock Exchange. **Stock exchange symbol:** MOT. **Number of employees worldwide:** 111,000.

NEC AMERICA INC.

6535 North Street, Highway 161, Irving TX 75039. 214/262-2000. **Contact:** Human Resources Department. **World Wide Web address:** http://www.nec.com. **Description:** Manufactures communications systems and equipment, computers, industrial electronics systems, electronics devices, and home electronics products. **Listed on:** NASDAQ. **Stock exchange symbol:** NIPNY.

NOKIA MOBILE PHONES INC.

6000 Connection Drive, Irving TX 75039. 972/894-5000. **Contact:** Human Resources. **World Wide Web address:** http://www.nokia. com. **Description:** A leading manufacturer and supplier of mobile phones as well as a supplier of mobile, broadband, and IP networks.

Listed on: New York Stock Exchange. **Stock exchange symbol:** NOK. **Number of employees worldwide:** 52,700.

RF MONOLITHICS, INC.
4347 Sigma Road, Dallas TX 75244. 972/233-2903. **Contact:** Human Resources. **World Wide Web address:** http://www.rfm.com. **Description:** Designs, develops, manufactures, and sells a broad range of radio frequency components and modules for the low-power wireless, high-frequency timing, and telecommunications markets. The company's products are based on surface acoustic wave reduced power consumption. The company markets its line of more than 500 resonators, filters, delay lines, and related modules to original equipment manufacturers worldwide. **Corporate headquarters location:** This location. **Listed on:** NASDAQ. **Stock exchange symbol:** RFMI.

SUSQUEHANNA RADIO CORP.
3500 Maple Avenue, Suite 1600, Dallas TX 75219. 214/526-2400. **Fax:** 214/520-4343. **Contact:** Human Resources. **World Wide Web address:** http://www.dfwradio.com. **Description:** Operates four radio stations in the Dallas - Fort Worth area: 99.5 The Wolf, Big Talk 570, Merge 93.3 Net, and The Ticket Sports Radio. **Corporate headquarters location:** York PA.

TELLABS TEXAS INC.
6565 MacArthur, Suite 225, Irving TX 75039. 972/869-4114. **Contact:** Human Resources. **World Wide Web address:** http://www.tellabs.com. **Description:** Tellabs designs and builds voice and data communication equipment used primarily by telephone companies. **Corporate headquarters location:** Naperville IL. **Operations at this facility include:** This location is a sales office. **Parent company:** Tellabs Operations Inc. **Listed on:** NASDAQ. **Stock exchange symbol:** TLAB.

VERIZON COMMUNICATIONS
P.O. Box 152013, Irving TX 75015-2013. 972/717-7700. **Physical address:** 500 East John Carpenter Freeway, Irving TX 75062. **Contact:** Human Resources. **World Wide Web address:** http://www.verizon.com. **Description:** A full-service communications services provider. Verizon offers residential local and long distance telephone services and Internet access; wireless service plans, cellular phones, and data services; a full-line of business services including Internet access, data services, and telecommunications

equipment and services; and government network solutions including Internet access, data services, telecommunications equipment and services, and enhanced communications services. **NOTE:** Resumes must be submitted via the Website: http://www.verizon.com/careers. **Corporate headquarters location:** New York NY. **Listed on:** New York Stock Exchange. **Stock exchange symbol:** VZ.

VERIZON COMMUNICATIONS

1255 Corporate Drive, Irving TX 75038. 972/507-5000. **Contact:** Human Resources. **World Wide Web address:** http://www.verizon. com. **Description:** A full-service communications services provider. Verizon offers residential local and long distance telephone services and Internet access; wireless service plans, cellular phones, and data services; a full-line of business services including Internet access, data services, and telecommunications equipment and services; and government network solutions including Internet access, data services, telecommunications equipment and services, and enhanced communications services. **NOTE:** Resumes must be submitted via the Website: http://www.verizon.com/careers. **Corporate headquarters location:** New York NY. **Listed on:** New York Stock Exchange. **Stock exchange symbol:** VZ.

VERIZON COMMUNICATIONS

2701 South Johnson Street, San Angelo TX 76904. 915/944-5511. **Contact:** Human Resources. **World Wide Web address:** http://www. verizon.com. **Description:** A full-service communications services provider. Verizon offers residential local and long distance telephone services and Internet access; wireless service plans, cellular phones, and data services; a full-line of business services including Internet access, data services, and telecommunications equipment and services; and government network solutions including Internet access, data services, telecommunications equipment and services, and enhanced communications services. **NOTE:** Resumes must be submitted via the Website: http://www.verizon.com/careers. **Corporate headquarters location:** New York NY. **Listed on:** New York Stock Exchange. **Stock exchange symbol:** VZ.

WORLDCOM

2400 North Glenville Drive, Richardson TX 75082. 972/729-7000. **Contact:** Human Resources. **World Wide Web address:** http://www. wcom.com. **Description:** One of the world's largest suppliers of local, long-distance, and international telecommunications services, and a global Internet service provider. **Corporate headquarters location:** Clinton MS. **Other U.S. locations:** Nationwide. **International locations:** Worldwide. **Parent company:** MCI Communications Corporation.

XEROX CORPORATION
1301 Ridgeview Drive, Lewisville TX 75057. 972/830-4000. **Contact:** Human Resources. **World Wide Web address:** http://www. xerox.com. **Description:** Xerox Corporation is a leader in the global document market providing document solutions that enhance business productivity. Xerox develops, manufactures, markets, sells, and services a full range of document processing products. **Corporate headquarters location:** Stamford CT. **Operations at this facility include:** This location is a sales and service office. **Listed on:** New York Stock Exchange. **Stock exchange symbol:** XRX.

COMPUTER HARDWARE, SOFTWARE, AND SERVICES

You can expect to find the following types of companies in this chapter: *Computer Components and Hardware Manufacturers • Consultants and Computer Training Companies • Internet and Online Service Providers • Networking and Systems Services • Repair Services/Rental and Leasing • Resellers, Wholesalers, and Distributors • Software Developers/Programming Services • Web Technologies*

ANALYSTS INTERNATIONAL CORPORATION (AIC)

3030 LBJ Freeway, Suite 820, Dallas TX 75234. 972/243-2001. **Fax:** 972/243-7468. **Contact:** Human Resources. **World Wide Web address:** http://www.analysts.com. **Description:** An international computer consulting firm. The company assists clients in developing systems in a variety of industries using different programming languages and software. Founded in 1966. **Corporate headquarters location:** Minneapolis MN. **Other U.S. locations:** Nationwide. **International locations:** Canada; England. **Listed on:** NASDAQ. **Stock exchange symbol:** ANLY.

AVNET, INC.

11333 Pagemill Road, Dallas TX 75243. 214/343-5000. **Fax:** 214/343-5054. **Recorded jobline:** 800/459-1225. **Contact:** Human Resources. **World Wide Web address:** http://www.avnet.com. **Description:** Avnet, Inc. is one of the nation's largest distributors of electronic components and computer products for industrial and military customers. The company also produces and distributes electronic, electrical, and video communications products. **Corporate headquarters location:** Chandler AZ. **Operations at this facility include:** This location is engaged in the distribution of company-manufactured electronics products. **Listed on:** New York Stock Exchange. **Stock exchange symbol:** AVT.

BANCTEC, INC.

2701 East Grauwyler Road, Irving TX 75061. 972/579-6000. **Fax:** 972/579-6877. **Contact:** Human Resources Manager. **E-mail address:** jobs@banctec.com. **World Wide Web address:** http://www.banctec. com. **Description:** Engaged in systems integration and specializes in document management solutions. The company also provides network support services and develops image management software. **Corporate headquarters location:** Dallas TX. **Listed on:** Privately held. **Number of employees worldwide:** 4,000.

CALYX SOFTWARE

718 North Buckner Boulevard, Suite 416-104, Dallas TX 75218. 214/320-3668. **Contact:** Personnel. **World Wide Web address:** http://www.calyxsoftware.com. **Description:** Designs and markets POINT for Windows, a processing application for mortgage professionals, and POINTMan, a processing application for loan agents. **Corporate headquarters location:** San Jose CA.

COMPAQ COMPUTER CORPORATION

5310 Harvest Hill Road, Suite 200, Dallas TX 75240. 972/702-4000. **Contact:** Human Resources. **World Wide Web address:** http://www. hp.com. **Description:** Compaq Computer Corporation designs, manufactures, sells, and services computers and associated peripheral equipment, software, and supplies. Applications and programs include scientific research, computation, communications, education, data analysis, industrial control, time sharing, commercial data processing, graphic arts, word processing, health care, instrumentation, engineering, and simulation. **NOTE:** Compaq is now part of Hewlett Packard. See the Website for more information. **Other U.S. locations:** Nationwide. **Operations at this facility include:** This location is a sales and service office.

COMPUCOM SYSTEMS, INC.

7171 Forest Lane, Dallas TX 75230. 214/265-3600. **Contact:** Human Resources. **World Wide Web address:** http://www.compucom.com. **Description:** A leading PC integration services company providing product procurement, advanced configuration, network integration, and support services. **Positions advertised include:** Call Center Team Leader; EDI Developer/Programmer. **Corporate headquarters location:** This location. **Other U.S. locations:** Nationwide. **Listed on:** NASDAQ. **Stock exchange symbol:** CMPC. **Number of employees nationwide:** 3,800.

COMPUTER ASSOCIATES INTERNATIONAL, INC.

5465 Legacy Drive, Plano TX 75024. 214/473-1000. **Contact:** Human Resources Manager. **World Wide Web address:** http://www. cai.com. **Description:** Computer Associates International is one of the world's leading developers of client/server and distributed computing software. The company develops, markets, and supports enterprise management, database and applications development, business applications, and consumer software products for a broad range of mainframe, midrange, and desktop computers. Computer Associates International serves major business, government, research, and educational organizations. Founded in 1976. **Positions advertised include:** Assistant Teacher; Divisional Quality Manager; Facilities Coordinator; Level 2 Support Manager; Sales Executive. **Special programs:** Internships; Co-ops. **Corporate headquarters location:** Islandia NY. **Other U.S. locations:** Nationwide. **Operations at this facility include:** This location develops and sells software, and offers support services. **Listed on:** New York Stock Exchange. **Stock exchange symbol:** CA. **Number of employees worldwide:** 18,200.

COMPUTER HORIZONS CORPORATION
5205 North O'Connor Boulevard, 6th Floor, Irving TX 75039-3789. 973/831-5200. **Toll-free phone:** 800/890-2421. **Fax:** 972/831-5905. **Contact:** Human Resources. **World Wide Web address:** http://www. computerhorizons.com. **Description:** A full-service technology solutions company offering contract staffing, outsourcing, re-engineering, and network management. **Corporate headquarters location:** Mountain Lakes NJ. **Listed on:** NASDAQ. **Stock exchange symbol:** CHRZ.

COMPUTER SCIENCES CORPORATION (CSC)
5525 LBJ Freeway, Dallas TX 75240. 972/386-0020. **Fax:** 972/386-0315. **Contact:** Human Resources. **World Wide Web address:** http:// www.csc.com. **Description:** Computer Sciences Corporation helps clients in industry and government use information technology to achieve strategic and operational objectives. The company tailors solutions from a broad suite of integrated service and technology offerings including e-business strategies and technologies, management and IT consulting, systems development and integration, application software, and IT and business process outsourcing. Founded in 1959. **Positions advertised include:** Third Party Administrator; Life Claims Examiner; Data Entry Clerk; Data Imaging Processor; Business Developer. **Corporate headquarters location:** El Segundo CA. **Operations at this facility include:** This location develops and markets software for financial institutions. **Listed on:** New York Stock Exchange. **Stock exchange symbol:** CSC. **Number of employees worldwide:** 68,000.

COMPUTER SCIENCES CORPORATION (CSC)
7800 North Simmons Freeway, Suite 800, Dallas TX 75247. 214/ 672-7400. **Contact:** Human Resources. **World Wide Web address:** http://www.csc.com. **Description:** CSC is in the Information Technology services industry, offering a broad array of professional services to clients in the global commercial and government

markets. **Positions advertised include:** Third Party Administrator; Life Claims Examiner; Data Entry Clerk; Data Imaging Processor; Business Developer. **Corporate headquarters location:** El Segundo CA. **International locations:** Worldwide. **Listed on:** New York Stock Exchange. **Stock exchange symbol:** CSC. **Number of employees worldwide:** 68,000.

COMPUTER SCIENCES CORPORATION (CSC)
12001 North Central Expressway, Suite 500, Dallas TX 75243. 972/778-7000. **Contact:** Human Resources. **World Wide Web address:** http://www.csc.com. **Description:** CSC is in the Information Technology services industry, offering a broad array of professional services to clients in the global commercial and government markets. **Positions advertised include:** Third Party Administrator; Life Claims Examiner; Data Entry Clerk; Data Imaging Processor; Business Developer. **Corporate headquarters location:** El Segundo CA. **International locations:** Worldwide. **Operations at this facility include:** This location is a sales office. **Listed on:** New York Stock Exchange. **Stock exchange symbol:** CSC. **Number of employees worldwide:** 68,000.

COREL, INC.
8144 Walnut Hill Lane, Suite 1050, Dallas TX 75231. 469/232-1000. **Fax:** 469/232-1194. **Contact:** Human Resources. **World Wide Web address:** http://www.corel.com. **Description:** Develops, markets, and supports a line of graphic application software products for IBM PCs and compatibles running under the Microsoft Windows operating environment. Products are designed for both business and professional use and include professional illustration, basic drawing and charting products, data-driven graphics, image editing, and reusable clip-art libraries. Corel, Inc. also offers systems software products designed to enhance the Windows and OS/2 operating environments. **Positions advertised include:** Account Manager. **Corporate headquarters location:** Ottawa, Canada. **Listed on:** NASDAQ. **Stock exchange symbol:** CORL. **Number of employees worldwide:** 889.

DNS-SOLUTIONS
4455 LBJ Freeway, Suite 810, Dallas TX 75244. 972/788-2160. **Contact:** Human Resources. **World Wide Web address:** http://www. dns-solutions.com. **Description:** Performs custom computer programming for multilevel marketing firms.

EDS (ELECTRONIC DATA SYSTEMS CORPORATION)
5400 Legacy Drive, Mail Slot H4-GB-35, Plano TX 75024. 972/605-2700. **Fax:** 800/562-6241. **Contact:** Human Resources. **E-mail address:** careers@eds.com. **World Wide Web address:** http://www.eds.com. **Description:** Provides consulting, systems development, systems integration, and systems management services for large-scale and industry-specific applications. Founded in 1962. **NOTE:** Entry-level positions are offered. **Positions advertised include:** Marketing Communications Specialist. **Special programs:** Internships; Training. **Corporate headquarters location:** This location. **Listed on:** New York Stock Exchange. **Stock exchange symbol:** EDS. **Annual sales/revenues:** More than $100 million.

EXECUTRAIN OF TEXAS
5455 Belt Line Road, Dallas TX 75240. 972/387-1212. **Contact:** Human Resources. **World Wide Web address:** http://www.executrain.com/dallas. **Description:** Trains businesses in the use of computer software and offers IT certification. **Other U.S. locations:** Nationwide. **International locations:** Worldwide.

FARSIGHT COMPUTER
1219 West University Boulevard, Odessa TX 79764-7119. 915/335-0879. **Fax:** 915/335-8411. **Contact:** Human Resources. **World Wide Web address:** http://www.farsweb.com. **Description:** A computer wholesaler, specializing in custom-built PCs.

FUJITSU NETWORK COMMUNICATIONS (FNC)
2801 Telecom Parkway, Richardson TX 75082. 972/690-6000. **Contact:** Recruiting. **World Wide Web address:** http://www.fnc.fujitsu.com. **Description:** Fujitsu Network Communications develops and manufactures broadband transmission and switching technologies to deliver voice, video, and data capabilities. **Operations at this facility include:** This location is engaged in the repair of cellular telephones.

HEWLETT-PACKARD COMPANY
3000 Waterview Parkway, Richardson TX 75080. 972/497-4000. **Contact:** Human Resources. **World Wide Web address:** http://www.hp.com. **Description:** Hewlett-Packard is engaged in the design and manufacture of measurement and computation products and systems used in business, industry, engineering, science, health care, and education. Principal products are integrated instrument and computer systems (including hardware and software), peripheral

products, and electronic medical equipment and systems. **NOTE:** Jobseekers are encouraged to apply via the Website: http://www. jobs.hp.com. **Positions advertised include:** Financial Specialist; Commodity Manager; Strategic Program Manager; Remote Application Engineer; Client Manager; Pre-sale Consultant. **Special programs:** Internships. **Corporate headquarters location:** Palo Alto CA. **Operations at this facility include:** This location builds supercomputers. **Listed on:** New York Stock Exchange. **Stock exchange symbol:** HPQ.

IBM CORPORATION

1605 LBJ Freeway, Dallas TX 75234. 972/280-5290. **Toll-free phone:** 800/426-4968. **Recorded jobline:** 800/964-4473. **Contact:** IBM Staffing Services. **World Wide Web address:** http://www.ibm. com. **Description:** IBM is a developer, manufacturer, and marketer of advanced information processing products including computers and microelectronic technology, software, networking systems, and information technology-related services. **NOTE:** Jobseekers should send a resume to IBM Staffing Services, 1DPA/051, 3808 Six Forks Road, Raleigh NC 27609. **Corporate headquarters location:** Armonk NY. **International locations:** Worldwide. **Operations at this facility include:** This location is a regional sales and marketing office. **Subsidiaries include:** IBM Credit Corporation; IBM Instruments, Inc.; IBM World Trade Corporation. **Listed on:** New York Stock Exchange. **Stock exchange symbol:** IBM.

I.T. PARTNERS, INC.

2735 Villa Creek Drive, Suite 175, Dallas TX 75234. 972/484-5300. **Fax:** 972/484-5605. **Contact:** Personnel. **E-mail address:** employment@itpartners.com. **World Wide Web address:** http:// www.itpartners.net. **Description:** Offers computer consulting services, software training, network implementation, and Web services (Web hosting and development). **Positions advertised include:** IT Professional.

I2 TECHNOLOGIES

One i2 Place, 11701 Luna Road, Dallas TX 75234. **Toll-free phone:** 800/800-3288. **Fax:** 214/860-6060. **Contact:** Recruiting. **World Wide Web address:** http://www.i2.com. **Description:** Develops and provides e-commerce, business-to-business, and open marketplace solutions. Founded in 1988. **Positions advertised include:** Senior Revenue Analyst; Senior Director of Corporate Accounting; Senior Financial Analyst; Director of Human Resources. **Corporate**

headquarters location: This location. **Other U.S. locations:** Nationwide. **International locations:** Worldwide. **Listed on:** NASDAQ. **Stock exchange symbol:** ITWO.

INTERPHASE CORPORATION

2901 North Dallas Parkway, Dallas TX 75093. 214/654-5000. **Toll-free phone:** 800/777-3722. **Fax:** 214/654-5500. **Contact:** Human Resources. **E-mail address:** iphase.resumes@iphase.com. **World Wide Web address:** http://www.iphase.com. **Description:** A developer, manufacturer, and marketer of networking and mass storage controllers, as well as stand-alone networking devices for computer systems. Networking products are primarily sold to original equipment manufacturers, value-added resellers, systems integrators, and large end users. **Corporate headquarters location:** This location. **Operations at this facility include:** Administration; Manufacturing; Research and Development; Sales. **Listed on:** NASDAQ. **Stock exchange symbol:** INPH.

INTERVOICE-BRITE, INC.

17811 Waterview Parkway, Dallas TX 75252. 972/454-8000. **Fax:** 972/454-8408. **Contact:** Human Resources. **World Wide Web address:** http://www.intervoice.com. **Description:** Develops, sells, and services interactive voice response systems that allow individuals to access a computer database using a telephone keypad, computer keyboard, or human voice. Applications are functioning in industries including insurance, banking, higher education, government, utilities, health care, retail distribution, transportation, and operator services. **Positions advertised include:** Senior Engineer; Engineer. **Listed on:** NASDAQ. **Stock exchange symbol:** INTV. **Corporate headquarters location:** This location.

ITAC SYSTEMS, INC.

3113 Benton Street, Garland TX 75042. 972/494-3073. **Fax:** 972/494-4159. **Contact:** Human Resources. **World Wide Web address:** http://www.mousetrak.com. **Description:** Manufactures the mouse-trak trackball, a computer peripheral product. Founded in 1993. **NOTE:** Entry-level positions are offered. **Corporate headquarters location:** This location. **Listed on:** Privately held.

KANEB SERVICES, INC.

2435 North Central Expressway, Suite 700, Richardson TX 75080. 972/699-4023. **Fax:** 972/699-4025. **Contact:** Personnel. **E-mail address:** employment@kaneb.com. **World Wide Web address:**

http://www.kaneb.com. **Description:** A holding company with subsidiaries that are engaged in various technical applications as well as the refining of petroleum products. **Corporate headquarters location:** This location. **Subsidiaries include:** InformaTech's Medical Services Division provides information technology services for medical information systems and applications. InformaTech's Information Technology Division is engaged in network design and installation, secure network architecture, seat management, custom computer design, and cabling; Kaneb Pipe Line Partners, LP owns and operates several thousand miles of pipeline, transports refined petroleum products, and terminals independent liquids. Kaneb Pipe Line operates more than 60 facilities in the United States and the United Kingdom. **Listed on:** New York Stock Exchange. **Stock exchange symbol:** KSL. **Annual sales/revenues:** More than $100 million.

LINX DATA TERMINALS, INC.
625 Digital Drive, Suite 100, Plano TX 75075. 972/964-7090. **Contact:** Human Resources. **World Wide Web address:** http://www. linxdata.com. **Description:** A manufacturer of networked data collection terminals and host connectivity software.

MERLIN SOFTWARE SERVICES, INC.
1800 Jay Ell Drive, Suite 100, Richardson TX 75081. 972/235-9551. **Contact:** Human Resources. **World Wide Web address:** http://www. merlinss.com. **Description:** Designs and installs software. The company also provides training services.

MESQUITE COMMUNITY HOSPITAL
3500 Interstate 30, Mesquite TX 75150. 972/698-3300. **Fax:** 972/698-2580. **Recorded jobline:** 972/698-2465. **Contact:** Human Resources. **World Wide Web address:** http://www.mchtx.com. **Description:** A hospital with 172 beds. Founded in 1978. **Positions advertised include:** Ambulatory Care Technician; Dietician; Facilities Manager; Medical Technologist; Registered Nurse; Rehabilitation Technician; Admitting Clerk.

MICRO COMPUTER SYSTEMS, INC.
6335 North State Highway 161, Irving TX 75039-2402. 214/262-3530. **Fax:** 214/262-3531. **Contact:** Personnel. **World Wide Web address:** http://www.mcsdallas.com. **Description:** Develops software including Local Area Network (LAN) communication systems and

configuration utilities for EISA computers. **Parent company:** NEC America.

NCR CORPORATION
450 East John Carpenter Freeway, Irving TX 75062. 972/650-2710. **Contact:** Human Resources Consultant. **World Wide Web address:** http://www.ncr.com. **Description:** NCR Corporation is a worldwide provider of computer products and services. The company provides computer solutions to three targeted industries: retail, financial, and communication. NCR Computer Systems Group develops, manufactures, and markets computer systems. NCR Financial Systems Group is an industry leader in financial delivery systems, relationship banking data warehousing solutions, and payments systems/item processing. NCR Retail Systems Group is a world leader in end-to-end retail solutions serving the food, general merchandise, and hospitality industries. NCR Worldwide Services provides data warehousing services solutions; end-to-end networking services; and designs, implements, and supports complex open systems environments. NCR Systemedia Group develops, produces, and markets a complete line of information products to satisfy customers' information technology needs including transaction processing media, auto identification media, business form communication products, managing documents and media, and a full line of integrated equipment solutions. **Corporate headquarters location:** Dayton OH. **Other U.S. locations:** Nationwide. **Operations at this facility include:** This location is a sales and service office. **Listed on:** New York Stock Exchange. **Stock exchange symbol:** NCR. **Number of employees worldwide:** 30,400.

NETWORK ASSOCIATES, INC.
13465 Midway Road, Dallas TX 75244. 972/308-9960. **Contact:** Human Resources. **World Wide Web address:** http://www.nai.com. **Description:** Designs, manufactures, markets, and supports software-based analysis and monitoring tools primarily for managing enterprisewide computer networks. Products include McAfee antivirus, Gauntlet firewall, PGP encryption, Sniffer network analyzers, and Magic Help Desk applications. Founded in 1989. **Listed on:** New York Stock Exchange. **Stock exchange symbol:** NET.

OPENCONNECT SYSTEMS, INC.
2711 LBJ Freeway, Suite 700, Dallas TX 75234. 972/484-5200. **Contact:** Human Resources. **World Wide Web address:** http://www. oc.com. **Description:** A leading provider of e-business solutions.

Founded in 1981. **Corporate headquarters location:** This location. **Listed on:** Privately held.

PER-SE TECHNOLOGIES, INC.
9441 LBJ Freeway, Suite 400, Dallas TX 75243. 972/664-6900. **Contact:** Human Resources. **World Wide Web address:** http://www. per-se.com. **Description:** A leading provider of comprehensive business management services, financial and clinical software, and Internet solutions to physicians and other healthcare professionals. **Corporate headquarters location:** Atlanta GA. **Listed on:** NASDAQ. **Stock exchange symbol:** PSTI.

RVSI ACUITY CIMATRIX
6311 North O'Connor Road, Suite N50, Irving TX 75039. 972/869-7684. **Contact:** Human Resources. **World Wide Web address:** http://www.rvsi.com. **Description:** RVSI Acuity CiMatrix provides data collection integrators with complete solutions including scanning components, networking, software tools, and support services. Customers are primarily involved in materials handling and factory automation environments, and include systems integrators, original equipment manufacturers, value-added resellers, and end users performing in-house systems integration. Products and related services fall into four major categories: omnidirectional scanning systems, intelligent fixed position line scanners, data collection terminals, and networking products. RVSI's foreign subsidiaries are located in Canada, Belgium, England, France, and Germany. **NOTE:** Send resumes to Human Resources, 5 Shawmut Road, Canton MA 02021. **Corporate headquarters location:** Canton MA. **Other U.S. locations:** Mission Viejo CA; San Jose CA; West Hartford CT; Roswell GA; Schaumburg IL; Southfield MI; Cincinnati OH. **Operations at this facility include:** This location is a sales office. **Listed on:** NASDAQ. **Stock exchange symbol:** ROBV.

RAYTHEON SYSTEMS COMPANY
P.O. Box 660023, Dallas TX 75266. 972/272-0515. **Contact:** Human Resources Department. **E-mail address:** resume@ rayjobs.com. **World Wide Web address:** http://www.raytheon.com. **Description:** Raytheon Systems designs, manufactures, and installs state-of-the-art communications and integrated command-and-control systems for military and industrial customers worldwide. **Parent company:** Raytheon Company is a diversified, international, multi-industry technology-based company ranked among the 100 largest U.S. industrial corporations. Raytheon has 110 facilities in 28 states

and the District of Columbia. Overseas facilities and representative offices are located in 26 countries, principally in Europe, the Middle East, and the Pacific Rim. The company's four business segments include Electronics, Major Appliances, Aircraft Products, and Energy and Environmental. **Operations at this facility include:** This location develops high-technology software. **Listed on:** New York Stock Exchange. **Stock exchange symbol:** RTN.

SIEMENS BUSINESS SERVICES, INC.
16801 Addison, Suite 400, Dallas TX 75001. 972/380-5111. **Contact:** Human Resources. **World Wide Web address:** http://www. sbs-usa.siemens. **Description:** Provides systems integration, help desk, and PC repair services to *Fortune* 1000 companies and federal clients. The company also resells hardware and software products. **Corporate headquarters location:** Rye Brook NY. **Parent company:** Siemens Corporation.

SOFTWARE SPECTRUM INC.
2140 Merritt Drive, Garland TX 75041. 972/840-6600. **Fax:** 972/864-3219. **Contact:** Human Resources. **World Wide Web address:** http://www.softwarespectrum.com. **Description:** Resells microcomputer software and services to businesses and government agencies. Software Spectrum also offers technical support and volume software license services. **Positions advertised include:** Account Executive; Customer Care Representative; Senior Accountant. **Corporate headquarters location:** This location. **Other U.S. locations:** Nationwide. **International locations:** Worldwide. **Subsidiaries include:** Spectrum Integrated Services. **Operations at this facility include:** Administration; Sales; Service. **Listed on:** NASDAQ. **Stock exchange symbol:** SSPE. **Number of employees worldwide:** 2,000.

SOURCESUITE LLC
5601 Executive Drive, Suite 200, Irving TX 75038. 972/701-5400. **Contact:** Human Resources. **World Wide Web address:** http:// www.srcm.com. **Description:** A leader in interactive content and navigation for interactive television. **Corporate headquarters location:** This location. **Parent company:** Insight Communications Company, Inc.

STORNET
624 Krona Drive, Suite 160, Plano TX 75074. 972/424-2800. **Contact:** Human Resources. **World Wide Web address:** http://

www.stornet.com. **Description:** The largest vendor-independent data-storage service company in the United States.

S2 SYSTEMS, INC.
4965 Preston Park Boulevard, Suite 800, Plano TX 75093. 972/458-3800. **Contact:** Human Resources. **World Wide Web address:** http://www.s2systems.com. **Description:** A provider of data communications middleware and related professional services that bridge the gap between open distributed systems and legacy mainframe and midrange systems used for online applications. **Corporate headquarters location:** This location.

TANDY WIRE AND CABLE COMPANY
3500 McCart Avenue, Fort Worth TX 76110. 817/415-1500. **Contact:** Marianne Wiestner, Human Resources Manager. **Description:** Engaged in the manufacture of wire and cable including computer cable. **Parent company:** Tandy Corporation. **Operations at this facility include:** Manufacturing.

THINKSPARK
4835 LBJ Freeway, Suite 1100, Dallas TX 75244. 972/392-0955. **Toll-free phone:** 888/262-6043. **Contact:** Human Resources. **World Wide Web address:** http://www.thinkspark.com. **Description:** Offers services in four main areas: Database Services, which includes database administration and monitoring services; E-Business Solutions, which includes knowledge management, enterprise resource planning, and e-commerce; System Services, which includes systems integration and interface design; and Education Services. Founded in 1987. **Positions advertised include:** Territory Manager.

UNITED STATES DATA CORPORATION (USDATA)
2435 North Central Expressway, Suite 100, Richardson TX 75080-2722. 972/680-9700. **Fax:** 972/669-0563. **Contact:** Human Resources. **E-mail address:** careers@usdata.com. **World Wide Web address:** http://www.usdata.com. **Description:** Develops, markets, and supports application-enabler software products that customers configure to implement a wide range of real-time monitoring, analysis, information management, and control solutions in worldwide industrial automation markets. USData also develops, markets, and supports integrated hardware, software, and systems solutions for automated identification and data collection applications that are sold to a broad base of customers throughout

North America. The company also acts as a full-service distributor and value-added remarketer for manufacturers of bar code equipment. **Special programs:** Internships. **Corporate headquarters location:** This location. **Other U.S. locations:** Atlanta GA; Chicago IL; Boston MA; Seattle WA. **Operations at this facility include:** Administration; Divisional Headquarters; Research and Development; Sales; Service. **Listed on:** NASDAQ. **Stock exchange symbol:** USDC.

EDUCATIONAL SERVICES

You can expect to find the following types of facilities in this chapter:
Business/Secretarial/Data Processing Schools •
Colleges/Universities/Professional Schools • Community Colleges/Technical
Schools/Vocational Schools • Elementary and Secondary Schools •
Preschool and Child Daycare Services

ABILENE CHRISTIAN UNIVERSITY
ACU Station, Box 29106, Abilene TX 79699-9106. 915/674-2000.
Contact: Human Resources. **Recorded jobline:** 915/674-5621.
World Wide Web address: http://www.acu.edu. **Description:** A
university with 117 undergraduate programs, 39 graduate fields of
study, and one doctoral program in theology. Approximately 4,800
students are enrolled in the university. **Positions advertised include:**
Administrative Secretary; Administrative Coordinator; Director of
Instructor and Faculty Development; Assistant Text Book Manager;
Multimedia Services Trainer; Developments Program Manager.

AMARILLO COLLEGE
P.O. Box 447, Amarillo TX 79178. 806/371-5000. **Contact:** Human
Resources. **World Wide Web address:** http://www.actx.edu.
Description: A two-year community college. Approximately 7,300
students are enrolled at this location. Amarillo College has three
other campuses in Amarillo.

ANGELO STATE UNIVERSITY
2601 West Avenue N, Box 11009, ASU Station, San Angelo TX
76909. 915/942-2168. **Contact:** Personnel Director. **World Wide
Web address:** http://www.angelo.edu. **Description:** A state university
offering 45 bachelor's degree and 21 master's degree programs.
Angelo State University has an enrollment of approximately 6,300
students. Founded in 1976.

THE ART INSTITUTE OF DALLAS
2 North Park East, 8080 Park Lane, Dallas TX 75231. 214/692-8080.
Fax: 214/361-0178. **Contact:** Human Resources. **World Wide Web
address:** http://www.aid.aii.edu. **Description:** A two-year accredited
institute with associate degree programs in art, fashion, photography,
interior design, and music and video production. **Positions
advertised include:** Assistant Director of Admissions; Digital Media
Lead Instructor; Supply Store Manager.

BAYLOR UNIVERSITY
P.O. Box 97053, 2nd Floor, Clifton Robinson Tower, 700 University Parks Drive, Waco TX 76798. 254/710-2219. **Fax:** 254/710-3819. **Contact:** Human Resources. **World Wide Web address:** http://www. baylor.edu. **Description:** One of the largest Baptist universities in the nation. Baylor University has over 13,000 students enrolled in a wide range of undergraduate and graduate programs. Founded in 1845. **Corporate headquarters location:** This location.

BROOKHAVEN COLLEGE
3939 Valley View Lane, Farmers Branch TX 75244. 972/860-4813. **Contact:** Human Resources Department. **World Wide Web address:** http://www.dcccd.edu. **Description:** A two-year community college offering a full range of transferable, freshman- and sophomore-level college courses. The college serves the northern portion of Dallas County, including North Dallas, Carrollton, Farmers Branch, Addison, Lewisville, Flower Mound, and The Colony. Brookhaven College serves 2,400 international students representing more than 100 countries and 65 languages. Founded in 1978. **Corporate headquarters location:** This location.

CISCO JUNIOR COLLEGE
841 North Judge Ely, Abilene TX 79601. 915/673-4567. **Contact:** Human Resources. **World Wide Web address:** http://www.cisco. cc.tx.us. **Description:** A junior college. **NOTE:** Jobseekers should address inquiries to Human Resources, Rural Route 3, Box 3, Cisco TX 76437.

COLLIN COUNTY COMMUNITY COLLEGE DISTRICT
4800 Preston Park Boulevard, P.O. Box 869055, Plano TX 75074. 972/881-5660. **Physical address:** 2200 West University Drive, McKinney TX 75070-8001. **Fax:** 972/985-3778. **Recorded jobline:** 972/881-5627. **Contact:** Kim Russell, Director of Human Resources. **World Wide Web address:** http://www.ccccd.edu. **Description:** A community college offering courses in computer science, humanities, international studies, fine arts, mathematics/natural science, health sciences, education, and engineering. **Positions advertised include:** Lifeguard; Associate Professor of English; Associate Professor of German; Safety and Security Officer; Accounts Payable Supervisor; Classroom Assistant; Corporate Trainer; Grant Coordinator. **Special programs:** Internships. **Corporate headquarters location:** This location.

DALLAS BAPTIST UNIVERSITY

3000 Mountain Creek Parkway, Dallas TX 75211-9299. 214/333-7100. **Contact:** Human Resources. **World Wide Web address:** http://www.dbu.edu. **Description:** An accredited university offering 34 undergraduate majors and eight master's programs.

DALLAS CHRISTIAN COLLEGE

2700 Christian Parkway, Dallas TX 75234. 972/241-3371. **Contact:** Ray Kelley, Academic Dean. **World Wide Web address:** http://www.dallas.edu. **Description:** Offers undergraduate programs in religious studies. Degree programs include pastoral ministry, youth ministry, education, music, and counseling.

DALLAS PUBLIC SCHOOLS

3807 Ross Avenue, Dallas TX 75204. 972/925-3700. **Contact:** Human Resources. **Description:** Administrative offices for the local school district. Dallas Public Schools is comprised of 154 elementary schools and 63 middle and high schools.

DEVRY INSTITUTE OF TECHNOLOGY

4800 Regent Boulevard, Irving TX 75063. 972/929-6777. **Fax:** 972/929-6678. **Contact:** Mr. R. Glyn Williams, Human Resources Manager. **E-mail address:** gwilliams@dal.devry.edu. **World Wide Web address:** http://www.dal.devry.edu. **Description:** Devry Institute of Technology is a fully-accredited college offering baccalaureate degrees in business and technology. **Corporate headquarters location:** Oakbrook Terrace IL. **Listed on:** New York Stock Exchange. **Stock exchange symbol:** DV.

EASTFIELD COLLEGE

3737 Motley Drive, Mesquite TX 75150. 972/860-7100. **Contact:** Human Resources. **World Wide Web address:** http://www.efc.dcccd.edu. **Description:** A community college.

EL CENTRO COLLEGE

801 Main Street, Dallas TX 75212. 214/860-2037. **Contact:** Human Resources. **World Wide Web address:** http://www.dcccd.edu. **Description:** A two-year community college. El Centro College operates as part of the Dallas County Community College District, which is comprised of seven area colleges.

FLIGHTSAFETY INTERNATIONAL, INC.
8900 Trinity Boulevard, Hurst TX 76053. 817/276-7500. **Fax:** 817/276-7501. **Contact:** Phyllis Lovelace, Manager of Human Resources. **World Wide Web address:** http://www.flightsafety.com. **Description:** Provides high-technology training to operators of aircraft and ships. Total training systems are used including sophisticated simulators and training devices, computer-based training, and professional instructors. **Corporate headquarters location:** Flushing NY. **Other U.S. locations:** Nationwide. **Listed on:** New York Stock Exchange. **Number of employees nationwide:** 2,000.

HARDIN-SIMMONS UNIVERSITY
HSU Box 16030, Abilene TX 79698. 915/670-1507. **Physical address:** 2200 South Hickory Street, Abilene TX 79601. **Fax:** 915/670-5874. **Contact:** Earl T. Garrett, Director of Human Resources. **World Wide Web address:** http://www.hsutx.edu. **Description:** A Southern Baptist university offering both graduate and undergraduate degrees. **Positions advertised include:** Administrative Assistant; Assistant Professor of Political Science; Assistant Professor of Sociology; Coordinator of Graduate Admissions; University Police Officer. **Corporate headquarters location:** This location. **Operations at this facility include:** Administration. **Number of employees at this location:** 300.

McMURRY UNIVERSITY
McMurry Station, P.O. Box 308, Abilene TX 79697. 915/793-3800. **Contact:** Human Resources. **World Wide Web address:** http://www.mcm.edu. **Description:** A four-year university offering undergraduate degrees. Approximately 1,425 students attend McMurry University.

MIDWESTERN STATE UNIVERSITY
3410 Taft Boulevsard, Wichita Falls TX 76308. 940/397-4221. **Fax:** 940/397-4780. **Contact:** Steve Holland, Director of Human Resources. **E-mail address:** steve.holland@nexus.mwsu.edu. **World Wide Web address:** http://www.mwsu.edu. **Description:** A state university with approximately 6,000 students enrolled in its undergraduate and graduate degree programs. **Positions advertised include:** Custodian; Storekeeper; University Nurse; Assistant Nursing Professor; Respiratory Care Professional. **Corporate headquarters location:** This location.

NORTH LAKE COLLEGE
5001 North MacArthur Boulevard, Irving TX 75038. 972/273-3000. **Contact:** Human Resources Department. **World Wide Web address:** http://www.dcccd.edu/nlc. **Description:** A two-year community college offering technical occupational courses as well as general studies. Approximately 6,200 students are enrolled. North Lake College operates as part of the Dallas County Community College District.

RICHLAND COLLEGE
12800 Abrams Road, Dallas TX 75243-2199. 972/238-6240. **Contact:** Personnel Director. **World Wide Web address:** http://www. rlc.dcccd.edu. **Description:** A junior college offering one- and two-year associate's degrees and certificates to approximately 12,500 students. Richland College operates as part of the Dallas County Community College District.

SOUTH PLAINS COLLEGE
1401 South College Avenue, Levelland TX 79336. 806/894-9611. **Fax:** 806/894-6880. **Contact:** Human Resources. **World Wide Web address:** http://www.spc.cc.tx.us. **Description:** A two-year, state-funded college. South Plains College offers majors in education, arts and sciences, nursing, and continuing education. The college has an enrollment of approximately 5,400 students.

SOUTHERN METHODIST UNIVERSITY
P.O. Box 750232, Dallas TX 75275-0232. 214/768-2000. **Contact:** Employment Office. **World Wide Web address:** http://www.smu. edu. **Description:** A university offering bachelor's, master's, professional, and doctoral degrees to approximately 9,700 students. **Special programs:** Internships. **Corporate headquarters location:** This location

SOUTHWEST COLLEGIATE INSTITUTE FOR THE DEAF
3200 Avenue C, Big Spring TX 79720-9960. 915/264-3700. **Fax:** 915/264-3707. **Contact:** Dr. Ron Brasel, Provost. **World Wide Web address:** http://www.hc.cc.tx.us. **Description:** A college for the deaf with an enrollment of approximately 105 students. The institute offers courses in liberal arts, technical, vocational/occupational, and developmental studies. The institute also offers numerous support services such as career advisement and job placement assistance. Founded in 1980. **Positions advertised include:** Secretary. **Parent company:** Howard County Junior College.

SOUTHWESTERN ADVENTIST UNIVERSITY

100 Hillcrest Drive, P.O. Box 567, Keene TX 76059. 817/645-3921. **Contact:** Human Resources. **World Wide Web address:** http://www. swau.edu. **Description:** A college affiliated with the Seventh Day Adventist Church and offering 40 undergraduate programs and two graduate-level programs. Over 1,100 students are enrolled.

SOUTHWESTERN BAPTIST THEOLOGICAL SEMINARY

P.O. Box 22000, Fort Worth TX 76122. 817/923-1921. **Contact:** Office of Church/Minister Relations. **World Wide Web address:** http://www.swbts.edu. **Description:** A seminary college offering a variety of religious training programs.

TARLETON STATE UNIVERSITY

Mail Stop T-510, Tarleton Station, Stephenville TX 76402. 254/968-9905. **Fax:** 254/968-9590. **Contact:** Ms. Mary Chenault, Human Resources Assistant. **World Wide Web address:** http://www. tarleton.edu. **Description:** A four-year state university offering bachelor's and master's degrees to approximately 6,300 students. Tarleton State University operates as part of the Texas A&M University System. **Corporate headquarters location:** College Station TX. **Operations at this facility include:** Administration.

TARRANT COUNTY JUNIOR COLLEGE

1500 Houston Street, Fort Worth TX 76102. 817/515-5100. **Contact:** Human Resources. **World Wide Web address:** http://www.tcjc. cc.tx.us. **Description:** A two-year college offering associate's degrees and certificates. **Corporate headquarters location:** This location. **Operations at this facility include:** Administration.

TEXAS A&M UNIVERSITY

P.O. Box 3011, East Texas Station, Commerce TX 75429. 903/886-5668. **Fax:** 903/886-5670. **Recorded jobline:** 903/886-5665. **Contact:** Human Resources. **World Wide Web address:** http://www. amu-commerce.edu. **Description:** A university that offers a wide range of undergraduate degree programs, master's degree programs, and doctoral and professional programs. **Positions advertised include:** Accountant; Administrative Assistant; Analytical Chemist; Assistant Research Scientist; Business Coordinator; Custodial Worker; Mechanical Equipment Foreman. **Corporate headquarters location:** College Station TX.

TEXAS CHRISTIAN UNIVERSITY

P.O. Box 298200, Fort Worth TX 76129. 817/257-7790. **Contact:** John Weif, Director of Employee Relations. **World Wide Web address:** http://www.tcu.edu. **Description:** A university offering undergraduate and graduate programs to approximately 7,000 students. **Positions advertised include:** Media Relations Intern; Administrative Assistant; Computer Hardware Technician; Service Assistant; Child Development Instructor; Student Teacher. **Corporate headquarters location:** This location.

TEXAS TECH UNIVERSITY

P.O. Box 41097, Lubbock TX 79409-1097. 806/742-2011. **Contact:** Jim Brown, Personnel Director. **World Wide Web address:** http://www.ttu.edu. **Description:** A state university. The university offers undergraduate and graduate degrees in liberal arts, law, applied health, and medicine. **Corporate headquarters location:** This location.

TEXAS WESLEYAN UNIVERSITY

1201 Wesleyan Street, Fort Worth TX 76105. 817/531-4403. **Fax:** 817/531-4402. **Contact:** Human Resources. **World Wide Web address:** http://www.txwesleyan.edu. **Description:** A small, private university affiliated with the United Methodist Church. Texas Wesleyan University offers a variety of undergraduate and graduate degrees to approximately 3,000 students. Founded in 1890. **Corporate headquarters location:** This location.

UNIVERSITY OF NORTH TEXAS

P.O. Box 311010, Denton TX 76203-1010. 940/565-2281. **Contact:** Human Resources. **World Wide Web address:** http://www.unt.edu. **Description:** A university offering undergraduate and graduate programs of study in numerous fields. Enrollment at the university is approximately 25,000.

UNIVERSITY OF NORTH TEXAS HEALTH SCIENCE AT FORT WORTH

3500 Camp Bowie Boulevard, Suite 735, Fort Worth TX 76107-2699. 817/735-2000. **Jobline:** 817/735-2675. **Contact:** Human Resources. **E-mail address:** hr_ase@hsc.unt.edu. **World Wide Web address:** http://www.hsc.unt.edu. **Description:** A health science education center. **Positions advertised include:** Clinical Services Representative; Clinical/Business Services Supervisor; Medical Assistant; Outreach Worker; Senior Licensed Vocational Nurse.

Corporate headquarters location: This location. **Operations at this facility include:** Administration; Education; Research and Development.

UNIVERSITY OF TEXAS AT ARLINGTON

1225 West Mitchell Street, Suite 112, Box 19176, Arlington TX 76019. 817/272-3461. **Fax:** 817/272-5798. **Contact:** Human Resources. **E-mail address:** employment@uta.edu. **World Wide Web address:** http://www.uta.edu. **Description:** A state university offering 55 bachelor's, 60 master's, and 19 doctoral degrees to approximately 20,000 students. Founded in 1895. **Positions advertised include:** President; Dean of Liberal Arts; Staff Nurse; Staff Auditor; Program Specialist; Counseling Specialist; Student Development Specialist; Secretary; Senior Administrative Clerk; Training Specialist; Building Attendant. **Special programs:** Internships. **Corporate headquarters location:** Austin TX. **Operations at this facility include:** Administration; Research and Development; Sales; Service.

UNIVERSITY OF TEXAS AT DALLAS

Mail Station AD 35, P.O. Box 830688, Richardson TX 75083-0688. 972/883-2221. **Contact:** Human Resources. **E-mail address:** jobs@ utdalla.edu. **World Wide Web address:** http://www.utdallas.edu. **Description:** A state university offering programs at the undergraduate, graduate, and doctoral levels. Enrollment at the university is approximately 10,000. **NOTE:** Part-time jobs are offered. **Positions advertised include:** Associate Director of Admissions.

UNIVERSITY OF TEXAS AT EL PASO

500 West University Avenue, El Paso TX 79968. 915/747-5000. **Contact:** Director of Human Resources. **World Wide Web address:** http://www.utep.edu. **Description:** One location of the state university. **Positions advertised include:** Special Events/Ticketing Coordinator; Education Coordinator; Equipment Manager; Data Manager; Network Analyst; Admissions Coordinator; Biological Safety Manager.

UNIVERSITY OF TEXAS AT TYLER

3900 University Boulevard, Tyler TX 75799. 903/566-7234. **Fax:** 903/566-5690. **Contact:** Human Resources. **World Wide Web address:** http://www.uttyl.edu. **Description:** A state university offering undergraduate and graduate programs of study. **Positions**

advertised include: Biology Lecturer; Assistant Professor of Chemistry; Electrical Engineering Professor.

ELECTRONIC/INDUSTRIAL ELECTRICAL EQUIPMENT

You can expect to find the following types of companies in this chapter:
Electronic Machines and Systems • Semiconductor Manufacturers

ARROW ELECTRONICS, INC.
6340 International Parkway, Suite 100, Plano TX 75093. 972/380-6464. **Toll-free phone:** 800/262-6064. **Contact:** Human Resources. **World Wide Web address:** http://www.arrow.com. **Description:** A distributor of electronic components, systems, and related items through a network in North America, Europe, and Asia. The company operates 150 marketing facilities, 10 primary distribution centers, and over 4,000 remote computer terminals that supply components to about 125,000 original equipment manufacturers and commercial customers. Semiconductors account for more than half of Arrow Schweber's sales. **Corporate headquarters location:** Melville NY. **Subsidiaries include:** Arrow Bell; Arrow CMS; Arrow Richey; Arrow Semiconductor; Arrow/Zeus Electronics; Marubun/Arrow USA, LLC. **Listed on:** New York Stock Exchange. **Stock exchange symbol:** ARW.

AVO INTERNATIONAL
4271 Bronze Way, Dallas TX 75237. 214/333-3201. **Contact:** Manager of Human Resources. **World Wide Web address:** http://www.avointl.com. **Description:** Manufactures test equipment and measurement instruments for electric power applications. **Corporate headquarters location:** This location.

DALLAS SEMICONDUCTOR CORPORATION
4401 South Beltwood Parkway, Dallas TX 75244-3292. 972/371-4000. **Contact:** Staffing Department. **World Wide Web address:** http://www.dalsemi.com. **Description:** Manufactures semiconductors. **NOTE:** Entry-level positions are offered. **Positions advertised include:** Analog/Mixed Signal Design Engineer; Corporate Applications Engineer; Failure Analysis Engineer; Metal Equipment Engineer; Senior Cost Accountant. **Listed on:** NASDAQ. **Stock exchange symbol:** MXIM.

DATAMATIC.COM, LTD.
3600 Kave Street, Plano TX 75074. 972/234-5000. **Toll-free phone:** 800/880-2878. **Fax:** 972/234-1134. **Contact:** Human Resources. **Description:** Supplies test and measurement systems to investor-

owned utilities and municipalities. Founded in 1977. **Office hours:** Monday - Friday, 8:00 a.m. - 5:00 p.m.

FAS TECHNOLOGIES

10480 Markison Road, Dallas TX 75238. 214/553-9991. **Fax:** 214/343-5364. **Contact:** Human Resources Manager. **E-mail address:** personnel@fas.com. **World Wide Web address:** http://www.fas.com. **Description:** Manufactures semiconductor processing equipment. Founded in 1988. **Corporate headquarters location:** This location. **International locations:** Japan. **Subsidiaries include:** FAS-Asia, Ltd. **Listed on:** Privately held.

FUJI SEMICONDUCTOR, INC.

P.O. Box 702708, Dallas TX 75370. 972/733-1700. **Physical address:** 2532 Highlander Way, Carrollton TX 75006. **Contact:** Human Resources. **World Wide Web address:** http://www.fujisemiconductor.com. **Description:** Manufactures and distributes semiconductors.

GEOTECH INSTRUMENTS, LLC

10755 Sanden Drive, Dallas TX 75238. 214/221-0000. **Contact:** Human Resources. **World Wide Web address:** http://www.geoinstr.com. **Description:** Manufactures earthquake monitoring equipment.

HONEYWELL SENSING AND CONTROL

830 East Arapaho Road, Richardson TX 75081. 972/470-4271. **Contact:** Jim Francis, Personnel Director. **World Wide Web address:** http://www.honeywell.com. **Description:** Honeywell is engaged in the research, development, manufacture, and sale of advanced technology products and services in the fields of chemicals, electronics, automation, and controls. The company's major businesses are home and building automation and control, performance polymers and chemicals, industrial automation and control, space and aviation systems, and defense and marine systems. **Parent company:** Honeywell is engaged in the research and development, manufacture, and sale of advanced technology products and services in satellite technology. **Operations at this facility include:** This location manufactures several different optoelectronics and fiber-optic systems and components including light-emitting and sensing devices/systems; and optical switches and isolators applicable to data transmission and automation of the

computer industry and the military worldwide. **Listed on:** New York Stock Exchange. **Stock exchange symbol:** HON.

HOWELL INSTRUMENTS, INC.
P.O. Box 985001, Fort Worth TX 76185-5001. 817/336-7411x223. **Physical address:** 3479 West Vickery Boulevard, Fort Worth TX 76107. **Fax:** 817/336-7874. **Contact:** Nell Whaylen, Personnel Manager. **E-mail address:** nmwhaylen@howellinst.com. **World Wide Web address:** http://www.howellinst.com. **Description:** Manufacturer of turbine engine instrumentation and test equipment for military, commercial, and private aviation applications. **NOTE:** Entry-level positions are offered. **Positions advertised include:** Field Engineer; Mechanical Engineer. **Corporate headquarters location:** This location.

INTEGRATED DEVICE TECHNOLOGY, INC.
15851 Dallas Parkway, Suite 335, Addison TX 75001-6064. 972/490-6167. **Contact:** Human Resources. **World Wide Web address:** http://www.idt.com. **Description:** Integrated Device Technology, Inc. designs, manufactures, and markets high-speed CMOS VLSI integrated circuits. The company focuses its efforts on four product areas: SRAM cache, specialty memory products, logic, and RISC microprocessors that are used in the desktop/server, data communications, and office automation markets.

NATIONAL SEMICONDUCTOR CORPORATION
1111 West Bardin Road, Arlington TX 76017. 817/468-6300. **Contact:** Human Resources. **World Wide Web address:** http://www.national.com. **Description:** Designs, develops, and manufactures microprocessors, consumer products, integrated circuits, memory systems, computer products, telecommunication systems, and high-speed bipolar circuits. **Positions advertised include:** Engineering Technician; Field Applications Engineer; Circuit Design Engineer; Senior Sales Engineer. **Corporate headquarters location:** Santa Clara CA. **International locations:** Scotland. **Listed on:** New York Stock Exchange. **Stock exchange symbol:** NSM.

NORTHROP GRUMMAN ELECTRONIC SYSTEMS
3414 Herrmann Drive, Garland TX 75041. 972/840-5600. **Contact:** Human Resources. **World Wide Web address:** http://www.littoneos.com. **Description:** Manufactures a diverse line of military equipment and electro-optical systems including guided-missile launchers, optical sighting and fire control equipment, laser range finders, night-

vision sights, and systems for weapons and high-intensity searchlights. **NOTE:** Entry-level positions and second and third shifts are offered. **Other U.S. locations:** Tempe AZ. **Parent company:** Northrop Grumman. **Operations at this facility include:** Administration; Manufacturing; Research and Development; Sales. **Listed on:** New York Stock Exchange. **Stock exchange symbol:** NOC.

OPTEK TECHNOLOGY INC.

1215 West Crosby Road, Carrollton TX 75006. 972/323-2200. **Contact:** Human Resources Manager. **World Wide Web address:** http://www.optekinc.com. **Description:** Produces fiber-optic, log-wavelength, light-emitting diodes; hybrid components; gallium arsenide and gallium aluminum arsenide circuits; and related products.

RAYTHEON SYSTEMS COMPANY

P.O. Box 6056, Greenville TX 75403-6056. 903/455-3450. **Contact:** Human Resources. **World Wide Web address:** http://www.raytheon. com. **Description:** Raytheon Systems designs, manufactures, and installs state-of-the-art communications and integrated command-and-control systems for military and industrial customers worldwide. **Parent company:** Raytheon Company is a diversified, international, multi-industry technology-based company ranked among the 100 largest U.S. industrial corporations. Raytheon has 110 facilities in 28 states and the District of Columbia. Overseas facilities and representative offices are located in 26 countries, principally in Europe, the Middle East, and the Pacific Rim. The company's four business segments include Electronics, Major Appliances, Aircraft Products, and Energy and Environmental. **Operations at this facility include:** This location manufactures electronic equipment for the military and commercial electronics industries. Military products include reconnaissance and surveillance equipment; command, control, and communications equipment; navigation and control systems; and aircraft maintenance and navigation systems. Nonmilitary products include mass media storage equipment, medical imaging devices, and data handling products. **Listed on:** New York Stock Exchange. **Stock exchange symbol:** RTN.

REXEL INC.

P.O. Box 9085, Addison TX 75001. 972/387-3600. **Contact:** Human Resources. **World Wide Web address:** http://www.rexel.com. **Description:** One of the world's largest distributors of electronic parts and supplies. **NOTE:** Resumes should be sent to Human Resources, 6700 LBJ Freeway, Suite 3700, Dallas TX 75240. **Corporate headquarters location:** This location. **Parent company:** Pinault-Printemps-Redoute. **Operations at this facility include:** Administration.

ROBINSON NUGENT, INC.
2640 Tarna Drive, Dallas TX 75229. 972/241-1738. **Contact:** Human Resources Manager. **World Wide Web address:** http://www. robinsonnugent.com. **Description:** Manufactures electronic connectors and integrated circuit sockets for the electronics industry. **NOTE:** Second and third shifts are offered. **Corporate headquarters location:** New Albany IN. **Parent company:** 3M Worldwide. **Operations at this facility include:** Manufacturing.

ROCHESTER GAUGES, INC.
11616 Harry Hines Boulevard, Dallas TX 75229. 972/241-2161. **Contact:** Barbara Nitishin, Personnel. **World Wide Web address:** http://www.rochestergauges.com. **Description:** A manufacturer of gauges, thermometers, and measuring devices. **NOTE:** Entry-level positions are offered. **Corporate headquarters location:** This location. **Operations at this facility include:** Manufacturing. **Listed on:** Privately held.

ST MICROELECTRONICS
1310 Electronics Drive, Carrollton TX 75006. 972/466-6000. **Contact:** Human Resources. **World Wide Web address:** http://www. us.st.com. **Description:** ST Microelectronics designs, develops, manufactures, and markets a broad range of semiconductor integrated circuits and discrete devices used in a variety of microelectronic applications. These applications include telecommunications systems, computer systems, consumer products, automotive products, and industrial automation and control systems. Founded in 1987. **Corporate headquarters location:** Montgomeryville PA. **Operations at this facility include:** This location manufactures microchips. **Listed on:** New York Stock Exchange. **Stock exchange symbol:** STM.

SIEMENS DEMATIC
P.O. Box 95080, Arlington TX 76005-1080. 817/640-5690. **Contact:** Human Resources. **World Wide Web address:** http://www.pa. siemens-dematic.com. **Description:** Designs, manufactures, integrates, and services high-speed automated document-processing,

materials-handling, mobile data, and voice communications systems. Primary customers are the U.S. Postal Service and other government agencies. **Parent company:** Siemens Corporation.

TECCOR ELECTRONICS INC.

1800 Hurd Drive, Irving TX 75038. 972/580-1515. **Contact:** Human Resources Department. **World Wide Web address:** http://www. teccor.com. **Description:** Manufactures electronic power controls and related equipment. A second plant (also at this location) manufactures semiconductor power devices, solid-state relays, and a variety of silicon chips and rectifiers. **Positions advertised include:** Supplier Quality Manager; Operations Design Support Engineer; 2nd Shift Supervisor; Channel Manager; Service Coordinator; Project Manager. **Corporate headquarters location:** This location. **Parent company:** Invensys Company.

THERMALLOY INC.

2700 Research Drive, Suite 200, Plano TX 55074. 972/633-9371. **Contact:** Human Resources. **World Wide Web address:** http://www. thermalloy.com. **Description:** Produces a variety of electronics components and systems, plastics, and machined products including ceramic electrical products, electronic semiconductor equipment, semiconductor insulating covers, screw machine products, plastic injected molding products for electronics use, and printed circuit board guides. **Positions advertised include:** Strategic Account Sales Engineer. **Parent company:** Aavid Thermalloy.

TRANSCORE INC.

19111 Dallas Parkway, Suite 300, Dallas TX 75287. 972/733-6600. **Fax:** 972/733-6699. **Contact:** Human Resources Department. **World Wide Web address:** http://www.transcore.com. **Description:** Manufactures electronic identification equipment. **Corporate headquarters location:** This location. **Listed on:** New York Stock Exchange.

ULTRAK INC.

1301 Waters Ridge Drive, Lewisville TX 75057. 972/353-6500. **Contact:** Human Resources. **World Wide Web address:** http://www. ultrak.com. **Description:** Manufactures security surveillance equipment. **Listed on:** NASDAQ. **Stock exchange symbol:** ULTK.

ZIMMERMAN SIGN COMPANY

9846 Highway 31 East, Tyler TX 75705-2329. 903/535-7400. **Contact:** Human Resources Manager. **World Wide Web address:** http://www.zimmermansign.com. **Description:** Manufactures electric signs. **Corporate headquarters location:** This location. **Other U.S. locations:** Jacksonville; Longview TX. **Operations at this facility include:** Administration; Manufacturing; Sales; Service.

ENVIRONMENTAL AND WASTE MANAGEMENT SERVICES

You can expect to find the following types of companies in this chapter:
Environmental Engineering Firms • Sanitary Services

ADS ENVIRONMENTAL SERVICES INC.

4144 North Central Expressway, Dallas TX 75238. 214/823-3930. **Contact:** Human Resources Department. **World Wide Web address:** http://www.adsenv.com. **Description:** Provides diagnostic testing services of water and wastewater, flow monitoring, and sewer system evaluation. Founded in 1974. **Positions advertised include:** Field Manager; Field Representative; Equipment Coordinator. **NOTE:** Send resumes to: ADS Corporation, 5030 Bradford Drive, Building One, Suite 210, Huntsville AL 35805. **Parent company:** ADS Corporation.

GEO-MARINE, INC.

550 East 15th Street, Plano TX 75074. 972/423-5480. **Contact:** Human Resources. **Fax:** 972/422-2736. **World Wide Web address:** http://www.geo-marine.com. **Description:** An environmental, engineering, consulting firm that provides services to government, business, and industry. Geo-Marine specializes in hazardous materials/waste management, natural resources management, energy management, and utility privatization, and NEPA Consulting. **Positions advertised include:** Project Manager; Associate Project Manager; Principal Investigator; Project Manager; Electrical & Mechanical Engineer. **Corporate headquarters location:** This location.

SAFETY-KLEEN CORPORATION

1722 Cooper Creek Road, Denton TX 76208. 940/483-5200. **Contact:** Human Resources. **World Wide Web address:** http://www. safety-kleen.com. **Description:** The company offers treatment, recycling, and disposal services. **Operations at this facility include:** This location is a recycling center for hazardous waste.

FABRICATED/PRIMARY METALS AND PRODUCTS

You can expect to find the following types of companies in this chapter:
Aluminum and Copper Foundries • Die-Castings • Iron and Steel Foundries • Steel Works, Blast Furnaces, and Rolling Mills

AMERIMAX BUILDING PRODUCTS, INC.
5208 Tennyson Parkway, Suite 100, Plano TX 75024. 469/366-3200. **Contact:** Human Resources Manager. **World Wide Web address:** http://www.amerimaxbp.com. **Description:** Fabricates building products of aluminum, steel, and vinyl. The company sells its products to manufacturers of recreational vehicles and prefabricated housing, retail building products suppliers, construction firms, and others. Amerimax's facilities include 15 fabrication plants located throughout the United States. Founded in 1954. **Corporate headquarters location:** This location. **Operations at this facility include:** Administration; Manufacturing; Research and Development; Sales.

ASARCO INC.
P.O. Box 1111, El Paso TX 79999-1111. 915/541-1800. **Physical address:** 2301 West Paisano Drive, El Paso TX 79922. **Contact:** Human Resources. **World Wide Web address:** http://www.asarco.com. **Description:** Asarco is one of the world's leading producers of nonferrous metals, primarily copper, lead, zinc, and silver, from its own mines and through its interest in Southern Peru Copper Corporation. Asarco also produces specialty chemicals and construction aggregates and provides environmental services. Asarco's copper operations consist of its Mission and Ray mines in Arizona, smelters in Hayden AZ and El Paso TX, and a refinery in Amarillo TX. In Missouri, the company operates an integrated lead circuit consisting of West Fork and Sweetwater mines, which provide over 90 percent of the feed for the nearby Glover smelter and refinery. The Tennessee mines division accounts for 57 percent of the total zinc concentrates produced by the company. The remaining 43 percent is produced as a coproduct at the West Fork and Sweetwater lead mines in Missouri and at the Leadville mine in Colorado. **International locations:** Australia; Mexico; Peru. **Operations at this facility include:** This location smelts copper. **Parent Company:** Grupo Mexico S.A. de C.V.

BWAY CORPORATION

3737 Miller Park Drive, Garland TX 75042. 972/535-1100. **Fax:** 972/535-1110. **Contact:** Human Resources. **E-mail address:** hr@ bwaycorp.com. **World Wide Web address:** http://www.bwaycorp. com. **Description:** Manufactures metal containers. **NOTE:** Second and third shifts are offered. **Corporate headquarters location:** Atlanta GA. **Other U.S. locations:** Nationwide. **Operations at this facility include:** Administration; Manufacturing; Sales; Service. **Listed on:** New York Stock Exchange. **Stock exchange symbol:** BY.

CHAPARRAL STEEL COMPANY

300 Ward Road, Midlothian TX 76065. 972/775-8241. **Contact:** Human Resources. **World Wide Web address:** http://www.chaparral steel.com. **Description:** A steel works company. Founded in 1975. **Listed on:** New York Stock Exchange. **Stock exchange symbol:** TXI.

G.H. HENSLEY INDUSTRIES, INC.

2108 Joe Field Road, Dallas TX 75229. 972/241-2321. **Contact:** Tom McCormack, Personnel Director. **World Wide Web address:** http://www.hensleyind.com. **Description:** Operates a steel foundry producing steel castings and construction equipment parts. **Corporate headquarters location:** This location. **Parent company:** Komatsu Ltd.

LEWIS & LAMBERT METAL

P.O. Box 14439, Haltom City TX 76117. 817/834-7146. **Contact:** Human Resources. **Description:** A leader in sheet metal installation and fabrication.

THE LOFLAND COMPANY

P.O. Box 35446, Dallas TX 75235. 214/631-5250. **Fax:** 213/631-2044. **Contact:** Gail Wachtendorf, Personnel Manager. **E-mail address:** gwachten@loftlandco.com. **World Wide Web address:** http://www.loflandcompany.com. **Description:** A steel fabricator and distributor of construction materials. **Corporate headquarters location:** This location. **Other U.S. locations:** AR; LA. **Operations at this facility include:** Administration; Manufacturing; Sales; Service.

LONE STAR STEEL COMPANY

P.O. Box 803546, Dallas TX 75380-3546. 972/386-3981. **Contact:** Human Resources. **World Wide Web address:** http://www.lonestar steel.com. **Description:** Manufactures steel tubular goods used for oil and gas drilling. **Positions advertised include:** Auditor; Engineer; Driver; Laborer. **Corporate headquarters location:** This location.

TEXAS STEEL COMPANY
3901 Hemphill Street, Fort Worth TX 76110. 817/923-4611. **Contact:** Hope Shukers, Personnel Supervisor. **Description:** Manufactures carbon, stainless steel, alloy castings, and other metal products for use in construction. **Corporate headquarters location:** This location.

THORNTON STEEL COMPANY INC.
2700 West Pafford, Fort Worth TX 76110. 817/926-3324. **Fax:** 817/926-0758. **Contact:** Hiring. **Description:** A structural steel fabricator. **Corporate headquarters location:** This location. **Operations at this facility include:** Manufacturing; Sales. **Number of employees at this location:** 15.

TRINITY INDUSTRIES, INC.
P.O. Box 7596, Fort Worth TX 76111. 817/625-4161. **Contact:** Human Resources. **World Wide Web address:** http://www.trin.net. **Description:** Manufactures an assortment of railroad and construction equipment and replacement parts. Trinity Industries also offers related services for the transportation, construction, aerospace, commercial, and industrial markets. Products include railcars, gas processing systems, petroleum transportation systems, guardrails, bridge girders and beams, airport boarding bridges, barges, tug boats, military marine vessels, and precision welding products. Trinity Industries also manufactures concrete and aggregates and produces metal components for the petrochemical, industrial, processing, and power markets. **Corporate headquarters location:** Dallas TX. **Operations at this facility include:** This location builds rail cars. **Listed on:** New York Stock Exchange. **Stock exchange symbol:** TRN.

TRINITY INDUSTRIES, INC.
Route 13, Box 175, Longview TX 75602. 903/758-0761. **Contact:** Human Resources. **World Wide Web address:** http://www.trin.net. **Description:** Manufactures an assortment of railroad and construction equipment and replacement parts. Trinity Industries also offers related services for the transportation, construction, aerospace, commercial, and industrial markets. Products include railcars, gas processing systems, petroleum transportation systems, guardrails, bridge girders and beams, airport boarding bridges,

barges, tug boats, military marine vessels, and precision welding products. Trinity Industries also manufactures concrete and aggregates and produces metal components for the petrochemical, industrial, processing, and power markets. **Positions advertised include:** Sales Management Trainee. **Corporate headquarters location:** Dallas TX. **Operations at this facility include:** This location builds tank cars. **Listed on:** New York Stock Exchange. **Stock exchange symbol:** TRN.

TRINITY INDUSTRIES, INC.
P.O. Box 568887, Dallas TX 75356-8887. 214/631-4420. **Contact:** Human Resources Department. **World Wide Web address:** http://www.trin.net. **Description:** Manufactures an assortment of railroad and construction equipment and replacement parts. Trinity Industries also offers related services for the transportation, construction, aerospace, commercial, and industrial markets. Products include railcars, gas processing systems, petroleum transportation systems, guardrails, bridge girders and beams, airport boarding bridges, barges, tug boats, military marine vessels, and precision welding products. Trinity Industries also manufactures concrete and aggregates and produces metal components for the petrochemical, industrial, processing, and power markets. **Positions advertised include:** Sales Management Trainee; Health and Welfare Benefits Director; Accounting Manager. **Corporate headquarters location:** This location. **Operations at this facility include:** Administration; Sales; Service. **Listed on:** New York Stock Exchange. **Stock exchange symbol:** TRN.

FINANCIAL SERVICES

You can expect to find the following types of companies in this chapter:
Consumer Finance and Credit Agencies • Investment Specialists •
Mortgage Bankers and Loan Brokers •
Security and Commodity Brokers, Dealers, and Exchanges

AMERICREDIT CORPORATION
801 Cherry Street, Suite 3900, Fort Worth TX 76102. 817/302-7000.
Fax: 817/302-7934. **Contact:** Personnel. **World Wide Web address:**
http://www.americredit.com. **Description:** A national consumer
finance company specializing in the purchasing, securitizing, and
servicing of automobile loans. **Corporate headquarters location:**
This location. **Other U.S. locations:** Nationwide. **Listed on:** New
York Stock Exchange. **Stock exchange symbol:** ACF.

BEAR, STEARNS & COMPANY, INC.
300 Crescent Court, Suite 200, Dallas TX 75201. 214/979-7900.
Contact: Human Resources. **World Wide Web address:** http://www.
bearstearns.com. **Description:** A leading worldwide investment
banking, securities trading, and brokerage firm. The firm's business
includes corporate finance, mergers and acquisitions, public finance,
institutional equities, fixed income sales and trading, private client
services, foreign exchange, future sales and trading, derivatives, and
asset management. **Corporate headquarters location:** New York NY.
Other U.S. locations: Nationwide. **Parent company:** The Bear
Stearns Companies Inc. also operates Bear, Stearns Securities
Corporation, providing professional and correspondent clearing
services including securities lending; and Custodial Trust Company,
providing master trust, custody, and government securities services.
Listed on: New York Stock Exchange. **Stock exchange symbol:** BSC.

CENTEX CORPORATION
P.O. Box 199000, Dallas TX 75219. 214/981-5000. **Contact:**
Human Resources. **E-mail address:** human.resources@checmail.
com. **World Wide Web address:** http://www.centex.com.
Description: Provides home building, mortgage banking,
contracting, and construction products and services. **Positions
advertised include:** Branch Support Specialist; Loan Officer.
Corporate headquarters location: This location. **Subsidiaries
include:** Centex Homes is one of America's largest homebuilders.
CTX Mortgage Company is among the top retail originators of single-
family home mortgages. Centex Construction Company, Inc. is one

of the largest general building contractors in the United States, as well as one of the largest constructors of health care facilities. Centex Construction Products, Inc., which manufactures and distributes cement, ready-mix concrete, aggregates, and gypsum wallboard, is one of the largest U.S.-owned cement producers. Centex Development Company, LP conducts real estate development activities. **Listed on:** New York Stock Exchange. **Stock exchange symbol:** CTX.

CITIGROUP
6400 Las Calinas Boulevard, Irving TX 75039. 972/652-4000. **Contact:** Human Resources Department. **World Wide Web address:** http://www.citigroup.com. **Description:** Citigroup offers financial solutions with home mortgages, credit cards, personal loans, insurance, business financing, banking and investments. **Other U.S. locations:** Nationwide. **Listed on:** New York Stock Exchange. **Stock exchange symbol:** C.

A.G. EDWARDS & SONS
2305 Cedars Spring Road, Suite 300, Dallas TX 75201. 214/954-1999. **Contact:** Human Resources. **World Wide Web address:** http://www.agedwards.com. **Description:** An investment firm offering bonds, money market accounts, mutual funds, IRAs, annuities, estate planning, and related services. Founded in 1887. **Corporate headquarters location:** St. Louis MO.

FIDELITY INVESTMENTS
400 East Las Colinas Boulevard, Mail Zone CP7I, Irving TX 75039. 972/584-7000. **Fax:** 972/584-7275. **Contact:** Human Resources. **World Wide Web address:** http://www.fidelity.com. **Description:** One of the nation's leading investment counseling and mutual fund/discount brokerage firms. **NOTE:** Entry-level positions and second and third shifts are offered. **Positions advertised include:** Principal Operating Systems Consultant. **Special programs:** Internships. **Internship information:** The company has an MIS internship program. Applications must be submitted by March 1st via e-mail or in writing. **Corporate headquarters location:** Boston MA. **Other U.S. locations:** Nationwide. **Listed on:** Privately held.

THE FINANCE COMPANY
2201 South W.S. Young Drive, Suite 106C, Killeen TX 76543. 254/526-8390. **Contact:** Human Resources. **Description:** Engaged primarily in buying and servicing installment contracts originated by

used car dealers. Most of The Finance Company's income comes from interest charged on contracts and from the discounts at which it purchases contracts. The company also receives revenue from the commissions received on ancillary products, such as credit insurance, limited physical damage insurance, and product warranties offered by the company and underwritten by third-party vendors. **NOTE:** Send resumes to: The Finance Company, Human Resources, P.O. Box 10306, Norfolk VA 23513.

FIRST SOUTHWEST COMPANY
1700 Pacific Avenue, Suite 500, Dallas TX 75201-4652. 214/953-4000. **Fax:** 214/953-8790. **Contact:** Personnel. **World Wide Web address:** http://www.firstsw.com. **Description:** Offers a full line of investment services including public, private, and corporate banking; funds management; trading of debt and equity securities; institutional sales; and clearing. **Corporate headquarters location:** This location. **Other area locations:** Abilene TX; Austin TX; Fort Worth TX; Houston TX; Lubbock TX; San Antonio TX. **Other U.S. locations:** AR; FL

FIRST UNION SECURITIES INC.
500 North Akard Street, Suite 1515, Lincoln Plaza, Dallas TX 75201. 214/740-3200. **Contact:** Personnel. **World Wide Web address:** http://www.firstunionsec.com. **Description:** Provides a broad range of financial services including asset management, lending, trust services, and investment banking. **Parent company:** Wachovia Securities.

J.P. MORGAN CHASE & COMPANY
P.O. Box 250, Arlington TX 76004-0250. 817/856-3277. **Contact:** Human Resources. **World Wide Web address:** http://www.jp morganchase.com. **Description:** Specializes in global financial services and retail banking. J.P. Morgan Chase and Company's services include asset management, cardmember services, community development, commercial banking for middle market companies, diversified consumer lending, global markets, home finance, investment banking, private banking, private equity, regional consumer and small business banking, and treasury and securities services. **Positions advertised include:** Personal Financial Advisor; Account Executive; Case Workflow Leader. **NOTE:** Job seekers are encouraged to apply via the Website: http://careers.jpmorganchase.com. **Listed on:** New York Stock Exchange. **Stock exchange symbol:** JPM.

JEFFERIES & COMPANY, INC.

13355 Noel Road, Suite 1400, Dallas TX 75240. 972/701-3000. **Contact:** Human Resources. **World Wide Web address:** http://www.jefco.com. **Description:** Engaged in equity, convertible debt and taxable fixed income securities brokerage and trading, and corporate finance. Jefferies & Company is one of the leading national firms engaged in the distribution and trading of blocks of equity securities primarily in the third market. Founded in 1962. **Parent company:** Jefferies Group, Inc. is a holding company which, through its primary subsidiaries Jefferies & Company; Investment Technology Group; Inc., Jefferies International Limited; and Jefferies Pacific Limited, is engaged in securities brokerage and trading, corporate finance, and other financial services.

MERRILL LYNCH

701 South Taylor Street, Suite 100, Amarillo TX 79101. 806/376-4861. **Contact:** Hiring Manager. **World Wide Web address:** http://www.ml.com. **Description:** Brokers in securities, option contracts, commodities, financial futures contracts, and insurance. **NOTE:** Please call for specific information on where to mail a resume. **Other U.S. locations:** Nationwide. **Listed on:** New York Stock Exchange. **Stock exchange symbol:** MER.

RBC DAIN RAUSCHER

2711 North Haskell Avenue, Suite 2400, Dallas TX 75204. 214/989-1000. **Contact:** Human Resources. **World Wide Web address:** http://www.rbcdain.com. **Description:** A financial consulting and securities firm. The company also provides real estate syndication and property investment services, as well as data processing services. **Corporate headquarters location:** Minneapolis MN.

SECURITY CAPITAL GROUP INC.

7777 Market Center Avenue, El Paso TX 79912. 915/877-1781. **Fax:** 915/877-5192. **Contact:** Pam Hynes, Manager of Recruiting. **World Wide Web address:** http://www.securitycapital.com. **Description:** Provides accounting, finance, MIS, internal audit, tax, cash management, human resources, and risk management. **NOTE:** Entry-level positions are offered. **Special programs:** Internships. **Listed on:** New York Stock Exchange. **Stock exchange symbol:** SCZ.

SOUTHWEST SECURITIES GROUP, INC.

1201 Elm Street, Suite 3500, Dallas TX 75270-2180. 214/651-1800. **Contact:** Human Resources. **World Wide Web address:** http://www.

southwestsecurities.com. **Description:** Southwest Securities Group, Inc. is a holding company with subsidiaries engaged in providing securities brokerage, investment banking, and investment advisory services. Founded in 1972. **Corporate headquarters location:** This location. **Other U.S. locations:** Chicago IL; Albuquerque NM; Santa Fe NM. **Listed on:** New York Stock Exchange. **Stock exchange symbol:** SWS. **Number of employees worldwide:** 1,100.

TRADESTAR INVESTMENTS
8201 Preston Road, Suite 270, Dallas TX 75209. 214/373-0066. **Toll-free phone:** 800/622-5484. **Contact:** Human Resources. **World Wide Web address:** http://www.selecttrade.com. **Description:** A regional brokerage firm.

UBS PAINEWEBBER, INC.
100 Crescent Court, Suite 600, Dallas TX 75201. 214/220-0400. **Contact:** Branch Manager. **World Wide Web address:** http://www. ubspainewebber.com. **Description:** A full-service securities firm with over 300 offices nationwide. Services include investment banking, asset management, merger and acquisition consulting, municipal securities underwriting, estate planning, retirement programs, and transaction management. Clients include corporations, governments, institutions, and individuals. Founded in 1879. **Positions advertised include:** Experienced Financial Advisor. **Corporate headquarters location:** New York NY. **Other U.S. locations:** Nationwide.

VALERO ENERGY CORPORATION
CREDIT CARD CENTER
P.O. Box 300, Amarillo TX 79105. 806/324-4601. **Contact:** Human Resources. **World Wide Web address:** http://www.valero.com. **Description:** Valero Energy Corporation has an extensive refining system with a throughput capacity of nearly 2 million barrels per day. The company's geographically diverse refining network stretches from Canada to the U.S. Gulf Coast, and West Coast. Valero has almost 5,000 retail sites in the United States and Canada, branded as Valero, Diamond Shamrock, Ultramar, Beacon, and Total. Valero is a leading producer of premium environmentally clean products, such as reformulated gasoline, (CARB) Phase II gasoline, low-sulfur diesel and oxygenates. **Positions advertised include:** Associate Systems Analyst; Credit Card Risk & Collections Manager; Customer Service Associate; Senior Credit Card Operations Systems Marketing Manager. **Corporate headquarters location:** San Antonio TX. **Operations at this facility include:** This location is the

credit card center servicing over 500,000 accounts. **Listed on:** New York Stock Exchange. **Stock exchange symbol:** VLO. **Number of employees worldwide:** 22,000.

VALERO ENERGY CORPORATION
MCKEE REFINERY

6701 FM 119, HCR Box 36, Sunray TX 79086-2013. 806/935-2141. **Contact:** Tonja Bilbrey, Human Resources Director. **Description:** Valero Energy Corporation has an extensive refining system with a throughput capacity of nearly 2 million barrels per day. The company's geographically diverse refining network stretches from Canada to the U.S. Gulf Coast, and West Coast. Valero has almost 5,000 retail sites in the United States and Canada, branded as Valero, Diamond Shamrock, Ultramar, Beacon, and Total. Valero is a leading producer of premium environmentally clean products, such as reformulated gasoline, (CARB) Phase II gasoline, low-sulfur diesel and oxygenates. The company also operates a credit card program with over 500,000 active accounts. **Corporate headquarters location:** San Antonio TX. **Operations at this facility include:** This location is an oil refinery. **Listed on:** New York Stock Exchange. **Stock exchange symbol:** VLO. **Number of employees worldwide:** 22,000.

FOOD AND BEVERAGES/ AGRICULTURE

You can expect to find the following types of companies in this chapter:
Crop Services and Farm Supplies • Dairy Farms • Food
Manufacturers/Processors and Agricultural Producers •
Tobacco Products

ANCHOR WEST INC.

P.O. Box 608, Pecos TX 79772. 915/447-2828. **Fax:** 915/447-4747.
Contact: Mr. Jesse Manciaz, Senior Human Resources Manager.
World Wide Web address: http://www.anchorfoods.com.
Description: Manufactures a variety of food products including
onion rings, sweet corn nuggets, bell pepper rings, zucchini slices,
okra slices, and beer batter products. **Parent company:** Anchor Food
Products (Appleton WI).

BEST MAID

P.O. Box 1809, Fort Worth TX 76101-1809. 817/335-5494. **Contact:**
Personnel Manager. **World Wide Web address:** http://www.best
maidproducts.com. **Description:** Manufactures and distributes
pickled fruits and vegetables.

BIMBO BAKERIES USA

P.O. Box 937, 515 Jones Street, Fort Worth TX 76101. 817/212-
2000. **Contact:** Rachel Gerragauch, Accounts Receivable
Coordinator. **World Wide Web address:** http://www.bimbobakeries
usa.com. **Description:** Manufactures, distributes, and markets bread,
cakes and cookies. **Corporate headquarters location:** This location.
Parent company: Grupo Bimbo.

BRUCE FOODS CORPORATION

8000 Ashley Road, El Paso TX 79934. 915/821-2500. **Contact:**
Human Resources. **World Wide Web address:** http://www.bruce
foods.com. **Description:** Processes a wide range of foods. Products
include Bruce's Yams, Cajun King, Casa Fiesta, Louisiana Gold,
Louisiana Hot Sauce, and Mexene Chili Products.

BUNGE FOODS GROUP

P.O. Box 163289, Fort Worth TX 76161-3289. 817/625-2331.
Contact: Human Resources. **World Wide Web address:** http://www.
bungefoods.com. **Description:** Produces shortening and margarine.
Corporate headquarters location: St. Louis MO. **Parent company:**

Bunge Corporation. **Operations at this facility include:** Administration; Manufacturing; Sales.

CACTUS FEEDERS INC.
P.O. Box 3050, Amarillo TX 79116. 806/373-2333. **Contact:** Kevin Hazelwood, Director of Employment. **E-mail address:** jobs@cactusfeeders.com. **World Wide Web address:** http://www.cactusfeeders.com. **Description:** Feeds and prepares cattle for delivery to meat packing plants and slaughterhouses.

CAMPBELL SOUP COMPANY
P.O. Box 9016, Paris TX 75461-9016. 903/737-2282. **Contact:** Human Resources. **World Wide Web address:** http://www.campbellsoup.com. **Description:** Campbell Soup Company produces commercial soups, juices, pickles, frozen foods, canned beans, canned pasta products, spaghetti sauces, and baked goods. The company's products are distributed worldwide. U.S. brand names include Campbell's, Vlasic, V8, Chunky, Home Cookin', Prego, Pepperidge Farm, LeMenu, and Swanson. European foods are sold under brand names such as Pleybin, Biscuits Delacre, Freshbake, Groko, Godiva, and Betis. **Positions advertised include:** Brand Manager; Finance Manager; Sales Representative. **Corporate headquarters location:** Camden NJ. **Other U.S. locations:** Sacramento CA; Maxton NC; Napoleon OH. **Operations at this facility include:** This location produces and cans soup. **Subsidiaries include:** Arnotts Biscuits of Australia. **Listed on:** New York Stock Exchange. **Stock exchange symbol:** CPB. **Number of employees nationwide:** 24,000.

COCA-COLA BOTTLING COMPANY OF NORTH TEXAS
P.O. Box 132008, Dallas TX 75313. 214/357-1781. **Physical address:** 6011 Lemmon Avenue, Dallas TX 75209. **Recorded jobline:** 214/902-2634. **Contact:** Human Resources. **World Wide Web address:** http://www.coca-cola.com. **Description:** Coca-Cola Bottling Company of North Texas is a regional subsidiary of Coca-Cola Enterprises. **Special programs:** Internships. **Corporate headquarters location:** Atlanta GA. **Other U.S. locations:** Nationwide. **Parent company:** Coca-Cola Enterprises Inc. is in the liquid, nonalcoholic refreshment business, which includes traditional carbonated soft drinks, still and sparkling waters, juices, isotonics, and teas. The company operates in 38 states, the District of Columbia, the U.S. Virgin Islands, the Islands of Tortola and Grand Cayman, and the Netherlands. **Operations at this facility include:**

This location houses executive offices. **Listed on:** New York Stock Exchange. **Stock exchange symbol:** KO.

DANKWORTH PACKAGING
P.O. Box 584, Ballinger TX 76821. 915/365-3553. **Fax:** 915/365-2367. **Contact:** Danny Hamilton, Plant Manager. **Description:** A meat packaging plant. **Corporate headquarters location:** This location.

DARLING INTERNATIONAL INC.
251 O'Connor Ridge Boulevard, Suite 300, Irving TX 75038. 972/717-0300. **Contact:** Mike Campbell, Director of Human Resources. **World Wide Web address:** http://www.darlingii.com. **Description:** Recycles animal by-products including fats and proteins into tallow, protein meals, and yellow grease. **Listed on:** American Stock Exchange. **Stock exchange symbol:** DAR.

DR PEPPER/7-UP COMPANY
P.O. Box 869077, Plano TX 75086-9077. 972/673-7000. **Physical address:** 5301 Legacy Drive, Plano TX 75024. **Contact:** Human Resources. **World Wide Web address:** http://www.drpepper.com. **Description:** Dr Pepper/7-Up Company manufactures, markets, and distributes soft drink syrups, concentrates, and extracts to bottlers. A food service segment distributes products to restaurants and convenience stores. **Parent company:** Cadbury Schweppes PLC. **Operations at this facility include:** This location houses the company's U.S. headquarters. **Listed on:** New York Stock Exchange. **Stock exchange symbol:** CSG.

FLEMING COMPANIES, INC.
P.O. Box 299013, Lewisville TX 75057. 972/840-4400. **Physical address:** 1945 Lakepointe Drive, Lewisville TX 75057. **Contact:** Human Resources. **World Wide Web address:** http://www.fleming. com. **Description:** A wholesale distributor of a wide variety of groceries, meats, dairy and delicatessen products, frozen foods, fresh produce, and general merchandise. **Corporate headquarters location:** This location.

FRITO-LAY, INC.
701 North Wildwood, Irving TX 75061. 972/579-2111. **Contact:** Human Resources. **World Wide Web address:** http://www.fritolay. com. **Description:** A worldwide manufacturer and wholesaler of a wide range of snack products including Fritos Corn Chips, Doritos

Tortilla Chips, Lays Potato Chips, Ruffles Potato Chips, Cracker Jack caramel popcorn, Chee-tos, and Smartfood Popcorn. **Positions advertised include:** Sales Manager; Production Manager; Maintenance Mechanic; Technical Manager Designate; Tractor/Trailer Mechanic. **Special programs:** Internships. **Corporate headquarters location:** Plano TX. **Other U.S. locations:** Nationwide. **Parent company:** PepsiCo, Inc. (Purchase NY) consists of Frito-Lay Company, Pepsi-Cola Company, Quaker Oats, and Tropicana Products, Inc. **Listed on:** New York Stock Exchange. **Stock exchange symbol:** PEP.

FRITO-LAY, INC.
P.O. Box 660634, Dallas TX 75266-0634. 972/334-7000. **Physical address:** 7701 Legacy Drive, Plano TX 75024-4099. **Fax:** 972/334-2019. **Contact:** Staffing. **World Wide Web address:** http://www.fritolay.com. **Description:** A worldwide manufacturer and wholesaler of a wide range of snack products including Fritos Corn Chips, Doritos Tortilla Chips, Lays Potato Chips, Ruffles Potato Chips, Cracker Jack caramel popcorn, Chee-tos, and Smartfood Popcorn. **Positions advertised include:** Sales Manager; Mobile Maintenance Technician; Technical Manager Designate; District Sales Leader. **Special programs:** Internships. **Corporate headquarters location:** This location. **Other U.S. locations:** Nationwide. **Parent company:** PepsiCo, Inc. (Purchase NY) consists of Frito-Lay Company, Pepsi-Cola Company, Quaker Oats, and Tropicana Products, Inc. **Listed on:** New York Stock Exchange. **Stock exchange symbol:** PEP.

FRITO-LAY, INC.
3203 Avenue B, Lubbock TX 79404. 806/762-7700. **Contact:** Human Resources Director. **World Wide Web address:** http://www.fritolay.com. **Description:** A worldwide manufacturer and wholesaler of a wide range of snack products including Fritos Corn Chips, Doritos Tortilla Chips, Lays Potato Chips, Ruffles Potato Chips, Cracker Jack caramel popcorn, Chee-tos, and Smartfood Popcorn. **Positions advertised include:** Sales Manager; Maintenance Business Unit Leader; Operations Resource Manager. **Corporate headquarters location:** Plano TX. **Other U.S. locations:** Nationwide. **Parent company:** PepsiCo, Inc. (Purchase NY) consists of Frito-Lay Company, Pepsi-Cola Company, Quaker Oats, and Tropicana Products, Inc. **Listed on:** New York Stock Exchange. **Stock exchange symbol:** PEP.

FRITO-LAY, INC.
P.O. Box 225458, Dallas TX 75222-5458. 817/861-1784. **Contact:** Staffing. **World Wide Web address:** http://www.fritolay.com. **Description:** A worldwide manufacturer and wholesaler of a wide range of snack products including Fritos Corn Chips, Doritos Tortilla Chips, Lays Potato Chips, Ruffles Potato Chips, Cracker Jack caramel popcorn, Chee-tos, and Smartfood Popcorn. **Positions advertised include:** Sales Manager; Mobile Maintenance Technician; Technical Manager Designate; District Sales Leader. **Special programs:** Internships. **Corporate headquarters location:** Plano TX. **Other U.S. locations:** Nationwide. **Parent company:** PepsiCo, Inc. (Purchase NY) consists of Frito-Lay Company, Pepsi-Cola Company, Quaker Oats, and Tropicana Products, Inc. **Operations at this facility include:** Divisional Headquarters; Research and Development. **Listed on:** New York Stock Exchange. **Stock exchange symbol:** PEP.

GANDY'S DAIRIES INC.
P.O. Box 992, San Angelo TX 76902. 915/655-6965. **Physical address:** 332 Pulliam Street, San Angelo TX 76903. **Contact:** Human Resources. **Description:** A milk distribution company. Gandy's Dairies Inc. does not process milk. **Parent company:** Dean Foods (Franklin Park IL).

HARVEST STATES FOODS
899 North Houston Street, Fort Worth TX 76106. 817/624-2123. **Contact:** Pam Harris, Personnel Director. **World Wide Web address:** http://www.harveststates.com. **Description:** Produces a line of frozen Mexican foods.

HOLLY SUGAR CORPORATION
P.O. Drawer 1778, Hereford TX 79045. 806/364-2590. **Contact:** Human Resources Manager. **World Wide Web address:** http://www. hollysugar.com. **Description:** Grows, harvests, and processes sugar beets into granulated sugar. Sugar is packaged at this location year round. **Parent company:** Imperial Holly Corporation (Sugar Land TX).

HORMEL FOODS CORPORATION
700 Highlander Boulevard, Suite 200, Arlington TX 76015. 817/465-4772. **Contact:** Office Manager. **World Wide Web address:** http:// www.hormel.com. **Description:** One of the leading processors and marketers of branded, value-added meat and food products. Principal products of the company are branded, processed meat and

food entrees, which are sold fresh, frozen, cured, smoked, cooked, and canned. These include sausages, hams, franks, bacon, canned luncheon meats, shelf-stable microwaveable entrees, stews, chili, hash, meat spreads, and frozen processed products. The majority of the company's products are sold under the Hormel brand name. Other trademarks of the company include Farm Fresh, Little Sizzlers, Quick Meal, Kid's Kitchen, Chi-Chi's, House of Tsang, Mary Kitchen, Dinty Moore, Light & Lean, Chicken by George, Black Label, and SPAM. **Positions advertised include:** Staff Accountant; Engineer; Computer Analyst; Production Manager. **Corporate headquarters location:** Austin MN. **Other U.S. locations:** CA; GA; IA; KS; NE; OK; WI. **International locations:** Australia; England; Japan; Korea; Panama; Philippines. **Subsidiaries include:** Dan's Prize, Inc.; Dubuque Foods; Farm Fresh Catfish Company; Jennie-O Foods. **Listed on:** New York Stock Exchange. **Stock exchange symbol:** HRL. **Number of employees nationwide:** 14,700.

IBP INC.
P.O. Box 30500, Amarillo TX 79187. 806/335-1531. **Contact:** Human Resources Department. **World Wide Web address:** http://www.ibpinc.com. **Description:** A slaughterhouse and meat packing plant. **Positions advertised include:** Truck Driver. **NOTE:** Send resumes to: Corporate Recruiter, IBP, Inc. World Headquarters, 800 Stevens Port Drive, Suite 818, Dakota Dunes SD 57049.

KARGILL
P.O. Box 20788, Waco TX 76702. 254/799-6211. **Contact:** Human Resources. **World Wide Web address:** http://www.plantation-foods.com. **Description:** A turkey processor.

KRAFT FOODS, INC.
2340 Forest Lane, Garland TX 75042. 972/272-7511. **Contact:** Human Resources Supervisor. **World Wide Web address:** http://www.kraftfoods.com. **Description:** Kraft Foods, Inc. is one of the largest producers of packaged grocery products in North America. Major brands include Jell-O, Post, Kool-Aid, Crystal Light, Entenmann's, Miracle Whip, Stove Top, and Shake 'n Bake. Kraft markets a number of products under the Kraft brand name including natural and processed cheeses, and dry packaged dinners. The company's products are supplied to more than 100 countries worldwide. **Parent company:** Philip Morris Companies is a holding company with principal wholly-owned subsidiaries Philip Morris Inc. (Philip Morris U.S.A.), Philip Morris International Inc., Kraft Foods,

Inc., Miller Brewing Company, and Philip Morris Capital Corporation. The Oscar Mayer unit markets processed meats, poultry, lunch combinations, and pickles under the Oscar Mayer, Louis Rich, Lunchables, and Claussen brand names. Kraft Foods Ingredients Corporation manufactures private-label and industrial food products for sale to other food processing companies. In the tobacco industry, Philip Morris U.S.A. and Philip Morris International together form one of the largest international cigarette operations in the world. U.S. brand names include Marlboro, Parliament, Virginia Slims, Benson & Hedges, and Merit. Miller Brewing Company brews beer under brand names including Molson Ice, Miller Genuine Draft, Miller High Life, Sharp's, Red Dog, Miller Lite, Icehouse, Foster's Lager, and Lowenbrau. Philip Morris Capital Corporation is engaged in financial services and real estate. **Operations at this facility include:** This location produces a variety of food products including barbecue sauce, mayonnaise, tartar sauce, Miracle Whip, Catalina dressing, and salad products. **Listed on:** New York Stock Exchange. **Stock exchange symbol:** KFT. **Number of employees nationwide:** 114,000.

LEON'S TEXAS CUISINE
P.O. Box 1850, McKinney TX 75070-1850. 972/529-5050. **Fax:** 972/529-2244. **Contact:** Cindy Stephens, Human Resources Director. **E-mail address:** cindy@texascuisine.com. **World Wide Web address:** http://www.texascuisine.com. **Description:** Produces corn dogs and other southwestern-style items that are sold and distributed to retail grocery stores nationwide. **NOTE:** Entry-level positions are offered. **Corporate headquarters location:** This location.

MILLER BREWING COMPANY
7001 South Freeway, Fort Worth TX 76134. 817/551-3200. **Contact:** Human Resources. **World Wide Web address:** http://www.miller brewing.com. **Description:** Miller Brewing Company produces and distributes beer and other malt beverages. Principal beer brands include Miller Lite, Lite Ice, Miller Genuine Draft, Miller Genuine Draft Light, Miller High Life, Miller Reserve, Lowenbrau, Milwaukee's Best, Meister Brau, Red Dog, and Icehouse. Miller also produces Sharp's, a nonalcoholic beer. **Corporate headquarters location:** Milwaukee WI. **Operations at this facility include:** This location brews a variety of beer brands. **Subsidiaries include:** Jacob Leinenkugel Brewing Company (Chippewa Falls WI) brews Leinenkugel's Original Premium, Leinenkugel's Light, Leinie's Ice,

Leinenkugel's Limited, Leinenkugel's Red Lager, and four seasonal beers: Leinenkugel's Genuine Bock, Leinenkugel's Honey Weiss, Leinenkugel's Autumn Gold, and Leinenkugel's Winter Lager. Molson Breweries U.S.A., Inc. (Reston VA) imports Molson beers from Canada, as well as Australia's Foster's Lager and many other brands. Miller is also majority owner of Celis Brewery Inc. (Austin TX). **Parent company:** Philip Morris Companies Inc. (New York). **Listed on:** New York Stock Exchange. **Stock exchange symbol:** MO.

MRS. BAIRD'S BAKERIES
P.O. Box 937, Fort Worth TX 76101. 214/526-7201. **Contact:** Human Resources. **World Wide Web address:** http://www.bimbo bakeriesusa.com. **Description:** Bakes bread and other goods. The company operates facilities located throughout Texas. **Parent company:** Bimbo Bakeries USA.

OWENS COUNTRY SAUSAGE INC.
P.O. Box 830249, Richardson TX 75083. 972/235-7181. **Contact:** Human Resources. **World Wide Web address:** http://www.owens inc.com. **Description:** Produces sausage and other pork products. **Corporate headquarters location:** This location.

PEPSI BOTTLING GROUP
4532 Highway 67, Mesquite TX 75150. 214/324-8500. **Contact:** Human Resources. **World Wide Web address:** http://www.pepsico.. com. **Description:** Bottles and distributes Pepsi-Cola beverages including the brand names Pepsi-Cola, Mountain Dew, Mug Root Beer, and Slice. **Parent company:** PepsiCo, Inc. (Purchase NY) consists of Frito-Lay Company, Gatorade/Tropicana North America, Pepsi-Cola Company, and Quaker Oats Company. **Listed on:** New York Stock Exchange. **Stock exchange symbol:** PEP.

PILGRIM'S PRIDE CORPORATION
P.O. Box 93, Pittsburg TX 75686-0093. 903/855-1000. **Contact:** Human Resources. **World Wide Web address:** http://www. pilgrimspride.com. **Description:** Produces chicken products and eggs for the restaurant, institutional, food service, grocery, and wholesale markets. The company's operations include breeding, hatching, growing, processing, packaging, and preparing poultry. Pilgrim's Pride Corporation also produces animal feeds and ingredients. The company is one of the largest producers of chicken products in the United States and Mexico. The company's primary domestic distribution is handled through restaurants and retailers in

central, southwestern, and western United States, and through the food service industry throughout the country. **Corporate headquarters location:** This location. **Other U.S. locations:** AR; AZ; OK. **Listed on:** New York Stock Exchange. **Stock exchange symbol:** CHX.

PILGRIM'S PRIDE CORPORATION
P.O. Box 1268, Mount Pleasant TX 75456-1268. 903/575-1000. **Contact:** Human Resources. **World Wide Web address:** http://www. pilgrimspride.com. **Description:** Pilgrim's Pride Corporation produces chicken products and eggs for the restaurant, institutional, food service, grocery, and wholesale markets. The company's operations include breeding, hatching, growing, processing, packaging, and preparing poultry. Pilgrim's Pride Corporation also produces animal feeds and ingredients. The company is one of the largest producers of chicken products in the United States and Mexico. The company's primary domestic distribution is handled through restaurants and retailers in central, southwestern, and western United States, and through the food service industry throughout the country. **Corporate headquarters location:** Pittsburg TX. **Other U.S. locations:** AR; AZ; OK. **Operations at this facility include:** This location manufactures animal feeds and prepared foods, and operates two slaughterhouses. **Listed on:** New York Stock Exchange. **Stock exchange symbol:** CHX.

PRICE'S CREAMERIES
600 North Piedras Street, El Paso TX 79923. 915/565-2711. **Contact:** Human Resources. **World Wide Web address:** http://www.prices milk.com. **Description:** A creamery that manufactures and distributes ice cream, milk, and fruit juices.

THE QUAKER OATS COMPANY
2822 Glenfield Avenue, Dallas TX 75233. 214/340-0370. **Contact:** Personnel Director. **World Wide Web address:** http://www.quake roats.com. **Description:** The Quaker Oats Company is best known for Old Fashioned Quaker Oats. Other products include Aunt Jemima syrups and pancacke mixes, and Rice-A-Roni instant rice. The Quaker Oats Company is also the primary producer of Gatorade, one of the leading sports beverages in the United States. **Corporate headquarters location:** Chicago IL. **Operations at this facility include:** This location is a distribution center. **Parent company:** PepsiCo. **Listed on:** New York Stock Exchange. **Stock exchange symbol:** PEP.

REPUBLIC BEVERAGE
1010 Isuzu Parkway, Grand Prairie TX 75050. 972/595-6100. **Contact:** Human Resources. **World Wide Web address:** http://www. republicbeverage.com. **Description:** A wine and alcohol wholesale distributor. **Positions advertised include:** Area Wine Manager.

SARA LEE BAKERY GROUP
3500 Manor Way, Dallas TX 75235. 214/357-1754. **Fax:** 214/353-1408. **Contact:** Human Resources. **World Wide Web address:** http://www.saraleebakerygroup.com. **Description:** Bakes and distributes breads and other baked goods. **Corporate headquarters location:** St. Louis MO. **Operations at this facility include:** Administration; Manufacturing; Sales. **Listed on:** New York Stock Exchange. **Stock exchange symbol:** SLE. **Number of employees nationwide:** 22,300.

SEED RESOURCE, INC.
P.O. Box 326, Tulia TX 79088. 806/995-3882. **Contact:** Gary Regner, Manager. **World Wide Web address:** http://www.seed resource.com. **Description:** Distributes forage seed including Sorghum Sudans, which it produces, alfalfa, turf grass seed, and wheat seed. The company also produces wheat. **Parent company:** AgriBioTech, Inc. (ABT) is a specialized distributor of forage (hay crops) and turf grass seed. The forage and turf grass seed industry supplies seed to the forage and turf cash crop sectors. The company also distributes nonseed products including Bloatenz Plus, a liquid bloat preventative administered to the drinking water of cattle, permitting them to graze on alfalfa safely; and PDS-1000, marketed in conjunction with Bloatenz Plus, is a microprocessor-controlled precision dispensing system designed to dispense solutions into the drinking water of livestock at a preset dosage rate. Other subsidiaries of ABT include Scott Seed Company; Hobart Seed Company; Halsey Seed Company; and Sphar & Company. Combined, these companies cover the following distribution territories: IN; KY; NM; NY; OK; OR; PA; TX; WA.

SOUTHWEST COCA-COLA BOTTLING COMPANY
6101 Avenue A, Lubbock TX 79404. 806/472-3200. **Contact:** Human Resources. **World Wide Web address:** http://www.coca-cola.com. **Description:** A bottling company packaging Coca-Cola, Barq's, and Dr. Pepper. **Parent company:** Coca-Cola Enterprises, Inc. is in the liquid nonalcoholic refreshment business, which includes traditional carbonated soft drinks, still and sparkling waters, juices, isotonics, and teas. The company operates in 38 states, the District of

Columbia, the U.S. Virgin Islands, the Islands of Tortola and Grand Cayman, and the Netherlands. Coca-Cola Enterprises operates 268 facilities, approximately 24,000 vehicles, and over 860,000 vending machines, beverage dispensers, and coolers used to market, distribute, and produce the company's products. **Listed on:** New York Stock Exchange. **Stock exchange symbol:** KO.

SUIZA FOODS

2515 McKinney Avenue, Suite 1200, Dallas TX 75201. 214/303-3400. **Fax:** 214/303-3499. **Contact:** Personnel. **World Wide Web address:** http://www.deanfoods.com. **Description:** Manufactures and distributes fresh milk and related dairy products, shelf-stable and refrigerated food and beverage products, frozen food products, coffee, and plastic containers. **Corporate headquarters location:** This location. **Parent company:** Dean Foods. **Listed on:** New York Stock Exchange. **Stock exchange symbol:** DF.

TYSON FOODS INC.

1484 North East Loop 436, Carthage TX 75633. 903/693-7101. **Contact:** Human Resources. **World Wide Web address:** http://www.tyson.com. **Description:** Tyson Foods Inc. is one of the world's largest fully-integrated producers, processors, and marketers of poultry-based food products. The company also produces other entrees and convenience food items. Products include Tyson Holly Farms Fresh Chicken, Weaver, Louis Kemp Crab, Lobster Delights, Healthy Portion, Beef Stir Fry, Crab Delights Stir Fry, Chicken Fried Rice Kits, Pork Chops with Cinnamon Apples, Salmon Grill Kits, Fish'n Chips Kits, and Rotisserie Chicken. **Positions advertised include:** Category Manager; Complex Nurse Manager; Industrial Engineer. **Special programs:** Internships. **Corporate headquarters location:** Springdale AR. **Operations at this facility include:** This location is a poultry processing plant. **Listed on:** New York Stock Exchange. **Stock exchange symbol:** TSN. **Number of employees nationwide:** 124,000.

U.S. FOODSERVICE

4202 Dan Morton Drive, Suite 106, Dallas TX 75236. 972/780-2310. **Fax:** 972/283-6123. **Contact:** Personnel. **World Wide Web address:** http://www.usfoodservice.com. **Description:** An institutional food production and distribution company with clients in the restaurant and health care industries. **Corporate headquarters location:** Columbia MD. **Other U.S. locations:** Nationwide. **Parent** company: Royal Ahold. **Listed on:** New York Stock Exchange. **Stock exchange symbol:** AHO.

U.S. FOODSERVICE

P.O. Box 2804, Lubbock TX 79408. 806/747-5204. **Contact:** Personnel. **World Wide Web address:** http://www.usfoodservice. com. **Description:** An institutional food production and distribution company with clients in the restaurant and health care industries. **Positions advertised include:** Experienced Territory Sales Representative. **Corporate headquarters location:** Columbia MD. **Other U.S. locations:** Nationwide. **Parent company:** Royal Ahold. **Listed on:** New York Stock Exchange. **Stock exchange symbol:** AHO.

U.S. FOODSERVICE

P.O. Box 871389, Mesquite TX 75187. 214/388-7700. **Toll-free phone:** 800/827-7926. **Contact:** Personnel. **World Wide Web address:** http://www.usfoodservice.com. **Description:** An institutional food production and distribution company with clients in the restaurant and health care industries. **Corporate headquarters location:** Columbia MD. **Other U.S. locations:** Nationwide. **Parent company:** Royal Ahold. **Listed on:** New York Stock Exchange. **Stock exchange symbol:** AHO.

GOVERNMENT

You can expect to find the following types of agencies in this chapter:
Courts • Executive, Legislative, and General Government • Public Agencies (Firefighters, Military, Police) • United States Postal Service

DALLAS, CITY OF
2014 Main Street, Room 100, Dallas TX 75201. 214/670-3120. **Fax:** 214/670-5855. **Contact:** Human Resources. **World Wide Web address:** http://www.dallascityhall.com. **Description:** Nonprofit, local government agency. This location also hires seasonally. **NOTE:** Second and third shifts are offered. **Positions advertised include:** Call Taker; Chemist; Emergency Management Coordinator; Engineer Assistant; Engineer; Senior Engineer; Equipment Operator. **Special programs:** Training; Summer Jobs. **Corporate headquarters location:** This location.

DALLAS POLICE DEPARTMENT
2014 Main Street, Room 201, Dallas TX 75201. 214/670-4407. **Toll-free phone:** 800/527-2948. **Fax:** 214/670-5093. **Contact:** Warren Mitchell, Recruiting Sergeant. **World Wide Web address:** http://www.ci.dallas.tx.us/dpd. **Description:** Provides law enforcement services. **NOTE:** The department requires 45 semester hours from an accredited college or university with a C or better average. Entry-level positions and second and third shifts are offered.

DALLAS PUBLIC WORKS AND TRANSPORTATION DEPARTMENT
320 East Jefferson Boulevard, Room 208, Dallas TX 75203. 214/948-4200. **Contact:** Human Resources Division. **World Wide Web address:** http://www.dallascityhall.com. **Description:** Administrative offices for the city public works and transportation department. **Operations at this facility include:** Administration; Divisional Headquarters.

DALLAS SHERIFF'S DEPARTMENT
133 North Industrial Boulevard, Dallas TX 75207. 214/749-8641. **Contact:** Human Resources Department. **Description:** Enforces justice, public order, and safety for the city of Dallas.

EL PASO, CITY OF
2 Civic Center Plaza, El Paso TX 79901-1196. 915/541-4000. **Contact:** Human Resources. **World Wide Web address:** http://www. ci.el-paso.tx.us. **Description:** Administrative offices for the city of El

Paso. **Positions advertised include:** Treasury Services Manager; Transit Communication Dispatcher; Electrician; Public Services Librarian; Transportation Planner; Library Branch Manager; Archives and Records Manager.

PLANO, CITY OF
P.O. Box 860358, Plano TX 75086-0358. 972/941-7000. **Contact:** Human Resources. **World Wide Web address:** http://www.ci. plano.tx.us. **Description:** Administrative offices for the city of Plano.

TEXAS DEPARTMENT OF TRANSPORTATION
P.O. Box 150, Abilene TX 79604. 915/676-6800. **Toll-free phone:** 800/893-6817. **Recorded jobline:** 800/893-6848. **Contact:** Employment. **World Wide Web address:** http://www.dot.state.tx.us. **Description:** Designs, builds, and maintains roads and highways throughout the state of Texas. **Positions advertised include:** Contract Specialist; Summer Engineering Intern.

U.S. DEPARTMENT OF VETERANS AFFAIRS
VETERANS ADMINISTRATION MEDICAL CENTER
300 Veterans Boulevard, Big Spring TX 79720. 915/263-7361. **Contact:** Human Resources. **World Wide Web address:** http:// www.va.gov. **Description:** A medical center operated by the U.S. Department of Veterans Affairs. From 54 hospitals in 1930, the VA health care system has grown to include 171 medical centers; more than 364 outpatient, community, and outreach clinics; 130 nursing home care units; and 37 domiciliary residences. The VA operates at least one medical center in each of the 48 contiguous states, Puerto Rico, and the District of Columbia. With approximately 76,000 medical center beds, the VA treats nearly 1 million patients in VA hospitals; 75,000 in nursing home care units; and 25,000 in domiciliary residences. The VA's outpatient clinics register approximately 24 million visits per year. **NOTE:** The VA Medical Center hires current or former federal employees, veterans, and disabled veterans. The VA Medical Center is currently under hiring constraints. Applications from the general public are not accepted. **Corporate headquarters location:** Washington DC.

U.S. ENVIRONMENTAL PROTECTION AGENCY (EPA)
1445 Ross Avenue, Dallas TX 75202-2733. 214/665-6444. **Contact:** Human Resources **World Wide Web address:** http://www.epa.gov. **Description:** The EPA is dedicated to improving and preserving the quality of the environment, both nationally and globally, and

protecting human health and the productivity of natural resources. The agency is committed to ensuring that federal environmental laws are implemented and enforced effectively; U.S. policy, both foreign and domestic, encourages the integration of economic development and environmental protection so that economic growth can be sustained over the long term; and public and private decisions affecting energy, transportation, agriculture, industry, international trade, and natural resources fully integrate considerations of environmental quality. Founded in 1970. **Special programs:** Internships. **Corporate headquarters location:** Washington DC. **Other U.S. locations:** Nationwide.

HEALTH CARE: SERVICES, EQUIPMENT, AND PRODUCTS

You can expect to find the following types of companies in this chapter:
Dental Labs and Equipment • Home Health Care Agencies • Hospitals and Medical Centers • Medical Equipment Manufacturers and Wholesalers • Offices and Clinics of Health Practitioners • Residential Treatment Centers/Nursing Homes • Veterinary Services

ALLEGIANCE HEALTHCARE CORPORATION

One Butterfield Trail, El Paso TX 79906. 915/779-3681. **Contact:** Human Resources. **World Wide Web address:** http://www. allegiance.net. **Description:** Allegiance Healthcare Corporation is a producer, developer, and distributor of medical products and technologies for use in hospitals and other health care settings. **Operations at this facility include:** This location manufactures disposable hospital gowns and drapes.

BAPTIST ST. ANTHONY HEALTH SYSTEM

1600 Wallace Boulevard, Amarillo TX 79106. 806/212-2000. **Contact:** Human Resources Manager. **E-mail address:** hr@ bsahs.com. **World Wide Web address:** http://www.bsahs.com. **Description:** A 255-bed general hospital. Baptist St. Anthony Health System also offers home health services, a hospice program, a rehabilitation/skilled nursing facility, a senior health center and a sports and occupational health center. **Positions advertised include:** Registration Assistant; Housekeeper; Human Resources Clerk; Cashier; Dishwasher; Hospitality Aide; Registered Nurse.

BAYLOR MEDICAL CENTER AT GARLAND

2300 Marie Curie Boulevard, Garland TX 75042. 972/487-5000. **Contact:** Human Resources. **World Wide Web address:** http://www. baylorhealth.com. **Description:** A 206-bed acute care medical and surgical center. **Positions advertised include:** Certified Nurses Aide; Certified Occupational Therapy Assistant; Dietician/Nutritionist; EEG Technologist; EKG Technician; Emergency Medical Technician; Home Health Aide; Medical Records Technician; Nuclear Medicine Technologist; Occupational Therapist; Pharmacist; Physical Therapist; Physician; Radiological Technologist; Registered Nurse; Respiratory Therapist; Social Worker; Speech-Language Pathologist. **Parent company:** Baylor Health Care System.

BAYLOR MEDICAL CENTER AT IRVING

1901 North MacArthur Boulevard, Irving TX 75061. 972/579-8100. **Contact:** Human Resources Department. **World Wide Web address:** http://www.baylorhealth.com. **Description:** A 288-bed, full-service hospital. The hospital employs specialists in the areas of oncology, neurosurgery, neurology, cardiology, and gastroenterology. **Positions advertised include:** Certified Nurses Aide; Certified Occupational Therapy Assistant; Dietician/Nutritionist; EEG Technologist; EKG Technician; Emergency Medical Technician; Home Health Aide; Medical Records Technician; Nuclear Medicine Technologist; Occupational Therapist; Pharmacist; Physical Therapist; Physician; Radiological Technologist; Registered Nurse; Respiratory Therapist; Social Worker; Speech-Language Pathologist. **Parent company:** Baylor Health Care System.

BAYLOR SENIOR HEALTH CENTER

820 West Arapaho Road, Suite 200, Richardson TX 75080. 972/498-4500. **Contact:** Human Resources. **World Wide Web address:** http://www.baylorhealth.com. **Description:** An outpatient facility that offers comprehensive primary care services to senior citizens. Founded in 1995. **Parent company:** Baylor Health Care System.

BAYLOR UNIVERSITY MEDICAL CENTER

3500 Gaston Avenue, Dallas TX 75246. 214/820-2525. **Contact:** Human Resources. **World Wide Web address:** http://www.bhcs. com. **Description:** A full-service, tertiary, teaching hospital. As the flagship hospital of the Baylor Health Care System, Baylor University Medical Center is comprised of five connecting hospitals. Hospital departments include family medicine, neurosurgery, obstetrics, gynecology, oncology, ophthalmology, orthopedic surgery, pathology, pediatrics, physical rehabilitation, plastic and reconstructive surgery, psychiatry, radiology, urology, and anesthesiology. **NOTE:** This location also houses the Baylor Rehabilitation Center. The center can be reached at 214/826-7030. **Positions advertised include:** Certified Nurses Aide; Certified Occupational Therapy Assistant; Dietician/Nutritionist; EEG Technologist; EKG Technician; Emergency Medical Technician; Home Health Aide; Medical Records Technician; Nuclear Medicine Technologist; Occupational Therapist; Pharmacist; Physical Therapist; Physician; Radiological Technologist; Registered Nurse; Respiratory Therapist; Social Worker; Speech-Language Pathologist. **Operations at this facility include:** Administration; Research and Development.

BAYLOR/RICHARDSON MEDICAL CENTER

401 West Campbell Road, Richardson TX 75080. 972/498-4737. **Fax:** 972/498-4978. **Recorded jobline:** 972/498-4875. **Contact:** Employment Coordinator. **World Wide Web address:** http://www. baylorhealth.com. **Description:** A 174-bed, nonprofit medical, surgical, and psychiatric hospital. Hospital specialties include family medicine, pediatrics, women's services, oncology, emergency medicine, cardiology, radiology and imaging, chemical dependency, skilled nursing, respiratory therapy, and home health. **Positions advertised include:** Certified Nurses Aide; Certified Occupational Therapy Assistant; Dietician/Nutritionist; EEG Technologist; EKG Technician; Emergency Medical Technician; Home Health Aide; Medical Records Technician; Nuclear Medicine Technologist; Occupational Therapist; Pharmacist; Physical Therapist; Physician; Radiological Technologist; Registered Nurse; Respiratory Therapist; Social Worker; Speech-Language Pathologist.

BIG SPRING STATE HOSPITAL

1901 North Highway 87, Big Spring TX 79720. 915/268-7256. **Fax:** 915/268-7285. **Contact:** Human Resources. **World Wide Web address:** http://www.mhmr.state.tx.us/hospitals/bigsrpingsh/big springsh.html. **Description:** A nonprofit, state-governed facility that specializes in the treatment of patients with mental illness. **NOTE:** Entry-level positions and second and third shifts are offered. **Special programs:** Internships. **Corporate headquarters location:** Austin TX. **Parent company:** Texas Department of Mental Health and Mental Retardation. **Operations at this facility include:** Administration. **Number of employees at this location:** 730.

CHILDREN'S MEDICAL CENTER OF DALLAS

1935 Motor Street, Dallas TX 75235. 214/456-7000. **Recorded jobline:** 214/456-2895. **Contact:** Human Resources. **World Wide Web address:** http://www.childrens.com. **Description:** A private, 322-bed children's medical center operating through 50 specialty clinics. **Positions advertised include:** Claim Representative; Clinical Lab Technician; Computer Programmer; Customer Service Representative; EEG Technologist; EKG Technician; Emergency Medical Technician; Human Resources Manager; Medical Records Technician; Physical Therapist; Psychologist; Public Relations Specialist; Radiological Technologist; Registered Nurse; Respiratory Therapist; Social Worker; Speech-Language Pathologist; Surgical Technician; Systems Analyst.

CHRISTUS ST. JOSEPH'S HEALTH SYSTEM

P.O. Box 9070, Paris TX 75460. 903/737-3253. **Fax:** 903/737-3887. **Contact:** Human Resources. **World Wide Web address:** http://www. stjosephs.com. **Description:** A nonprofit, 216-bed, acute care hospital that provides comprehensive heart programs, inpatient and outpatient dialysis, rehabilitation services, oncology, radiation therapy, and nuclear medicine services. **Positions advertised include:** Cath Lab Technician; Certified Nurse Technician; Diagnostic Technician; Director of Performance Improvement; Fitness Instructor; Housekeeper; Licensed Vocational Nurse; Medical Technologist; Nuclear Medicine Technician.

COLUMBIA/HCA

6565 North MacArthur, Suite 350, Irving TX 75039. 972/401-8750. **Contact:** Human Resources. **World Wide Web address:** http://www. hcahealthcare.com. **Description:** Columbia/HCA owns several hundred surgical centers and hospitals. Founded in 1992. **Other U.S. locations:** Nationwide. **Operations at this facility include:** This location is a regional administrative office. **Number of employees at this location:** 5,000.

COOK CHILDREN'S MEDICAL CENTER

801 Seventh Avenue, Fort Worth TX 76104-2733. 817/885-4419. **Fax:** 817/885-3947. **Recorded jobline:** 817/885-4414. **Contact:** Human Resources. **World Wide Web address:** http://www.cook childrens.org. **Description:** A pediatric health care center. Founded in 1985. **NOTE:** Entry-level positions and second and third shifts are offered. **Positions advertised include:** Occupational Therapist; Registered Nurse; Administrative Director; Respiratory Therapist; Audiologist; Radiographer; Phlebotomist; Food Service Supervisor; Nurse Recruiter; Paramedic; Communications Clerk; Speech Pathologist.

DE SOTO ANIMAL HOSPITAL

200 North Hampton, De Soto TX 75115. 972/223-4840. **Contact:** Human Resources. **Description:** Provides general medical and surgical services to domestic animals. Other services include radiology, dentistry, behavior counseling, allergy testing, and boarding.

DOCTORS HOSPITAL

9440 Poppy Drive, Dallas TX 75218. 214/324-6297. **Fax:** 214/324-6547. **Recorded jobline:** 214/324-6700. **Contact:** Human Resources.

World Wide Web address: http://www.tenethealth.com. **Description:** A hospital. Founded in 1959. **Positions advertised include:** Legal Secretary; Registered Nurse; LPN; Therapist; Social Worker; Nurse Manager. **Special programs:** Internships. **Other U.S. locations:** Nationwide. **Parent company:** Tenet Healthcare Corporation owns and operates a network of hospitals and related businesses nationwide. **Operations at this facility include:** Administration. **Listed on:** New York Stock Exchange. **Stock exchange symbol:** THC.

EAST TEXAS MEDICAL CENTER
1000 South Beckham, Tyler TX 75701. 903/597-0351. **Recorded jobline:** 903/531-8016. **Contact:** Human Resources. **World Wide Web address:** http://www.etmc.org. **Description:** A 454-bed general hospital. Services include acute care rehabilitation, cardiovascular care, neurological services, obstetrical services, and a level-one trauma center. **Positions advertised include:** Medical Receptionist; Charge Entry Clerk; Collector; Insurance Specialist; Payment Entry Clerk; Medical Records Specialist. **Parent company:** East Texas Medical Center Regional Healthcare System.

ESSILOR GROUP
13515 North Stemmons Freeway, Dallas TX 75234. 972/241-4141. **Contact:** Human Resources. **World Wide Web address:** http://www.essilor.com. **Description:** A manufacturer of prescription optical lenses and ophthalmic products.

ETHICON, INC.
3348 Pulliam Street, San Angelo TX 76905-4430. 915/482-5200. **Contact:** Human Resources. **World Wide Web address:** http://www.ethiconinc.com. **Description:** Manufactures products for precise wound closure including sutures, ligatures, mechanical wound closure instruments, and related products. The company makes its own surgical needles and provides thousands of needle-suture combinations to surgeons. **Positions advertised include:** Master Black Belt; Regional Medical Services Manager; Pharmaceuticals Sales Representative. **Parent company:** Johnson & Johnson (New Brunswick NJ). **Listed on:** New York Stock Exchange. **Stock exchange symbol:** JNJ.

HARRINGTON CANCER CENTER
1500 Wallace Boulevard, Amarillo TX 79106. 806/359-4673. **Toll-free phone:** 800/274-HOPE. **Fax:** 806/354-5881. **Contact:** Human

Resources. **E-mail address:** jobs@harringtoncc.org. **World Wide Web address:** http://www.harringtoncc.org. **Description:** Provides various services to cancer patients who formerly had to travel hundreds of miles for treatment. Medical specialties include radiation services, medical oncology, blood diseases and hematology, supportive care, a women's center, and cancer prevention and education. **NOTE:** All interested jobseekers must fill out a job application to be considered for employment. Applications can be picked up in the Personnel Department or obtained online.

HARRIS METHODIST FORT WORTH HOSPITAL
1301 Pennsylvania Avenue, Fort Worth TX 76104. 817/882-2882. **Fax:** 817/882-2865. **Recorded jobline:** 800/477-7876. **Contact:** Human Resources. **World Wide Web address:** http://www.texas health.org. **Description:** A 606-bed, tertiary care facility that also houses a multidisciplinary cancer center. **NOTE:** Entry-level positions, part-time jobs, and second and third shifts are offered. **Positions advertised include:** Certified Nurses Aide; Certified Occupational Therapy Assistant; Dietician/Nutritionist; EEG Technologist; EKG Technician; Emergency Medical Technician; Home Health Aide; Medical Records Technician; Nuclear Medicine Technologist; Occupational Therapist; Pharmacist; Physical Therapist; Physician; Radiological Technologist; Registered Nurse; Respiratory Therapist; Social Worker; Speech-Language Pathologist. **Special programs:** Internships. **Office hours:** Monday - Friday, 8:00 a.m. - 5:00 p.m. **Parent company:** Harris Methodist Health System.

HEALTHSOUTH
2124 Research Row, Dallas TX 75235. 214/904-6100. **Contact:** Human Resources. **World Wide Web address:** http://www. healthsouth.com. **Description:** A comprehensive medical rehabilitation hospital specializing in orthopedic surgery. HealthSouth also operates an outpatient facility. **Positions advertised include:** Physical Therapist; Radiology Technician; Site Coordinator. **Corporate headquarters location:** Birmingham AL. **Other U.S. locations:** Nationwide. **Listed on:** New York Stock Exchange. **Stock exchange symbol:** HRC. **Number of employees worldwide:** 33,700.

HENDERSON MEMORIAL HOSPITAL
300 Wilson Street, Henderson TX 75652. 903/657-7541. **Toll-free phone:** 800/329-7541. **Fax:** 903/655-3931. **Recorded jobline:** 903/655-3773. **Contact:** Human Resources. **World Wide Web address:** http://www.hmhmychoice.com. **Description:** A private, nonprofit,

acute care hospital. **NOTE:** Entry-level positions and second and third shifts are offered. **Positions advertised include:** Registered Nurse; Ward Clerk; Telemetry Technician; Network Technician; Physical Therapist; PBX Operator; Scrub Technician; Performance Improvement Manager. **Special programs:** Internships; Apprenticeships. **Office hours:** Monday - Friday, 7:30 a.m. - 5:00 p.m. **Corporate headquarters location:** This location. **Operations at this facility include:** Administration; Service. **Listed on:** Privately held.

HENDRICK HEALTH SYSTEM
1242 North 19th Street, Abilene TX 79601-2316. 915/670-2000. **Contact:** Human Resources. **E-mail address:** hrdept@hendrick health.org. **World Wide Web address:** http://www.hendrickhealth. org. **Description:** Operates a 525-bed, general hospital. Founded in 1924. **Positions advertised include:** Accounting Clerk; Certified Technician; Clinical Education Supervisor; Construction Technician; Food Service Worker; Lead Social Worker; Occupational Therapist; Phlebotomist; Scheduling Specialist; Truck Driver. **Parent company:** Baptist General Convention of Texas.

HUGULEY MEMORIAL MEDICAL CENTER
11801 South Freeway, P.O. Box 6337, South Fort Worth TX 76115-0337. 817/551-2703. **Fax:** 817/551-2455. **Contact:** Human Resources. **E-mail address:** huguleyresumes@ahss.org. **World Wide Web address:** http://www.huguley.org. **Description:** A 213-bed acute care facility. Huguley Memorial Medical Center also owns Willow Creek (Arlington TX), a mental health facility. **Positions advertised include:** Central Services Technician; Floor Technician; Nursery Attendant; Dishroom Operator; Production Supervisor; Food Service Assistant. **Special programs:** Internships. **Operations at this facility include:** Administration; Service.

IHS HOSPITAL AT DALLAS
7955 Harry Heinz Boulevard, Dallas TX 75235. 214/637-0000. **Fax:** 214/905-0566. **Contact:** Jill Doire, Divisional Recruiter. **World Wide Web address:** http://www.ihs-inc.com. **Description:** A long-term, acute care hospital. **NOTE:** Entry-level positions and part-time jobs are offered. **Positions advertised include:** Administrator.

IHS OF EL PASO
2311 North Oregon Street, 5th Floor, El Paso TX 79902. 915/545-1823. **Contact:** Jill Doire, Divisional Recruiter. **World Wide Web**

address: http://www.ihs-inc.com. **Description:** A 181-bed, long-term, acute care hospital. **Positions advertised include:** Administrator.

JOHNSON & JOHNSON MEDICAL, INC.
2500 East Arbrook Boulevard, Arlington TX 76014. 817/262-3900. **Contact:** Human Resources. **E-mail address:** resume@medus.jnj. com. **World Wide Web address:** http://www.jnj.com. **Description:** Manufactures and markets an extensive line of disposable packs and gowns, surgical products, decontamination and disposal systems, latex gloves, and surgical antiseptics. **Positions advertised include:** Master Black Belt; Director of Professional Marketing; Franchise Business Analyst; Regional Medical Services Manager. **Special programs:** Internships. **Corporate headquarters location:** This location. **Other U.S. locations:** CA; CT; FL. **Parent company:** Johnson & Johnson (New Brunswick NJ). **Operations at this facility include:** Administration; Manufacturing; Research and Development; Sales. **Listed on:** New York Stock Exchange. **Stock exchange symbol:** JNJ.

JORDAN HEALTH SERVICES
P.O. Box 840, Mount Vernon TX 75457. 903/537-2376. **Contact:** John McAuley, Personnel Manager. **World Wide Web address:** http://www.jhsi.com. **Description:** A diversified home health care agency. **Positions advertised include:** Licensed Practical Nurse; Occupational Therapist; Physical Therapist; Registered Nurse; Respiratory Therapist; Social Worker; Speech-Language Pathologist. **Operations at this facility include:** Administration. **Listed on:** Privately held.

KIMBERLY-CLARK CORPORATION
P.O. Box 619100, Dallas TX 75261. 972/281-1200. **Contact:** Human Resources. **E-mail address:** opportunities@kc-careers.com. **World Wide Web address:** http://www.kimberly-clark.com. **Description:** Manufactures and markets products for personal, business, and industrial uses throughout the world. The name brands of Kimberly-Clark Corporation include Kleenex facial and bathroom tissue, Huggies diapers and baby wipes, Pull-Ups training pants, Kotex and New Freedom feminine care products, Depend and Poise incontinence care products, Hi-Dri household towels, Kimguard sterile wrap, Kimwipes industrial wipers, and Classic business and correspondence papers. Most of the company's products are made using advanced technologies in absorbency, fibers, and nonwovens. Kimberly-Clark Corporation has extensive overseas operations in

Europe and Asia. **Corporate headquarters location:** This location. **Listed on:** New York Stock Exchange. **Stock exchange symbol:** KMB.

LELAND MEDICAL PLAZA

2696 West Walnut Street, Garland TX 75042. 972/276-7116. **Contact:** Human Resources. **World Wide Web address:** http://www. lelandmedical.com. **Description:** A 113-bed hospital specializing in industrial, behavioral, orthopedic, plastic surgery, and surgical weight loss programs. **Parent company:** Leland Medical Centers.

LONGVIEW REGIONAL MEDICAL CENTER

P.O. Box 14000, Longview TX 75607. 903/758-1818. **Fax:** 903/232-3888. **Recorded jobline:** 903/232-3726. **Contact:** Human Resources. **World Wide Web address:** http://www.longviewregional.com. **Description:** A 164-bed, acute care, medical center providing cardiovascular, pediatric, dialysis, intensive care, intermediate care, outpatient care, and laboratory services. Founded in 1980. **NOTE:** Entry-level positions, part-time jobs, and second and third shifts are offered. **Positions advertised include:** Registered Nurse; LPN; Nursing Assistant; Cook; Laboratory Assistant; Sleep Study Technician; Housekeeper; Food Service Technician. **Corporate headquarters location:** Dallas TX. **Other U.S. locations:** Nationwide.

MEDICAL CENTER HOSPITAL/ODESSA

500 West Fourth Street, Odessa TX 79761. 915/640-4000. **Fax:** 915/640-1245. **Contact:** LaDonna Melson, Personnel Manager. **E-mail address:** lmelson@echd.org. **World Wide Web address:** http://www. odessamch.org. **Description:** A 396-bed, acute care hospital. Medical Center Hospital provides various services including a neonatal care nursery, skilled nursing facility, Intensive Care Unit, Critical Care Unit, and 24-hour emergency care. **Positions advertised include:** Admitting Clerk; Controller; Housekeeper; Phlebotomist; Pharmacy Technician; Occupational Therapist; Speech Therapist; PACS Coordinator; Respiratory Director; Shift Coordinator.

MEDICAL CENTER OF PLANO

3901 West 15th Street, Plano TX 75075. 972/596-6800. **Recorded jobline:** 972/596-5300. **Contact:** Human Resources Department. **World Wide Web address:** http://www.medicalcenterofplano.com. **Description:** A 400-bed medical center providing acute and residential care.

MEDICAL CITY DALLAS HOSPITAL
7777 Forest Lane, Building B, Suite D-250, Dallas TX 75230. 972/ 566-7070. **Toll-free phone:** 800/224-4733. **Contact:** Professional Recruiters. **World Wide Web address:** http://www.medicalcity hospital.com. **Description:** A full-service hospital. **NOTE:** Entry-level positions, part-time jobs, and second and third shifts are offered. **Positions advertised include:** Assistant Nurse Manager; Case Supply Technician; Central Sterile Technician; Clinical Dietician; Construction Project Manager; Cook; Director of Patient Access; Hospitality Representative; Maintenance Mechanic; Medical Physicist; Occupational Therapist; OR Assistant.

MEMORIAL HOSPITAL & MEDICAL CENTER
2200 West Illinois Avenue, Midland TX 79701. 915/685-1111. **Contact:** Richard Pehl, Assistant Director of Personnel. **Description:** A full-service, 300-bed health facility. Memorial Hospital & Medical Center houses a cancer center, maternity/child services, intensive care nursery, pediatrics, and a 24-hour emergency room. **Positions advertised include:** Manager of Inpatient Imaging Services; Medical Technologist; Pharmacist; Pharmacy Manager; Surgical Technician.

METHODIST MEDICAL CENTER
1441 North Beckley Avenue, Dallas TX 75203. 214/947-8181. **Contact:** Human Resources Department. **World Wide Web address:** http://www.mhd.com/mmc.html. **Description:** An acute care medical center licensed for 478 beds.

NORTHWEST TEXAS HEALTHCARE SYSTEM
1506 Coulter Street, Amarillo TX 79106. 806/354-1000. **Contact:** Human Resources. **World Wide Web address:** http://www.nwths. com. **Description:** Operates Northwest Texas Hospital and The Pavilion. Northwest Texas Hospital offers more than 35 medical specialties and subspecialties. The Pavilion is a full-service mental health facility that provides a comprehensive range of services to people of all ages.

NURSEFINDERS
3141 Hood Street, Suite 512, Dallas TX 75219. 214/520-8770. **Contact:** Human Resources. **World Wide Web address:** http://www. nursefinders.com. **Description:** A home health care agency. **Positions advertised include:** Registered Nurse; Home Health Care Nurse; Case Manager. **Other U.S. locations:** Nationwide.

NURSES TODAY INCORPORATED

4230 LBJ Freeway, Suite 110, Dallas TX 75244. 972/233-9966. **Toll-free phone:** 800/830-7616. **Fax:** 972/233-5354. **Contact:** Jo Elste, Human Resources Manager. **World Wide Web address:** http://www. nursestoday.com. **Description:** Provides home health care and case management services. Founded in 1982. **NOTE:** Part-time jobs are offered. **Positions advertised include:** Licensed Vocational Nurse; Registered Nurse; Certified Nurse Assistant; Mental Health Technician; Medical Receptionist; Occupational Health Nurse. **Office hours:** Monday - Friday, 8:00 a.m. - 5:00 p.m. **Corporate headquarters location:** This location.

ODESSA REGIONAL HOSPITAL

520 East Sixth Street, Odessa TX 79760. 915/334-8397. **Contact:** Human Resources. **World Wide Web address:** http://www. tenethealth.com. **Description:** A hospital offering specialized labor/delivery services, pediatrics, family care, and surgical services. **Positions advertised include:** Radiology Technician; Registered Nurse; Registrar; CT Scanner; Medical Staff Coordinator; Licensed Vocational Nurse; Pharmacist. **Parent company:** Tenet HealthSystem. **Listed on:** New York Stock Exchange. **Stock exchange symbol:** THC.

183 ANIMAL HOSPITAL

1010 West Airport Freeway, Irving TX 75062. 972/579-0115. **Contact:** Human Resources. **World Wide Web address:** http://www.183animalhospital.com. **Description:** Provides general medical and surgical services along with diagnostic testing, radiography, and dentistry for small animals.

ORTHOFIX INC.

1720 Bray Central Drive, McKinney TX 75069. 972/918-2511. **Fax:** 972/918-2511. **Contact:** Human Resources. **World Wide Web address:** http://www.orthofix.com. **Description:** Orthofix Inc. develops, manufactures, markets, and distributes medical devices to promote bone healing. Products are primarily used by orthopedic surgeons. **Positions advertised include:** Executive Administrative Assistant; Materials Analyst. **Operations at this facility include:** Administration; Divisional Headquarters; Manufacturing; Research and Development; Sales; Service.

PALO PINTO GENERAL HOSPITAL
400 SW 25th Avenue, Mineral Wells TX 76067. 940/328-6390. **Fax:** 940/328-6230. **Contact:** Human Resources. **World Wide Web address:** http://www.ppgh.com. **Description:** A 99-bed, nonprofit, acute care hospital. **NOTE:** Entry-level positions, part-time jobs, and second and third shifts are offered. **Positions advertised include:** Registered Vascular Technician; Physical Therapist; Medical Technologist; Registered Nurse; Licensed Vocational Nurse.

PARKLAND MEMORIAL HOSPITAL
5201 Harry Hines Boulevard, Dallas TX 75235. 214/590-8000. **Contact:** Employment Services. **World Wide Web address:** http:// www.pmh.org. **Description:** A Level I trauma center, and a 900-bed teaching hospital. **Positions advertised include:** Chief Information Officer; Accounting Assistant; Accounting Clerk; Administrative Assistant; Associate Unit Manager; Registered Nurse; Clinical Nurse Specialist; Lead Nurse; Staff Physician. **Note:** Non-nursing applications can be faxed to 214/590-2767. Nursing applications can be faxed to 214/590-8991. **Parent company:** Parkland Health & Hospital System includes Parkland Memorial Hospital, Community Oriented Primary Care, Parkland Community Health Plan, Inc., and the Parkland Foundation.

PEARLE VISION, INC.
2534 Royal Lane, Dallas TX 75229. 972/277-5000. **Fax:** 972/277-6415. **Contact:** Human Resources. **World Wide Web address:** http:// www.pearlevision.com. **Description:** Manufactures and retails prescription eyewear. **Corporate headquarters location:** This location. **Parent company:** Cole National Corporation. **Operations at this facility include:** Administration; Manufacturing. **Listed on:** New York Stock Exchange. **Stock exchange symbol:** CNJ.

PROVIDENCE HEALTH CENTER
P.O. Box 2589, Waco TX 76702. 254/751-4000. **Contact:** Human Resources. **World Wide Web address:** http://www.providence-waco. org. **Description:** A 170-bed, acute care hospital. Founded in 1905. **Corporate headquarters location:** This location. **Parent company:** Providence Healthcare Network (also at this location). **Positions advertised include:** Registered Nurse Supervisor; Pharmacy Technician; Counselor; RN Case Manager; OR Technician; Physical Therapist; Lab Technician; Occupational Therapist; Licensed Vocational Nurse; Nurse Practitioner.

QUEST MEDICAL, INC.
ATRION CORPORATION
One Allentown Parkway, Allen TX 75002-4211. 972/390-9800. **Fax:** 972/390-2881. **Contact:** Human Resources. **E-mail address:** hrstaffing@atrioncorp.com. **World Wide Web address:** http://www. atrioncorp.com. **Description:** Develops, manufactures, markets, sells, and distributes proprietary products to the healthcare industry. **Corporate headquarters location:** This location. **Parent company:** Atrion Corporation (also at this location) is a holding company that designs, develops, manufactures, markets, sells, and distributes proprietary products and components for the healthcare industry. Other subsidiaries of Atrion Corporation include Atrion Medical Products and Halkey-Roberts. **Listed on:** NASDAQ. **Stock exchange symbol:** ATRI. **Number of employees at this location:** 443.

RHD MEMORIAL MEDICAL CENTER
7 Medical Parkway, Dallas TX 75234. 972/247-1000. **Contact:** Personnel. **World Wide Web address:** http://www.rhdmemorial. com. **Description:** A 160-bed, acture care community hospital. **Parent company:** Tenet HealthSystem. **Positions advertised include:** Director of Health Information; Surgical Technician; Registered Nurse.

RIO VISTA REHABILITATION HOSPITAL
1740 Curie Drive, El Paso TX 79902. 915/544-3399. **Contact:** Human Resources. **World Wide Web address:** http://www.sphn. com. **Description:** An inpatient and outpatient rehabilitation facility that assists patients experiencing orthopedic problems, joint replacement, trauma, arthritis, or amputation. **Positions advertised include:** Registered Nurse; Licensed Vocational Nurse. **Parent company:** Tenet HealthSystem.

ROYAL OPTICAL U.S. VISION
1334 Inwood Road, Dallas TX 75247. 214/630-5791. **Contact:** Human Resources. **Description:** Manufactures frames, grinds lenses, and distributes a line of eyewear.

SHANNON MEDICAL CENTER
P.O. Box 1879, San Angelo TX 76902. 915/657-5243. **Fax:** 915/481-8521. **Recorded jobline:** 915/657-5298. **Contact:** Joyce Duncan, Employment Manager. **E-mail address:** joyceduncan@ shannonhealth.com. **World Wide Web address:** http://www.shannon health.com. **Description:** A 274-bed, nonprofit hospital offering

surgery, intensive care, orthopedic, oncology, telemetry, skilled nursing, and cardiac services. Shannon Medical Center also operates a Level II trauma and sleep disorder center. Founded in 1932. **NOTE:** Entry-level positions and second and third shifts are offered. **Company slogan:** We do what ordinary hospitals can't. **Positions advertised include:** Physical Therapist; Assistant Controller; Dietician; Nursing Assistant; Patient Care Manager; Pharmacist; Exercise Assistant; Grant Coordinator; RN Staffing Coordinator. **Special programs:** Training. **Office hours:** Monday - Friday, 8:00 a.m. - 5:00 p.m. **Corporate headquarters location:** This location.

TENET HEALTHCARE CORPORATION
P.O. Box 809088, Dallas TX 75380-9088. 469/893-2200. **Fax:** 469/893-1321. **Contact:** Manager of Recruitment. **World Wide Web address:** http://www.tenethealth.com. **Description:** A multibillion-dollar, multihospital corporation that, with its subsidiaries, owns or operates approximately 130 acute care facilities nationwide. **Positions advertised include:** Registered Nurse; Licensed Vocational Nurse; Case Manager; Phlebotomist. **Corporate headquarters location:** Santa Monica CA. **Other U.S. locations:** Nationwide. **Operations at this facility include:** Administration; Regional Headquarters. **Listed on:** New York Stock Exchange. **Stock exchange symbol:** THC. **Number of employees nationwide:** 106,900.

TEXAS HEALTH RESOURCES
611 Ryan Plaza Drive, Suite 200, Arlington TX 76011. 214/345-4251. **Toll-free phone:** 800/749-6877. **Recorded jobline:** 214/345-7863. **Contact:** Linda Ochoa, Employment Manager. **World Wide Web address:** http://www.texashealth.org. **Description:** One of the largest nonprofit health care systems in Texas including a nursing home, 11 acute care hospitals, clinics, and home health services. **NOTE:** Part-time jobs and second and third shifts are offered. **Positions advertised include:** Substance Abuse Coordinator; Dietician; Food Service Worker; Registered Nurse; Caterer; Laboratory Assistant; Teacher; Records Coordinator; Clinical Nursing Coordinator; Unit Secretary. **Corporate headquarters location:** This location. **Other area locations:** Greenville TX; Kaufman TX; Plano TX; Winnsboro TX.

TEXAS MEDICAL AND SURGICAL ASSOCIATES
8440 Walnut Hill Lane, Dallas TX 75231. 214/345-1400. **Contact:** Human Resources. **Description:** A private clinic. **Office hours:** Monday - Friday, 8:30 a.m. - 5:00 p.m.

TEXOMA MEDICAL CENTER (TMC)
1000 Memorial Drive, Denison TX 75020. 903/416-4050. **Fax:** 903/416-4087. **Recorded jobline:** 800/566-1211. **Contact:** Joni Horn, Employment Coordinator. **World Wide Web address:** http://www.thcs.org. **Description:** Texoma Medical Center (TMC) is an acute care hospital with 300 beds. TMC offers general medical and surgical services, intensive care, and pediatric care. Founded in 1965. **NOTE:** Second and third shifts are offered. **Positions advertised include:** Licensed Vocational Nurse; Nurse Aide; Nurse Manager; Nursing Service Manager. **Special programs:** Co-ops; Summer Jobs. **Corporate headquarters location:** This location. **Other U.S. locations:** OK. **Subsidiaries include:** Times Medical Equipment. **Parent company:** Texoma Healthcare Systems, Inc. (also at this location). **Operations at this facility include:** Administration; Support Services.

U.S. DEPARTMENT OF VETERANS AFFAIRS
CENTRAL TEXAS VETERANS HEALTHCARE SYSTEM
4800 Memorial Drive, Waco TX 76711. 254/752-6581. **Contact:** Personnel. **World Wide Web address:** http://www.va.gov. **Description:** A medical center. From 54 hospitals in 1930, the VA health care system has grown to include 171 medical centers; more than 360 outpatient, community, and outreach clinics; 130 nursing home care units; and more than 35 domiciliary residences. The VA operates at least one medical center in each of the 48 contiguous states, Puerto Rico, and the District of Columbia. With approximately 76,000 medical center beds, the VA treats nearly one million patients in VA hospitals; 75,000 in nursing home care units; and 25,000 in domiciliary residences. The VA's outpatient clinics register approximately 24 million visits per year. **NOTE:** Central Texas Veterans Healthcare System hires current or former federal employees, veterans, and disabled veterans. Central Texas Veterans Healthcare System is currently under hiring constraints. Applications from the general public are not accepted. **Parent company:** U.S. Department of Veterans Affairs.

U.S. DEPARTMENT OF VETERANS AFFAIRS
VETERANS ADMINISTRATION MEDICAL CENTER
6010 Amarillo Boulevard West, Amarillo TX 79106. 806/355-9703. **Contact:** Human Resources. **World Wide Web address:** http://www.va.gov. **Description:** A medical center operated by the U.S. Department of Veterans Affairs. From 54 hospitals in 1930, the VA health care system has grown to include 171 medical centers; more

than 364 outpatient, community, and outreach clinics; 130 nursing home care units; and 37 domiciliary residences. The VA operates at least one medical center in each of the 48 contiguous states, Puerto Rico, and the District of Columbia. With approximately 76,000 medical center beds, the VA treats nearly 1 million patients in VA hospitals; 75,000 in nursing home care units; and 25,000 in domiciliary residences. The VA's outpatient clinics register approximately 24 million visits per year. **NOTE:** The VA Medical Center hires current or former federal employees, veterans, and disabled veterans. The VA Medical Center is currently under hiring constraints. Applications from the general public are not accepted. **Corporate headquarters location:** Washington DC.

U.S. DEPARTMENT OF VETERANS AFFAIRS
VETERANS ADMINISTRATION NORTH TEXAS HEALTHCARE SYSTEM
4500 South Lancaster Road, Dallas TX 75216. 214/742-8387. **Contact:** Human Resources. **World Wide Web address:** http://www. va.gov. **Description:** From 54 hospitals in 1930, the VA health care system has grown to include 171 medical centers; more than 364 outpatient, community, and outreach clinics; 130 nursing home care units; and 37 domiciliary residences. The VA operates at least one medical center in each of the 48 contiguous states, Puerto Rico, and the District of Columbia. With approximately 76,000 medical center beds, the VA treats nearly one million patients in VA hospitals; 75,000 in nursing home care units; and 25,000 in domiciliary residences. The VA's outpatient clinics register approximately 24 million visits per year. **Special programs:** Internships. **Corporate headquarters location:** Washington DC. **Operations at this facility include:** This location houses administrative offices.

UNITED REGIONAL HEALTHCARE SYSTEMS
1600 Eighth Street, Wichita Falls TX 76301. 940/764-7000. **Toll-free phone:** 800/221-9750. **Fax:** 940/764-7820. **Recorded jobline:** 940/ 764-7802. **Contact:** Patra Linderkamp, Recruitment. **World Wide Web address:** http://www.urhcs.org. **Description:** A licensed, 300-bed, acute care facility. **Positions advertised include:** Certified Scrub Technician; Diagnostic Radiological Technician; Emergency Department Services Technician; Phlebotomist; Licensed Vocational Nurse; Occupational Therapist; Patient Care Associate; Pharmacist; Registered Nurse.

UNIVERSITY MEDICAL CENTER

602 Indiana Avenue, Lubbock TX 79415. 806/743-3111. **Recorded jobline:** 806/743-3352. **Contact:** Human Resources Manager. **World Wide Web address:** http://www.teamumc.org. **Description:** A 354-bed hospital operating through The Children's Hospital, The Southwest Cancer Center, Level I Trauma Center, a Pre-Hospital Emergency Service, a Burn Intensive Care Unit, and Community Outreach Programs. **Positions advertised include:** Patient Access Associate; Development Director; Coder; Clinical Application Specialist; Emergency Center Nurse Manager; Registered Nurse; Licensed Vocational Nurse. **Special programs:** Internships.

UNIVERSITY OF TEXAS HEALTH CENTER AT TYLER

11937 U.S. Highway 271, Tyler TX 75708-3154. 903/877-7740. **Fax:** 903/877-7729. **Recorded jobline:** 903/877-7071. **Contact:** Employment Services. **E-mail address:** jobs@uthct.edu. **World Wide Web address:** http://www.uthct.edu. **Description:** A nonprofit hospital engaged in patient care, education, and research. **Positions advertised include:** Administrative Director of Business Services; Charge Nurse; Staff Nurse; Medical Technologist; Research Associate; Compliance Specialist; Accountant; Surgical Technologist; Licensed Vocational Nurse; Hospital Technical Assistant.

UNIVERSITY OF TEXAS SOUTHWESTERN MEDICAL CENTER AT DALLAS

5323 Harry Hines Boulevard, Dallas TX 75139-9023. 214/648-3111. **Fax:** 214/648-9875. **Recorded jobline:** 214/648-5627. **Contact:** Personnel. **World Wide Web address:** http://www.swmed.edu. **Description:** An academic medical center affiliated with Southwestern Medical School, Southwestern Graduate School of Biomedical Sciences, and Southwestern Allied Health Sciences School. **NOTE:** Entry-level positions are offered. **Positions advertised include:** Senior Administrative Assistant; Office Assistant; Clinic Staff Assistant; Medical Office Assistant; Pathologist Assistant; Billing Coordinator; Phlebotomist; Senior Press Operator; Case Aide; Driver; Senior Animal Technician. **Special programs:** Internships. **Operations at this facility include:** Administration; Research and Development.

VERNON WICHITA FALLS STATE HOSPITAL

P.O. Box 300, Wichita Falls TX 76307. 940/552-9901. **Fax:** 940/689-5735. **Contact:** Staffing. **Description:** A nonprofit, forensic and mental health hospital. **Special programs:** Internships.

Corporate headquarters location: Austin TX. **Other area locations:** Vernon TX. **Parent company:** Texas Department of Mental Health. **Operations at this facility include:** Administration.

VISITING NURSE ASSOCIATION
1440 West Mockingbird Lane, Suite 500, Dallas TX 75247. 214/689-0000. **Contact:** Human Resources. **World Wide Web address:** http://www.vnatexas.org. **Description:** A home health care agency that provides intermittent in-home visits. **Positions advertised include:** Home Care Registered Nurse; Home Health Aide; Quality/Infection Control Analyst; Physical Therapist. **Other U.S. locations:** Nationwide.

WADLEY REGIONAL MEDICAL CENTER
1000 Pine Street, Texarkana TX 75501. 903/798-7160. **Fax:** 903/798-7177. **Recorded jobline:** 903/798-7161. **Contact:** Human Resources. **E-mail address:** resumes@wadleyrmc.com. **World Wide Web address:** http://www.wadleyrmc.com. **Description:** A nonprofit, acute care hospital with 448 beds. The services offered at Wadley Regional Medical Center include a skilled nursing facility, a Cancer Treatment & Diagnostic Imaging Center, a day surgery center, and a Community Oriented Medical Plan Clinic. Founded in 1959. **NOTE:** Second and third shifts are offered. **Company slogan:** To improve the health and healthcare of those we serve. **Positions advertised include:** Dietician; Diagnostic Technologist; Licensed Vocational Nurse; Pharmacy Technician; Phlebotomist; Coder; Cook/Baker; Housekeeper. **Special programs:** Summer Jobs.

ZALE LIPSHY UNIVERSITY HOSPITAL
UNIVERSITY OF TEXAS SOUTHWESTERN MEDICAL CENTER CAMPUS
5151 Harry Hines Boulevard, Dallas TX 75235-7786. 214/590-3150. **Fax:** 214/590-3193. **Contact:** Human Resources. **E-mail address:** response@zluh.org. **World Wide Web address:** http://www.zluh.org. **Description:** Zale Lipshy University Hospital at Southwestern Medical Center was built to serve University of Texas Southwestern Medical Center at Dallas as its private, nonprofit, adult referral hospital for specialized tertiary care. The facilities consist of 152 hospital beds (20 intensive care unit beds, 89 medical/surgical beds, 22 rehabilitation beds, and 21 psychiatric beds) and 12 operating room suites for specialized surgical care in the areas of neurological surgery, orthopedics, urology, gynecology, otorhinolaryngology (ear, nose, and throat), ophthalmology, cardiothoracic surgery, oral and

maxillofacial surgery, vascular surgery, and plastic and reconstructive surgery. Founded in 1989. **NOTE:** Second and third shifts are offered. **Positions advertised include:** Data Quality Technician; Registered Nurse; Assistant Clinical Nurse Manager; Laboratory Manager; Environmental Services Attendant Group Leader; Dishwasher; Buyer. **Operations at this facility include:** Administration; Service.

HOTELS AND RESTAURANTS

You can expect to find the following types of companies in this chapter:
Casinos • Dinner Theaters • Hotel/Motel Operators • Resorts • Restaurants

ACCOR HOTELS
14651 Dallas Parkway, Suite 500, Dallas TX 75254. 972/386-6161. **Contact:** Cheryl Beuttas, Director of Corporate Human Resources. **World Wide Web address:** http://www.accorhotel.com. **Description:** This location houses the administrative offices. Overall, Accor Hotels operates over 3,700 hotels, including Motel 6 and Red Roof Inn, in 90 countries. **Number of employees worldwide:** 147,000.

BFX HOSPITALITY GROUP, INC.
226 Bailey Avenue, Suite 101, Fort Worth TX 76107. 817/332-4761. **Fax:** 817/877-0420. **Contact:** Human Resources. **Description:** Owns and operates hotels and restaurants. **Corporate headquarters location:** This location. **Subsidiaries include:** American Food Classics, Inc.; Hotels of Distinction.

BRINKER INTERNATIONAL INC.
6820 LBJ Freeway, Dallas TX 75240. 972/980-9917. **Fax:** 972/770-9593. **Contact:** Corporate Recruiting. **World Wide Web address:** http://www.brinker.com. **Description:** Operates full-service, casual dining restaurants including Chili's Grill & Bar, Chili's Too, Cozymel's, On the Border, Romano's Macaroni Grill, and Spageddie's Italian Foods. **Positions advertised include:** Cost Analyst; Credit Card Accountant; Disbursement Exception Specialist; Fixed Asset Associate; Payroll Compliance Administrator; Payroll Project Analyst; Senior Payroll Business Analyst. **Corporate headquarters location:** This location. **Other U.S. locations:** Nationwide. **Listed on:** New York Stock Exchange. **Stock exchange symbol:** EAT. **Number of employees nationwide:** 90,000.

CEC ENTERTAINMENT INC.
dba CHUCK E. CHEESE
P.O. Box 152077, Irving TX 75015. 972/258-8507. **Fax:** 972/258-8545. **Contact:** Human Resources. **World Wide Web address:** http://www.chuckecheese.com. **Description:** Operates over 400 Chuck E. Cheese's pizza and amusement franchises throughout the United States and Canada. **Positions advertised include:** Director of Risk Management. **Corporate headquarters location:** This location. **Listed on:** New York Stock Exchange. **Stock exchange symbol:** CEC.

CARLSON RESTAURANTS WORLDWIDE INC.

7540 LBJ Freeway, Dallas TX 75251. 972/450-5400. **Fax:** 972/776-5468. **Contact:** Employee Relations. **World Wide Web address:** http://www.tgifridays.com. **Description:** Operates the TGI Friday's chain of casual-dining restaurants, which has over 500 locations. **Corporate headquarters location:** This location. **Parent company:** Carlson Companies, Inc. (Minneapolis MN).

CULINAIRE INTERNATIONAL, INC.

2121 San Jacinto Street, Suite 3100, Dallas TX 75201. 214/754-1880. **Fax:** 214/754-1894. **Contact:** Human Resources. **E-mail address:** recruit@culinaireintl.com. **World Wide Web address:** http://www.culinaireintl.com. **Description:** Provides the food and beverage services for a wide range of corporate clients. **Positions advertised include:** Restaurant Manager; Catering Sales Manager; Executive Chef; Food and Beverage Director; Catering Sales Manager. **Corporate headquarters location:** This location.

DAVE & BUSTER'S, INC.

2481 Manana Drive, Dallas TX 75220. 214/357-9588. **Contact:** Human Resources. **World Wide Web address:** http://www.daveandbusters.com. **Description:** An operator of 20 restaurant/entertainment complexes. Each location houses eating venues and amusement facilities including billiards, video games, and virtual reality games. Founded in 1982. **Corporate headquarters location:** This location. **Other U.S. locations:** Nationwide. **International locations:** Canada; Taiwan. **Listed on:** New York Stock Exchange. **Stock exchange symbol:** DAB.

EL CHICO RESTAURANTS, INC.

12200 Stemmons Freeway, Suite 100, Dallas TX 75234. 972/241-5500. **Fax:** 972/888-8150. **Contact:** Recruiter. **World Wide Web address:** http://www.elchico.com. **Description:** Operates a chain of full-service restaurants. **Corporate headquarters location:** This location. **Parent company:** Consolidated Restaurants Inc. (also at this location). **Operations at this facility include:** Administration; Manufacturing; Research and Development.

EMBASSY SUITES HOTEL

4250 Ridgemont Drive, Abilene TX 79606. 915/698-1234. **Contact:** Human Resources Department. **World Wide Web address:** http://www.embassy-suites.com. **Description:** A 176-room hotel.

FOUR SEASONS RESORT AND CLUB

4150 North MacArthur Boulevard, Irving TX 75038. 972/717-0700. **Recorded jobline:** 972/717-2544. **Contact:** Human Resources Manager. **World Wide Web address:** http://www.fourseasons.com. **Description:** A 357-room resort offering two championship golf courses, 12 tennis courts, a spa, and a conference center. The 18-hole TPC championship golf course is the site of the annual GTE Byron Nelson Classic on the PGA Tour. The 176,000-square-foot sports club and spa has a racquet sports center, indoor and outdoor pools and tracks, and complete personal training facilities. The 20,000-square-foot conference center includes 26 multipurpose meeting and function rooms. Overall, Four Seasons Hotels & Resorts operates approximately 50 luxury hotels and resorts in 22 countries. Founded in 1960. **NOTE:** Entry-level positions, part-time jobs, and second and third shifts are offered. **Special programs:** Training; Summer Jobs. **Corporate headquarters location:** Toronto, Canada. **Other U.S. locations:** Nationwide. **International locations:** Worldwide.

HARVEY HOTEL/DFW AIRPORT

4545 West John Carpenter Freeway, Irving TX 75063. 972/929-4500. **Fax:** 972/929-0733. **Contact:** Personnel. **World Wide Web address:** http://www.bristolhotels.com. **Description:** A 500-room hotel. Harvey Hotel's business center offers typing, copying, fax, car rental information, travel agency information, and word processing services. **NOTE:** Entry-level positions and second and third shifts are offered. **Special programs:** Internships; Training. **Corporate headquarters location:** Addison TX.

HYATT REGENCY DALLAS AT REUNION

300 Reunion Boulevard, Dallas TX 75207. 214/651-1234. **Contact:** Mark Spinelli, Human Resources Manager. **World Wide Web address:** http://www.hyatt.com. **Description:** A luxury hotel offering an 18-story atrium that houses dining and entertainment facilities including a pool, a fully-equipped fitness center, tennis and basketball courts, three restaurants, and a revolving rooftop lounge. **Corporate headquarters location:** Chicago IL. **Other U.S. locations:** Nationwide. **Parent company:** Hyatt Hotel Corporation.

MARRIOTT SOUTH CENTRAL REGIONAL OFFICE

5151 Beltline Road, Suite 500, Dallas TX 75254. 972/385-1600. **Contact:** Regional Director. **World Wide Web address:** http://www. marriott.com. **Description:** Marriott Corporation is a nationwide, diversified food service, retail merchandising, and hospitality company, doing business in more than 25 U.S. airports, as well as operating restaurants under various names nationwide. **Positions advertised include:** Staff Development Coordinator; Controller. **Special programs:** Internships. **Corporate headquarters location:** Washington DC. **Operations at this facility include:** This location houses the regional office for the hotel chain. **Listed on:** New York Stock Exchange. **Stock exchange symbol:** MAR.

METROMEDIA RESTAURANT GROUP
6500 International Parkway, Suite 1000, Plano TX 75093. 972/588-5000. **Fax:** 972/588-5467. **Contact:** Human Resources Manager. **World Wide Web address:** http://www.metromediarestaurants.com. **Description:** One of the largest, full-service, restaurant chain operators in the nation. The company operates nearly 1,000 restaurants in 45 states and two countries including Bennigan's, Bonanza, Ponderosa, And Steak and Ale. **Corporate headquarters location:** This location. **Listed on:** Privately held.

OMNI HOTELS
420 Decker Drive, Suite 200, Irving TX 75062-3952. 972/730-6664. **Fax:** 972/871-5669. **Contact:** Bethany Senger, Corporate Recruiting Manager. **World Wide Web address:** http://www.omnihotels.com. **Description:** Operates an international chain of hotels, motels, and resorts. **NOTE:** Entry-level positions are offered. **Special programs:** Internships; Training. **Corporate headquarters location:** This location. **Other U.S. locations:** Nationwide. **Operations at this facility include:** Administration. **Listed on:** Privately held. **Number of employees worldwide:** 10,000.

OMNI RICHARDSON HOTEL
701 East Campbell Road, Richardson TX 75081. 972/231-9600. **Contact:** Human Resources. **World Wide Web address:** http://www. omnihotels.com. **Description:** A 342-room hotel with two restaurants, meeting facilities, and a fitness center. **Corporate headquarters location:** Irving TX. **Parent company:** Omni Hotels. **Listed on:** Privately held. **Number of employees worldwide:** 10,000.

PANCHO'S MEXICAN BUFFET, INC.
P.O. Box 7407, Fort Worth TX 76111-0407. 817/831-0081. **Physical address:** 3500 Noble Street, Fort Worth TX 76111. **Contact:** Human Resources. **World Wide Web address:** http://www. panchosmexicanbuffet.com. **Description:** Pancho's Mexican Buffet

operates a chain of Mexican restaurants with a buffet-style format. Pancho's Mexican Buffet operates 47 restaurants in Texas, Arizona, Louisiana, New Mexico, and Oklahoma. Founded in 1966. **Corporate headquarters location:** This location. **Operations at this facility include:** This location houses administrative offices.

PIZZA INN INC.
3551 Plano Parkway, The Colony TX 75056. 469/384-5000. **Contact:** Human Resources. **E-mail address:** jobs@pizzainn.com. **World Wide Web address:** http://www.pizzainn.com. **Description:** Engaged primarily in operating and franchising restaurants serving pizza and complimentary foods and beverages. Pizza Inn operates more than 430 restaurants in 20 states. **Operations at this facility include:** Administration; Sales. **Listed on:** NASDAQ. **Stock exchange symbol:** PZZI.

SULLINS & ASSOCIATES, INC.
McDONALD'S CORPORATION
122 South 12th Street, Suite 105, Corsicana TX 75110. 903/872-5611. **Fax:** 903/872-5613. **Contact:** Human Resources. **Description:** A leader in the fast-food industry, McDonald's offers quick-service meals, specializing in hamburgers. **World Wide Web address:** http://www.mcdonalds.com. **Special programs:** Internships. **Other area locations:** Ennis TX; Greenville TX; Palestine TX; Terrell TX; Waxahachie TX.

TRIANGLE FOOD SERVICES
16970 Dallas Parkway, Suite 701, Dallas TX 75248. 972/248-4145. **Fax:** 972/248-8116. **Contact:** Human Resources Director. **Description:** A cafeteria chain with 68 locations in five states. **Corporate headquarters location:** This location. **Listed on:** Privately held.

WYNDHAM ANATOLE HOTEL
2201 Stemmons Freeway, Dallas TX 75207. 214/748-1200. **Contact:** Employment Manager. **World Wide Web address:** http://www.wyndham.com. **Description:** A luxury convention hotel with over 1,600 rooms. **Positions advertised include:** Executive Chef; Sous Chef. **Operations at this facility include:** Service.

INSURANCE

You can expect to find the following types of companies in this chapter:
Commercial and Industrial Property/Casualty Insurers • Health Maintenance Organizations (HMOs) • Medical/Life Insurance Companies

BLUE CROSS BLUE SHIELD OF TEXAS

P.O. Box 655730, Dallas TX 75265. 972/766-6900. **Physical address:** 901 South Central Expressway, Richardson TX 75080. **Fax:** 972/766-6102. **Recorded jobline:** 972/766-5364. **Contact:** Director of Employment. **World Wide Web address:** http://www.bcbstx.com. **Description:** A nonprofit health care insurance organization providing managed health care plans to both individuals and groups. Blue Cross and Blue Shield offers Point-of-Service, individual health, indemnity, PPO, and HMO plans. **Positions advertised include:** Master Clerk; Internal Auditor; Hospital Contract Representative; Senior Health Underwriter; Claims Examiner; Accounting Manager; Unit Manager; Interactive Designer.

CNA COMMERCIAL INSURANCE

P.O. Box 219011, Dallas TX 75221-9011. 214/220-1300. **Toll-free phone:** 877/261-6680. **Fax:** 214/220-1690. **Contact:** Human Resources. **World Wide Web address:** http://www.cna.com. **Description:** A property and casualty insurance writer, offering commercial and personal policies. **Positions advertised include:** Actuarial Analyst; Accounting Specialist; Claims Manager; Claims Specialist. **Corporate headquarters location:** Chicago IL. **Operations at this facility include:** This location specializes in commercial insurance policies including worker's compensation. **Listed on:** New York Stock Exchange. **Stock exchange symbol:** CNA.

CHUBB GROUP OF INSURANCE COMPANIES

2000 Brian Street, Suite 3400, Dallas TX 75201. 214/754-0777. **Contact:** Personnel Manager. **World Wide Web address:** http://www.chubb.com. **Description:** A property and casualty insurer with more than 130 offices in 32 countries worldwide. Chubb Group of Insurance Companies offers a broad range of specialty insurance services designed for individuals and businesses, serving industries including high-technology, financial institutions, and general manufacturers. Founded in 1882. **Number of employees worldwide:** 10,000.

CRUM & FORSTER INSURANCE
6404 International Parkway, Suite 1000, Plano TX 75093. 972/380-3000. **Contact:** Human Resources. **World Wide Web address:** http://www.cfins.com. **Description:** Offers property and casualty insurance to commercial customers.

GENERALCOLOGNE RE
8144 Walnut Hill Lane, Suite 1250, Dallas TX 75231-3309. 214/691-3000. **Contact:** Human Resources. **World Wide Web address:** http://www.gcre.com. **Description:** Provides property and casualty reinsurance to primary insurers on a direct basis.

INSPIRE INSURANCE SOLUTIONS
300 Burnett Street, Fort Worth TX 76113. 817/332-7761. **Contact:** Human Resources. **World Wide Web address:** http://www.nspr.com. **Description:** Provides administrative and consulting services to property and casualty insurance companies. **Corporate headquarters location:** This location.

LAWYERS TITLE INSURANCE CORPORATION
7557 Rambler Road, Suite 1200, Dallas TX 75231. 214/720-7600. **Contact:** Human Resources. **World Wide Web address:** http://www.landam.com. **Description:** Provides title insurance and other real estate-related services on commercial and residential transactions in the United States, Canada, the Bahamas, Puerto Rico, and the U.S. Virgin Islands. Lawyers Title Insurance Corporation also provides search and examination services and closing services for a broad-based customer group that includes lenders, developers, real estate brokers, attorneys, and homebuyers. This location covers Kansas, New Mexico, Oklahoma, and Texas. **Corporate headquarters location:** Richmond VA. **Other U.S. locations:** Nationwide. **Parent company:** Land America Financial Group. **Listed on:** New York Stock Exchange. **Stock exchange symbol:** LFG.

NATIONAL FOUNDATION LIFE INSURANCE COMPANY
110 West Seventh Street, Suite 300, Fort Worth TX 76102. 817/878-3300. **Contact:** Human Resources. **World Wide Web address:** http://www.nationalfoundation.net. **Description:** A life insurance company. **Corporate headquarters location:** This location. **Operations at this facility include:** Administration.

STATE FARM INSURANCE
17301 Preston Road, Dallas TX 75379. 972/732-5000. **Contact:** Human Resources. **World Wide Web address:** http://www. statefarm.com. **Description:** Offers automobile, health, homeowners, life, and renters insurance. **Corporate headquarters location:** Bloomington IL. **Operations at this facility include:** Regional Headquarters.

TRAVELERS PROPERTY CASUALTY COMPANY
P.O. Box 660456, Dallas TX 75266. 972/866-4748. **Physical address:** 7920 Beltline Road, Dallas TX 75240. **Contact:** Cheryl Powell, Human Resources Coordinator. **World Wide Web address:** http://www.travelers.com. **Description:** Offers a wide range of insurance products to commercial customers including workers' compensation, property, liability, and surety bonds. The company also provides homeowners and auto insurance to consumers. **Corporate headquarters location:** Hartford CT.

UNITED INSURANCE COMPANIES INC.
4001 McEwen, Suite 200, Dallas TX 75244. 972/392-6700. **Fax:** 972/392-6737. **Contact:** Human Resources. **World Wide Web address:** http://www.uici.net. **Description:** Offers health and life insurance. **NOTE:** Entry-level positions are offered. **Positions advertised include:** Outside Sales Representative; Underwriter. **Special programs:** Training. **Corporate headquarters location:** This location. **Other U.S. locations:** Glendale AZ; Lakewood CO; St. Petersburg FL; Norcross GA; Oklahoma City OK; Sioux Falls SD. **Operations at this facility include:** Administration; Service. **Listed on:** New York Stock Exchange. **Stock exchange symbol:** UCI.

WAUSAU INSURANCE COMPANIES
P.O. Box 152800, Irving TX 75015-2800. 972/650-1955. **Contact:** Human Resources. **World Wide Web address:** http://www.wausau. com. **Description:** Offers casualty, property, and group insurance products to commercial customers through 100 service offices located throughout the United States. **NOTE:** Entry-level positions are offered. **Positions advertised include:** Total Loss Claims Representative; Insurance Special Investigator; Business Market Sales Associate; Senior Broker Assistant; Field Investigator; Legal Secretary; Office Services Assistant; Claims Manager. **Corporate headquarters location:** Wausau WI. **Other U.S. locations:** Nationwide. **Operations at this facility include:** Administration; Divisional Headquarters; Sales.

LEGAL SERVICES

You can expect to find the following types of companies in this chapter:
Law Firms • Legal Service Agencies

ACKELS & ACKELS LLP
2777 Stemmons Freeway, Suite 879, Dallas TX 75207. 214/267-8600. **Fax:** 214/267-8605. **Contact:** Office Manager. **Description:** A law firm that specializes in civil, criminal, and commercial litigation, and also practices personal injury, juvenile, and entertainment law.

JOHN ATWOOD LAW OFFICE
3500 Oak Lawn Avenue Suite 400, Dallas TX 75219. 214/523-9520. **Contact:** Personnel Department. **Description:** A law firm that specializes in corporate, real estate, administrative, and taxation law.

BAKER BOTTS LLP
2001 Ross Avenue, Suite 600, Dallas TX 75201-2980. 214/953-6500. **Contact:** Human Resources. **World Wide Web address:** http://www.bakerbotts.com. **Description:** A law firm providing services in almost all areas of civil law. Baker Botts LLP is one of the nation's oldest and largest law firms. **Positions advertised include:** Clerk; Legal Assistant. **Corporate headquarters location:** Houston TX. **Other U.S. locations:** DC; NY. **International locations:** Azerbaijan; England; Russia; Saudi Arabia.

BARON & BUDD, P.C.
3102 Oak Lawn Avenue, Suite 1100, Dallas TX 75219-4281. 214/521-3605. **Contact:** Personnel. **World Wide Web address:** http://www.baronbudd.com. **Description:** A plaintiffs' law firm specializing in environmental and toxic tort litigation.

CANTEY & HANGER, LLP
801 Cherry Street, Suite 2100, Burnett Plaza, Fort Worth TX 76102. 817/877-2800. **Contact:** Personnel. **World Wide Web address:** http://www.canteyhanger.com. **Description:** A law firm specializing in corporate law.

DAVIS & MUNCK
900 Three Galleria Tower, 13155 Noel Road, Dallas TX 75240. 214/922-9221. **Contact:** Personnel. **World Wide Web address:** http://www.davismunck.com. **Description:** A law firm specializing in corporate, IPO, estate, and real estate law.

FRED MISKO, JR., P.C.

3811 Turtle Creek Boulevard, Suite 1000, Dallas TX 75219. 214/443-8000. **Contact:** Human Resources. **World Wide Web address:** http://www.misko.com. **Description:** A trial practice specializing in personal injury law.

THOMPSON & KNIGHT LLP

1700 Pacific Avenue, Suite 3300, Dallas TX 75201. 214/969-1700. **Contact:** Human Resources. **World Wide Web address:** http://www.tklaw.com. **Description:** A law firm specializing in a wide variety of law disciplines including bankruptcy, corporate, intellectual property, real estate, and environmental.

WEBB, STOKES & SPARKS, L.L.P.

P.O. Box 1271, San Angelo TX 76902. 915/653-6866. **Physical address:** 314 West Harris Avenue, San Angelo TX 76903. **Toll-free phone:** 800/727-4529. **Fax:** 915/655-1250. **Contact:** Human Resources Department. **World Wide Web address:** http://www.webbstokessparks.com. **Description:** A law office specializing in personal injury cases.

WINSTEAD SECHREST & MINICK P.C.

5400 Renaissance Tower, 1201 Elm Street, Dallas TX 75270. 214/745-5211. **Contact:** Patty Stewart, Human Resources Manager. **E-mail address:** pstewart@winstead.com. **World Wide Web address:** http://www.winstead.com. **Description:** A law firm offering services in a variety of practice areas including environmental, insurance, real estate, and tax.

OFFICES OF NORMAN A. ZABLE, P.C.

5757 Alpha Road, Suite 504, Dallas TX 75240. 972/386-6900. **Contact:** Human Resources Department. **Description:** A civil law practice specializing in business and bankruptcy law.

MANUFACTURING: MISCELLANEOUS CONSUMER

You can expect to find the following types of companies in this chapter:
Art Supplies • Batteries • Cosmetics and Related Products • Household Appliances and Audio/Video Equipment • Jewelry, Silverware, and Plated Ware • Miscellaneous Household Furniture and Fixtures • Musical Instruments • Tools • Toys and Sporting Goods

APW WYOTT FOOD SERVICE EQUIPMENT
729 Third Avenue, Dallas TX 75226. 214/421-7366. **Fax:** 214/565-0976. **Contact:** Human Resources. **World Wide Web address:** http://www.apwwyott.com. **Description:** Manufactures counter top equipment, equipment used in fabrication plans for restaurants or concessions, heavy-duty ovens, cooking equipment, and deck ovens.

ATLAS MATCH CORPORATION
P.O. Box 1227, Euless TX 76040. 817/267-1500. **Physical address:** 1801 South Airport Circle, Euless TX 76040. **Fax:** 817/354-7478. **Contact:** Human Resources. **World Wide Web address:** http://www. atlasmatch.com. **Description:** Manufactures a wide variety of matchbooks with advertisements.

DART CONTAINER CORPORATION
850 Solon Road, Waxahachie TX 75165. 972/937-7270. **Contact:** Human Resources. **World Wide Web address:** http://www.dart container.com. **Description:** Manufactures and wholesales Styrofoam cups, plates, and beverage coolers.

DESIGN SOURCE
P.O. Box 420406, Dallas TX 75342-1068. 214/742-8234. **Contact:** Human Resources. **Description:** A manufacturer of wooden and upholstered furniture for the home.

FOSSIL, INC.
2280 North Greenville Avenue, Richardson TX 75082-4412. 214/348-7400. **Contact:** Human Resources. **E-mail address:** jobs@ fossil.com. **World Wide Web address:** http://www.fossil.com. **Description:** Manufactures watches, leather accessories, T-shirts, and sunglasses. **Positions advertised include:** Account Representative; Product Manager; Configuration Manager; Merchandise Planner;

Senior Designer. **Listed on:** NASDAQ. **Stock exchange symbol:** FOSL.

HASBRO, INC.
8889 Gateway West, El Paso TX 79925. 915/590-0126. **Contact:** Human Resources. **World Wide Web address:** http://www.hasbro. com. **Description:** Hasbro is a major producer and marketer of toys including brand names GI Joe, My Little Pony, Tonka Trucks, Cabbage Patch Kids, Play-Doh, and Nerf. Affiliate Hasbro Playskool manufactures preschool toys, childcare products, play sets, and children's apparel. **Corporate headquarters location:** Pawtucket RI. **Listed on:** New York Stock Exchange. **Stock exchange symbol:** HAS.

HELEN OF TROY LTD.
One Helen of Troy Plaza, El Paso TX 79912. 915/225-8000. **Fax:** 915/225-8010. **Contact:** Human Resources. **World Wide Web address:** http://www.hotus.com. **Description:** Helen of Troy markets hair care appliances through major retail outlets worldwide. The company manufactures products under brand names including Vidal Sassoon, Revlon, Sable, and Helen of Troy. The company also services the professional retail market with an extensive collection of professional hair care appliances for salon use. **Corporate headquarters location:** This location. **Operations at this facility include:** This division serves as one of the primary development arenas for all corporate product lines. **Listed on:** NASDAQ. **Stock exchange symbol:** HELE.

JOSTENS, INC.
P.O. Box AC, Denton TX 76202-1836. 940/891-0434. **Contact:** Human Resources. **World Wide Web address:** http://www.jostens. com. **Description:** Jostens, Inc.'s primary business segments are School Products, Recognition, and Jostens Learning. The School Products segment is comprised of five businesses: Printing and Publishing, Jewelry, Graduation Products, U.S. Photography, and Jostens Canada. Products include yearbooks, commercial printing, desktop publishing curriculum kits, class rings, graduation accessories, diplomas, trophies, plaques and other awards, school pictures, group photographs for youth camps and organizations, and senior graduation portraits. This segment serves schools, colleges, and alumni associations in the United States and Canada through 1,100 independent sales representatives. Jostens also maintains an international sales force in approximately 50 countries for American schools and military installations. The Recognition segment provides

products and services that reflect achievements in service, sales, quality, productivity, attendance, safety, and retirements. It also produces awards for championship team accomplishments and affinity products for associations. This segment serves companies, professional and amateur sports teams, and special interest associations through an independent sales force of approximately 100 people. Jostens Learning produces educational software for children in kindergarten through grade 12, offering software-based curriculum in reading, mathematics, language arts, science programs, and early childhood instruction, as well as programs for at-risk learning and home learning. As one of the nation's largest providers of curriculum software, Jostens Learning serves more than 4 million students in 10,000 schools nationwide. Customers may purchase programs to meet specific instructional needs, add products in a modular approach, or choose to implement a comprehensive schoolwide solution. **Operations at this facility include:** This location manufactures jewelry, which is sold to consumers through independent contract salespeople.

JUMPKING INC.
1371 South Town East Boulevard, Mesquite TX 75149. 972/290-7300. **Contact:** Personnel. **World Wide Web address:** http://www. iconfitness.com. **Description:** Manufactures trampolines and related accessories.

KOHLER COMPANY
P.O. Box 1709, Brownwood TX 76804. 915/643-2661. **Contact:** Human Resources. **World Wide Web address:** http://www.kohler. com. **Description:** A large manufacturer of vitreous china. Kohler also has a plastics division that produces showers and baths. **Corporate headquarters location:** Kohler WI.

LASTING PRODUCTS
2115 West Valley View Lane, Suite 200, Farmers Branch TX 75234. 972/247-9696. **Contact:** Personnel. **World Wide Web address:** http://www.lastingproducts.com. **Description:** Manufactures decorative home products made of wood, metal, ceramic, and glass.

MARY KAY, INC.
16251 Dallas Parkway, Addison TX 75001. 972/687-6300. **Contact:** Human Resources. **World Wide Web address:** http://www.marykay. com. **Description:** Manufactures and distributes cosmetics and other health and beauty aids. Production and development is conducted at

a facility in Texas, while distribution is carried out by approximately 300,000 direct sales consultants. Products are sold in 16 countries.

NASH MANUFACTURING, INC.
315 West Ripy Street, Fort Worth TX 76110. 817/926-5225. **Contact:** Human Resources. **World Wide Web address:** http://www.nashmfg.com. **Description:** Manufactures sports and athletic equipment including skateboards and water skis.

NATIONAL BANNER COMPANY
11938 Harry Hines Boulevard, Dallas TX 75234. 972/241-2131. **Contact:** Human Resources. **World Wide Web address:** http://www.nationalbanner.com. **Description:** Manufactures and wholesales flags, banners, and pennants.

PRO-LINE CORPORATION
2121 Panoramic Circle, Dallas TX 75212. 214/631-4247. **Contact:** Human Resources. **World Wide Web address:** http://www.pralinecorp.com. **Description:** Manufactures hair care products including relaxers, botanicals, and perm repair products. **Corporate headquarters location:** This location.

RUBBERMAID, INC.
7121 Shelby Avenue, Greenville TX 75402. 903/455-0011. **Contact:** Human Resources. **World Wide Web address:** http://www.rubbermaid.com. **Description:** Rubbermaid manufactures and sells rubber and plastic products for the consumer and commercial markets. Products include over 2,500 items for home organization, kitchen and bath, household repairs/do-it-yourself, and agricultural, industrial, and institutional use. **Corporate headquarters location:** Wooster OH. **Operations at this facility include:** This location manufactures household products such as plastic food storage containers.

SAMSILL CORPORATION
4301 Mansfield Highway, Fort Worth TX 76119. 817/535-0203. **Contact:** Human Resources. **World Wide Web address:** http://www.samsill.com. **Description:** Manufactures office products such as plastic binders and sheet protectors.

SKEETER PRODUCTS INC.

P.O. Box 230, Kilgore TX 75662. 903/984-0541. **Contact:** Human Resources. **World Wide Web address:** http://www.skeeterboats.com. **Description:** Manufactures fishing boats.

SWEETHEART CUP COMPANY, INC.

4444 West Ledbetter Drive, Dallas TX 75236. 214/339-3131. **Contact:** Human Resources. **World Wide Web address:** http://www.sweetheart.com. **Description:** Manufactures and distributes a variety of food serviceware including plates, cups, bowls, drinking straws, and ice cream cones, as well as containers for use in packaging food and dairy products. **Positions advertised include:** Sales Representative; Marketing Associate. **Corporate headquarters location:** Chicago IL. **Operations at this facility include:** Manufacturing; Sales.

TEMTEX INDUSTRIES INC.

5400 LBJ Freeway, Suite 1375, Dallas TX 75240. 972/726-7175. **Contact:** Human Resources. **World Wide Web address:** http://www.temcofireplaces.com. **Description:** Manufactures ceramic logs for fireplaces. **Corporate headquarters location:** This location.

TEXAS RECREATION CORPORATION

P.O. Box 539, Wichita Falls TX 76307. 940/322-4463. **Contact:** Human Resources. **World Wide Web address:** http://www.texasrec.com. **Description:** Manufactures soft foam products including pool flotation devices.

MANUFACTURING: MISCELLANEOUS INDUSTRIAL

You can expect to find the following types of companies in this chapter:
Ball and Roller Bearings • Commercial Furniture and Fixtures • Fans, Blowers, and Purification Equipment • Industrial Machinery and Equipment • Motors and Generators/Compressors and Engine Parts • Vending Machines

ABCO INDUSTRIES INC.
P.O. Box 268, Abilene TX 79604. 915/677-2011. **Contact:** Human Resources. **World Wide Web address:** http://www.abcoboilers.com. **Description:** Manufactures industrial boilers.

BOOTH, INC.
P.O. Box 111754, Carrolton TX 75006-1754. 214/369-9085. **Contact:** Human Resources Department. **World Wide Web address:** http://www.boothair.com. **Description:** An industrial manufacturing company specializing in the production of air conditioning and heating systems. **Parent company:** Trane.

THE BRINKMANN CORPORATION
4215 McEwen Road, Dallas TX 75244. 972/387-4939. **Contact:** Human Resources Department. **World Wide Web address:** http://www.thebrinkmanncorp.com. **Description:** A diversified manufacturer producing items such as meat smokers, spotlights, and metal detectors. **Corporate headquarters location:** This location. **Operations at this facility include:** Manufacturing; Sales.

CONVEYORS, INC.
620 South Fourth Avenue, Mansfield TX 76063. 817/477-3155. **Contact:** Human Resources. **World Wide Web address:** http://www.conveyorsinc.net. **Description:** A manufacturer and retailer of conveyors and conveyor-related equipment.

FERGUSON MANUFACTURING AND EQUIPMENT
4900 Harry Hines Boulevard, Dallas TX 75235. 214/631-3000. **Contact:** Human Resources. **World Wide Web address:** http://www.fergusonrollers.com. **Description:** Manufactures and distributes construction machines and equipment.

FLOWSERVE CORPORATION
222 West Las Colinas Boulevard, Suite 1500, Irving TX 75039. 972/443-6500. **Contact:** Human Resources. **World Wide Web address:** http://www.flowserve.com. **Description:** Manufactures valves for the chemical and petroleum industries. **Corporate headquarters location:** This location. **Listed on:** New York Stock Exchange. **Stock exchange symbol:** FLS.

FORNEY CORPORATION
3405 Wiley Post Road, Carrollton TX 75006. 972/458-6100. **Contact:** Human Resources. **World Wide Web address:** http://www.forneycorp.com. **Description:** Manufactures industrial boiler burners, and burner and process control equipment and systems. **Parent company:** Kidde PLC.

HART & COOLEY
12504 Weaver Road, El Paso TX 79928. 915/852-9111. **Fax:** 915/852-1309. **Contact:** Human Resources. **World Wide Web address:** http://www.hartandcooley.com. **Description:** Manufactures registers and grills for heating and cooling systems. **Parent company:** Tomkins PLC.

HOBART CORPORATION
8120 Jetstar Drive, Suite 100, Irving TX 75063. 972/915-3822. **Contact:** Human Resources. **World Wide Web address:** http://www.hobartcorp.com. **Description:** Manufactures food equipment for restaurants and supermarkets. Products include slicers, mixers, scales, fryers, food cutters, and toasters. **Corporate headquarters location:** Troy OH. **Parent company:** Food Equipment Group. **Operations at this facility include:** Sales; Service.

INGERSOLL-RAND COMPANY
P.O. Box 462288, Garland TX 75040. 972/495-8181. **Contact:** Human Resources. **World Wide Web address:** http://www.ingersoll-rand.com. **Description:** Manufactures compressors, pumps, and other nonelectrical industrial equipment and machinery. Ingersoll-Rand Company's products include air compression systems, antifriction systems, construction equipment, air tools, bearings, locks, tools, and pumps. The company operates 93 production facilities throughout the world. **Listed on:** New York Stock Exchange. **Stock exchange symbol:** IR.

JOHN DEERE COMPANY
4040 McEwen, Suite 200, Dallas TX 75244-5032. 972/385-1701. **Contact:** Human Resources. **World Wide Web address:** http://www. deere.com. **Description:** John Deere manufactures, distributes, and finances the sale of heavy equipment and machinery for use in the agricultural equipment and industrial equipment industries. The agricultural equipment sector manufactures tractors, soil, seeding, and harvesting equipment. The industrial equipment segment manufactures a variety of earth moving equipment, tractors, loaders, and excavators; the consumer products division manufactures a variety of tractors and products for the homeowner. Financial services, including personal and commercial lines of insurance, retail, and managed health care services, are also offered. **Operations at this facility include;** This office is the agricultural equipment sales office for the region. **Listed on:** New York Stock Exchange. **Stock exchange symbol:** DE.

JOHNSON CONTROLS, INC.
3021 West Bend Drive, Irving TX 75063. 972/869-4494. **Contact:** Human Resources. **World Wide Web address:** http://www.johnson controls.com. **Description:** Manufactures and markets automobile, marine, and commercial storage batteries for sale to private labels. **Corporate headquarters location:** Milwaukee WI. **Operations at this facility include:** Manufacturing; Sales; Service. **Listed on:** New York Stock Exchange. **Stock exchange symbol:** JCI. **Number of employees worldwide:** 112,000.

MADIX INC.
P.O. Box 729, Terrell TX 75160-0729. 972/524-5744. **Contact:** Human Resources. **World Wide Web address:** http://www.madixinc. com. **Description:** A manufacturer of store fixtures such as grocery store shelving.

MARTIN SPROCKET & GEAR INC.
3100 Sprocket Drive, Arlington TX 76015. 817/467-5181. **Contact:** Personnel. **World Wide Web address:** http://www.martinsprocket. com. **Description:** Manufactures chain sprockets and gears. **Corporate headquarters location:** This location. **Other U.S. locations:** Nationwide. **Listed on:** Privately held.

MARTIN SPROCKET & GEAR INC.
P.O. Box 1038, Fort Worth TX 76101. 817/258-3000. **Contact:** Darrell Riddick, Personnel Manager. **World Wide Web address:**

http://www.martinsprocket.com. **Description:** Manufactures, installs, and services conveyor equipment. **Positions advertised include:** Sales Representative; Marketing Representative. **Corporate headquarters location:** Arlington TX. **Other U.S. locations:** Nationwide. **Listed on:** Privately held.

MYKROLIS CORPORATION

915 Enterprise Boulevard, Allen TX 75013-8003. 972/359-4000. **Contact:** Human Resources. **World Wide Web address:** http://www. mykrolis.com. **Description:** Manufactures pressure gauges used by pharmaceutical, agricultural, and oil and gas companies. **Corporate headquarters location:** Bedford MA. **Listed on:** New York Stock Exchange. **Stock exchange symbol:** MYK

NCH CORPORATION

P.O Box 152170, Irving TX 75015. **Toll-free phone:** 800/527-9919. **Fax:** 972/438-0707. **Recorded jobline:** 972/721-6116. **Contact:** Human Resources. **World Wide Web address:** http://www.nch.com. **Description:** Manufactures and supplies specialty chemicals, water treatment products, fasteners, welding supplies, plumbing and electronic parts, and safety supplies to a worldwide customer base. Founded in 1919. **NOTE:** Entry-level positions and part-time jobs are offered. **Company slogan:** World class products and services. **Special programs:** Internships; Training. **Corporate headquarters location:** This location. **Other U.S. locations:** El Segundo CA; Atlanta GA; Chicago IL; Paramus NJ; Seattle WA. **International locations:** Asia; Australia; Europe; South America.

NATIONAL OILWELL

P.O. Box 1101, Pampa TX 79066-1101. 806/665-3701. **Fax:** 806/665-3216. **Contact:** Human Resources. **World Wide Web address:** http://www.natoil.com. **Description:** Designs and manufactures a complete line of oil and gas drilling and workover rigs, related equipment, and accessories. Through its specialty steel division, the company produces a wide array of alloy steel forging and bar stock for use in industries ranging from aerospace to nuclear energy. Founded in 1925. **Other area locations:** Alice TX; Beaumont TX; Houston TX; Odessa TX. **International locations:** Moscow, Russia; United Kingdom. **Listed on:** New York Stock Exchange. **Stock exchange symbol:** NOI. **Number of employees at nationwide:** 6,200.

NOBLE CONSTRUCTION EQUIPMENT, INC.
1802 East 50th Street, Lubbock TX 79404. 806/747-4663. **Contact:** Human Resources. **World Wide Web address:** http://www.noblecei. com. **Description:** Manufactures and distributes industrial machinery and other industrial equipment. **International locations:** Mexico.

PARKER HANNIFIN CORPORATION
STRATOFLEX AEROSPACE/MILITARY CONNECTORS DIVISION
P.O. Box 10398, Fort Worth TX 76114. 817/738-6543. **Fax:** 817/ 738-0598. **Contact:** Human Resources. **World Wide Web address:** http://www.parker.com. **Description:** The company makes motion control products including fluid power systems, electromechanical controls, and related components. The Motion and Control Group manufactures hydraulic pumps, power units, control valves, accumulators, cylinders, actuators, and automation devices to remove contaminants from air, fuel, oil, water, and other fluids. The Fluid Connectors Group manufactures connectors, tube and hose fittings, hoses, and couplers that transmit fluid. The Seal Group manufactures sealing devices, gaskets, and packing materials that insure leak-proof connections. The Automotive and Refrigeration Groups manufacture components for use in industrial and automotive air conditioning and refrigeration systems. **Positions advertised include:** Technical Data Manager. **Corporate headquarters location:** Cleveland OH. **Operations at this facility include:** This location is a manufacturer of hose fittings and hose assemblies for the aerospace, military, and marine markets. **Listed on:** New York Stock Exchange. **Stock exchange symbol:** PH. **Number of employees worldwide:** 45,000.

PERRY EQUIPMENT CORPORATION
P.O. Box 640, Mineral Wells TX 76068-0640. 940/325-2575. **Contact:** Doug Harcourt, Vice President of Personnel. **World Wide Web address:** http://www.pecousa.com. **Description:** Manufactures filtration separation cartridges, flow-measurement systems, and systems for the oil, gas, and chemical processing industries. **Positions advertised include:** Field Engineer. **Corporate headquarters location:** This location. **Other area locations:** Amarillo TX; Houston TX. **Listed on:** Privately held.

STEELCASE INC.
3131 McKinney Avenue, Suite 300, Dallas TX 75204-2442. 214/871-3044. **Contact:** Human Resources. **World Wide Web address:** http://www.steelcase.com. **Description:** Manufactures metal

and wood office furniture. **Listed on:** New York Stock Exchange. **Stock exchange symbol:** SCS.

3M
P.O. Box 1669, Brownwood TX 76804. 915/646-3551. **Contact:** Human Resources. **World Wide Web address:** http://www.3m.com. **Description:** 3M manufactures products in three sectors: Industrial and Consumer; Information, Imaging, and Electronic; and Life Sciences. The Industrial and Consumer Sector manufactures a variety of products under brand names including 3M, Scotch, Post-it, Scotch-Brite, and Scotchgard. The Information, Imaging, and Electronic Sector is a leader in several high-growth global industries including telecommunications, electronics, electrical, imaging, and memory media. The Life Science Sector serves two broad market categories: health care, and traffic and personal safety. In the health care market, 3M is a leading provider of medical and surgical supplies, drug-delivery systems, and dental products; in traffic and personal safety, 3M is a leader in products for worker protection, vehicle and sign graphics, and out-of-home advertising. **Corporate headquarters location:** St. Paul MN. **Operations at this facility include:** This location makes highly reflective products for license plates and street signs. **Listed on:** New York Stock Exchange. **Stock exchange symbol:** MMM.

THE TRANE COMPANY
P.O. Box 814609, Dallas TX 75381. 972/406-6000. **Fax:** 972/243-1349. **Contact:** Human Resources. **E-mail address:** tranejobs@ netscape.net. **World Wide Web address:** http://www.trane.com. **Description:** Engaged in the development, manufacture, and sale of air conditioning equipment designed for use in central air conditioning systems for commercial, institutional, industrial, and residential buildings. The Trane Company's products are designed to cool water, and to cool, heat, humidify, dehumidify, move, and filter air. Other products include similar systems for buses and rapid transit vehicles, refrigeration equipment for trucks, and pollution control equipment. **NOTE:** Entry-level positions are offered. **Positions advertised include:** Customer Service Representative; HVAC Service Technician; Inventory Coordinator; Regional Safety and Health Coordinator. **Corporate headquarters location:** La Crosse WI. **Parent company:** American Standard.

TRAULSEN & COMPANY, INC.
4401 Blue Mound Road, Fort Worth TX 76106. 817/625-9671. **Contact:** Ana Flores, Human Resources Manager. **World Wide Web address:** http://www.traulsen.com. **Description:** Manufactures an extensive line of commercial refrigerators and freezers. **Corporate headquarters location:** This location.

TYLER PIPE INDUSTRIES, INC.
P.O. Box 2027, Tyler TX 75710. 903/882-5511. **Contact:** Human Resources. **World Wide Web address:** http://www.tylerpipe.com. **Description:** Manufactures and distributes soil pipe and pipe fittings. Tyler Pipe Industries, Inc. is also a national producer of both plastic and iron piping for large-volume users.

VECTA
1800 South Great SW Parkway, Grand Prairie TX 75051. 972/641-2860. **Contact:** Human Resources. **World Wide Web address:** http://www.vecta.com. **Description:** Custom manufactures office furniture.

VIRGINIA KMP CORPORATION
4100 Platinum Way, Dallas TX 75237. 214/330-7731. **Contact:** Vice President of Operations. **World Wide Web address:** http://www.virginiakmp.com. **Description:** Manufactures and sells chemicals, filter dryers, refrigeration accumulators, and air conditioners.

MINING/GAS/PETROLEUM/ENERGY RELATED

You can expect to find the following types of companies in this chapter:
Anthracite, Coal, and Ore Mining • Mining Machinery and Equipment• Oil and Gas Field Services • Petroleum and Natural Gas

AERIFORM CORPORATION

3813 County Road West, Odessa TX 79764. 915/335-4200. **Contact:** Human Resources. **World Wide Web address:** http://www. aeriform.com. **Description:** Aeriform ranks among the nation's largest independent suppliers of specialty gases, medical gases, welding equipment, and cryogenic products. **Positions advertised include:** Driver; Inside/Counter Sales Representative; Branch Manager; Customer Service Manager. **Corporate headquarters location:** Houston TX.

AMERADA HESS CORPORATION

6688 North Central Expressway, Suite 1400, Dallas TX 75206. 214/ 691-5200. **Contact:** Human Resources. **World Wide Web address:** http://www.ahc.com. **Description:** An international oil and gas exploration company. **Corporate headquarters location:** This location. **International locations:** Worldwide. **Operations at this facility include:** Administration. **Listed on:** New York Stock Exchange. **Stock exchange symbol:** AHC.

ATMOS ENERGY CORPORATION

P.O. Box 650205, Dallas TX 75265. 972/934-9227. **Fax:** 972/855-4039. **Contact:** Manager of Compensation and Employment. **E-mail address:** employment@atmosenergy.com. **World Wide Web address:** http://www.atmosenergy.com. **Description:** Distributes natural gas and propane. **Corporate headquarters location:** This location. **Other U.S. locations:** CO; KY; LA. **Subsidiaries include:** Energas; Greeley Gas; Trans Louisiana Gas; Western Kentucky Gas. **Operations at this facility include:** Administration. **Number of employees nationwide:** 2,300.

BP AMOCO PLC

P.O. Box 1610, Midland TX 79702. 915/688-5200. **Fax:** 915/688-5537. **Contact:** Human Resources. **World Wide Web address:** http:// www.bp.com. **Description:** A chemical processing plant. **Listed on:** New York Stock Exchange. **Stock exchange symbol:** BP.

COMPUTALOG
WIRELINE PRODUCTS, INC.
500 Winscott Road, Fort Worth TX 76126. 817/249-1391. **Fax:** 817/249-7284. **Contact:** Human Resources. **E-mail address:** jobs-usa@computalog.com. **World Wide Web address:** http://www. computalog.com. **Description:** Manufactures, sells, and services oilwell equipment for the oil field service industry. **Positions advertised include:** MWD Operator; Down Hole Surveyor; Junior Field Engineer. **Office hours:** Monday - Friday, 8:00 a.m. - 5:00 p.m.

ENSCO INTERNATIONAL INCORPORATED
1445 Ross Avenue, Suite 2700, Dallas TX 75202. 214/922-1500. **Contact:** Human Resources. **World Wide Web address:** http://www. enscous.com. **Description:** One of the world's largest offshore oil and gas drilling companies. **Corporate headquarters location:** This location. **Listed on:** New York Stock Exchange. **Stock exchange symbol:** ESV.

EXXONMOBIL CORPORATION
5959 Las Colinas Boulevard, Irving TX 75039-2298. 972/444-1000. **Fax:** 972/444-1348. **Contact:** Personnel. **World Wide Web address:** http://www.exxon.mobil.com. **Description:** An integrated oil company engaged in the worldwide marketing, refining, manufacturing, exploration, production, transportation, and research and development of petroleum and chemical products. Other products include fabricated plastics, films, food bags, housewares, garbage bags, and building materials. The company also has subsidiaries involved in real estate development and mining operations. **Corporate headquarters location:** This location. **Listed on:** New York Stock Exchange. **Stock exchange symbol:** XOM.

GAS EQUIPMENT COMPANY
11616 Harry Hines Boulevard, P.O. Box 29242, Dallas TX 75229. 972/241-2333. **Toll-free phone:** 800/821-1829. **Contact:** Human Resources Department. **World Wide Web address:** http://www.gas equipment.com. **Description:** A wholesale distributor of liquefied petroleum products. **Corporate headquarters location:** This location. **Listed on:** Privately held.

GEER TANK TRUCKS INC.
P.O. Drawer J, Jacksboro TX 76458. 940/567-2677. **Contact:** Human Resources. **World Wide Web address:** http://www.geertank

trucks.com. **Description:** A crude oil purchaser. The company also hauls various substances including oil and saltwater.

HARBISON-FISCHER MANUFACTURING COMPANY
P.O. Box 2477, Fort Worth TX 76113-2477. 817/297-2211. **Fax:** 817/297-4248. **Contact:** Leon Gregory, Personnel Director. **World Wide Web address:** http://www.hfpumps.com. **Description:** Manufactures subsurface oil well pumping equipment. **Corporate headquarters location:** This location. **Other area locations:** Odessa TX. **Subsidiaries include:** Challenger Tank (Whitehouse TX); National Steelcrafters (Eugene OR). **Operations at this facility include:** Administration; Manufacturing; Research and Development; Sales; Service.

HOLLY CORPORATION
100 Crescent Court, Suite 1600, Dallas TX 75201-6927. 214/871-3555. **Contact:** Human Resources. **World Wide Web address:** http://www.hollycorp.com. **Description:** A holding company that refines and markets petroleum products through its subsidiaries. The company also operates a jet fuel terminal in Idaho for the U.S. government. **Subsidiaries include:** Montana Refining Company (Great Falls MT); Navajo Refining Company (Artesia NM). **Listed on:** American Stock Exchange. **Stock exchange symbol:** HOC. **Number of employees nationwide:** 521.

HUNT OIL COMPANY
1445 Ross Avenue, Suite 1400, Dallas TX 75202. 214/978-8000. **Contact:** Human Resources. **World Wide Web address:** http://www. huntoil.com. **Description:** Refines and distributes petroleum and natural gas. **Positions advertised include:** Senior Production Operations Analyst; IT Technical Support Analyst; Security Officer; Senior Internal Auditor; Tax Staff Accountant. **Special programs:** Internships. **Corporate headquarters location:** This location. **Operations at this facility include:** Administration. **Listed on:** Privately held.

JRC HALLIBURTON ENERGY SERVICES, INC.
8432 South Interstate 35 S, Alvarado TX 76009. 817/790-2038. **Contact:** Human Resources Manager. **World Wide Web address:** http://www.halliburton.com. **Description:** Provides evaluation services in connection with the drilling and completion of gas and oil wells. The company also manufactures and sells the equipment and supplies required to perform these services. **Positions advertised**

include: Account Representative; Field Service Engineer. **Other U.S. locations:** Nationwide. **Parent company:** Halliburton Company. **Listed on:** New York Stock Exchange. **Stock exchange symbol:** HAL.

KERR McGEE CORPORATION

14311 Welch Road, Dallas TX 75244. 972/715-4000. **Contact:** Employment. **World Wide Web address:** http://www.kerr-mcgee. com. **Description:** Explores for, acquires, develops, produces, and sells oil and natural gas worldwide. **Listed on:** New York Stock Exchange. **Stock exchange symbol:** KMG.

PATTERSON DRILLING COMPANY, INC.

4105 South Chadbourne Street, San Angelo TX 76904. 915/655-6773. **Contact:** Human Resources. **Description:** Engaged in onshore drilling for oil and gas; and the exploration, development, and production of oil and gas. The company's operations are conducted primarily in the Permian Basin in western Texas and southeastern New Mexico, and in southern and southeastern Texas. Founded in 1978. **Corporate headquarters location:** Snyder TX.

PATTERSON DRILLING COMPANY, INC.

P.O. Drawer 1416, Snyder TX 79550. 915/573-1831. **Contact:** Human Resources. **Description:** Engaged in onshore drilling for oil and gas; and the exploration, development, and production of oil and gas. The company's operations are conducted primarily in the Permian Basin in western Texas and southeastern New Mexico, and in southern and southeastern Texas. **Corporate headquarters location:** This location.

PHILLIPS PETROLEUM COMPANY

4001 Penbrook Street, Odessa TX 79762. 915/368-1266. **Contact:** Human Resources Department. **World Wide Web address:** http:// www.phillips66.com. **Description:** Provides gas services including crude oil transportation, exploration, drilling, procurement, and regulation. Phillips Petroleum Company has offices in west Texas and New Mexico. **Listed on:** New York Stock Exchange. **Stock exchange symbol:** P.

PIONEER NATURAL RESOURCES

P.O. Box 3178, Midland TX 79702. 915/683-4768. **Contact:** Human Resources Department. **E-mail address:** recruiter@pioneernrc.com. **World Wide Web address:** http://www.pioneernrc.com. **Description:** Engaged in the exploration and production of oil and gas. **NOTE:** Send resumes to: Pioneer Natural Resources, Attn: Human Resources, 5205 North O'Connor Boulevard, Suite 1400, Irving TX 75039. **Special programs:** Internships; Summer Jobs. **Internship information:** Internships are offered in accounting, engineering, and geology. **Corporate headquarters location:** Irving TX. **International locations:** Buenos Aires, Argentina; Calgary, Canada. **Listed on:** New York Stock Exchange. **Stock exchange symbol:** PXD. **CEO:** Scott Sheffield. **Number of employees nationwide:** 900.

PIONEER NATURAL RESOURCES
5205 North O'Connor Boulevard, Suite 1400, Irving TX 75039-3747. 972/444-9001. **Contact:** Human Resources Department. **E-mail address:** recruiter@pioneernrc.com. **World Wide Web address:** http://www.pioneernrc.com. **Description:** Engaged in the exploration and production of petroleum oil and natural gas. **Corporate headquarters location:** This location. **International locations:** Buenos Aires, Argentina; Calgary, Canada. **Listed on:** New York Stock Exchange. **Stock exchange symbol:** PXD. **CEO:** Scott Sheffield. **Number of employees nationwide:** 900.

POOL COMPANY
P.O. Box 1117, Crane TX 79731. 915/558-2561. **Fax:** 915/558-2402. **Contact:** Employment Recruiter. **Description:** Engaged in pulling wells and hauling water. **Corporate headquarters location:** This location.

REPUBLIC SUPPLY COMPANY
5646 Milton Street, Suite 800, Dallas TX 75206. 214/987-9868. **Contact:** Human Resources. **Description:** Distributes oil field supplies and industrial machine equipment. **Corporate headquarters location:** This location. **Operations at this facility include:** Administration. **Listed on:** Privately held.

SANTA FE INTERNATIONAL CORPORATION
2 Lincoln Centre, 5420 LBJ Freeway, Suite 1100, Dallas TX 75240. 972/701-7300. **Contact:** Human Resources. **World Wide Web address:** http://www.sfdrill.com. **Description:** An oil well drilling company. **Positions advertised include:** Drilling Superintendent; Toolpusher; Tourpusher; Driller' Welder; Barge Supervisor; Paint Foreman; Blaster.

SOUTHWEST ROYALTIES, INC.

P.O. Box 11390, Midland TX 79702. 915/686-9927. **Contact:** Patty Hollums, Personnel Manager. **World Wide Web address:** http://www.swrinc.com. **Description:** Engaged in oil exploration and development. **Corporate headquarters location:** This location.

SOUTHWESTERN PETROLEUM CORPORATION

P.O. Box 961005, Fort Worth TX 76161. 817/332-2336. **Fax:** 817/877-4047. **Contact:** Human Resources. **World Wide Web address:** http://www.swepcousa.com. **Description:** Manufactures protective coatings and specialty lubricants for the energy industry. **Corporate headquarters location:** This location. **Listed on:** Privately held.

TIMBER SHARP DRILLING INC.

P.O. Drawer 10970, Midland TX 79702-7970. 915/699-5050. **Contact:** Human Resources. **Description:** Engaged in domestic onshore contract drilling of oil and gas wells for major and independent oil and gas producers and the exploration for, development, and production of oil and gas. The company's contract drilling activities are primarily conducted in the Permian Basin of western Texas and eastern New Mexico.

UTI DRILLING, LP

1950 Avenue S, Levelland TX 79336. 806/894-5479. **Fax:** 806/785-8400. **Contact:** Human Resources. **Description:** Operates oil and gas drilling rigs and provides contract drilling services to the oil and gas industry. **Parent company:** Patterson Energy.

PAPER AND WOOD PRODUCTS

You can expect to find the following types of companies in this chapter:
Forest and Wood Products and Services • Lumber and Wood Wholesale • Millwork, Plywood, and Structural Members • Paper and Wood Mills

BOISE CASCADE CORPORATION
10770 Bekay, Dallas TX 75238. 214/341-9000. **Contact:** Personnel Director. **World Wide Web address:** http://www.bc.com. **Description:** An integrated paper and forest products company with operations located nationwide. The company manufactures and distributes paper and paper products, office products, and building products; and owns and manages timberland to support these operations. Boise Cascade is one of the largest pulp and paper producers in the United States. The company has the capacity to produce 3.2 million tons of uncoated and coated papers, newsprint, containerboard, and pulp each year. Founded in 1957. **Corporate headquarters location:** Boise ID. **Listed on:** New York Stock Exchange. **Stock Exchange symbol:** BCC.

INTERNATIONAL PAPER COMPANY
P.O. Box 870, Texarkana TX 75504-0870. 903/796-7101. **Contact:** Human Resources. **World Wide Web address:** http://www. internationalpaper.com. **Description:** International Paper is a manufacturer of pulp and paper, packaging, and wood products, as well as a range of specialty products. The company is organized into five business segments: Printing Papers, in which principal products include uncoated papers, coated papers, bristles, and pulp; Packaging, which includes industrial packaging, consumer packaging, and kraft and specialty papers; Distribution, which includes sales of printing papers, graphic arts equipment and supplies, packaging materials, industrial supplies, and office products; Specialty Products, which includes imaging products, specialty panels, nonwovens, chemicals, and minerals; and Forest Products, which includes logs and wood products. **Corporate headquarters location:** Purchase NY. **Operations at this facility includes:** This location manufactures folding cartons. **Listed on:** New York Stock Exchange. **Stock exchange symbol:** IP. **Number of employees worldwide:** 100,000.

INTERNATIONAL PAPER COMPANY
9301 Billy the Kid Street, El Paso TX 79907. 915/858-8877. **Contact:** Human Resources. **World Wide Web address:** http://www.

internationalpaper.com. **Description:** A manufacturer of pulp and paper, packaging, and wood products as well as a range of specialty products. The company is organized into five business segments: Printing Papers, in which principal products include uncoated papers, coated papers, bristles, and pulp; Packaging, which includes industrial packaging, consumer packaging, and kraft and specialty papers; Distribution, which includes sales of printing papers, graphic arts equipment and supplies, packaging materials, industrial supplies, and office products; Specialty Products, which includes imaging products, specialty panels, nonwovens, chemicals, and minerals; and Forest Products, which includes logs and wood products. **Corporate headquarters location:** Purchase NY. **Listed on:** New York Stock Exchange. **Stock exchange symbol:** IP. **Number of employees worldwide:** 100,000.

MEADWESTVACO

5215 North O'Connor Boulevard, Suite 200, Irving TX 75039. 972/ 868-9060. **Contact:** Human Resources. **World Wide Web address:** http://www.meadwestvaco.com. **Description:** MeadWestvaco manufactures, sells, and markets pulp, paper, paperboard, shipping containers, packaging, lumber, school supplies, office supplies, stationery products, and electronic publishing and information retrieval systems. **Operations at this facility include:** This location is a sales office. **Listed on:** New York Stock Exchange. **Stock exchange symbol:** MWV.

ROCK-TENN COMPANY

1385 Northwestern Drive, El Paso TX 79912. 915/581-5492. **Contact:** Human Resources. **World Wide Web address:** http://www. rocktenn.com. **Description:** Manufactures recycled paperboard and paperboard products. Over two-thirds of paperboard production is used by the company's own converting plants to produce folding cartons, book and notebook covers, components for the furniture industry, and solid fiber partitions used in shipping glass and plastic containers. **Listed on:** New York Stock Exchange. **Stock exchange symbol:** RKT.

SMURFIT-STONE CONTAINER CORPORATION

6701 South Freeway, Fort Worth TX 76134. 817/568-3400. **Contact:** Human Resources. **World Wide Web address:** http://www.smurfit-stone.com. **Description:** Smurfit-Stone Container Corporation is one of the world's leading paper-based packaging companies. The company's main products include corrugated containers, folding cartons, and multiwall industrial bags. The company is also one of the world's largest collectors and processors of recycled products that are then sold to a worldwide customer base. Smurfit-Stone Container Corporation also operates several paper tube, market pulp, and newsprint production facilities. **Corporate headquarters location:** Chicago IL. **Other U.S. locations:** Nationwide. **International locations:** Worldwide. **Operations at this facility include:** This location manufactures corrugated fiberboard boxes.

TRIANGLE PACIFIC CORPORATION
16803 Dallas Parkway, Addison TX 75001. 972/931-3000. **Contact:** Human Resources. **World Wide Web address:** http://www.triangle pacific.com. **Description:** Manufactures hardwood dimension and flooring. Brand names include Bruce, Hartco, and Robbins flooring and cabinets. **Parent company:** Armstrong World Industries.

WEYERHAEUSER COMPANY
8800 Sterling Street, Irving TX 75063. 972/929-8581. **Contact:** Human Resources Manager. **World Wide Web address:** http://www.weyerhaeuser.com. **Description:** Weyerhaeuser Company's principal businesses are the growing and harvesting of timber; the manufacture, distribution, and sale of forest products including logs, wood chips, and building products; real estate development and construction; and financial services. Weyerhaeuser is one of the world's largest private owners of marketable softwood timber and one of the largest producers of softwood lumber and pulp. The company is also one of North America's largest producers of forest products and recyclers of office wastepaper, newspaper, and corrugated boxes. Weyerhaeuser Company also sells electricity to utility companies generated from its 15 trash-to-energy plants and six small cogeneration and recycling plants. The Water Division manufactures and operates facilities and systems for water purification, water treatment, and managed by-products. The Air Division designs, manufactures, and integrates air pollution emission control and measurement systems and related equipment. Founded in 1900. **Corporate headquarters location:** Federal Way WA. **Other U.S. locations:** Nationwide. **International locations:** Worldwide. **Listed on:** New York Stock Exchange. **Stock exchange symbol:** WY. **Number of employees worldwide:** 47,000.

PRINTING AND PUBLISHING

You can expect to find the following types of companies in this chapter:
Book, Newspaper, and Periodical Publishers • Commercial Photographers•
Commercial Printing Services • Graphic Designers

AMARILLO GLOBE -NEWS
P.O. Box 2091, Amarillo TX 79166. 806/376-4488. **Fax:** 806/345-3370. **Contact:** Human Resources. **World Wide Web address:** http://www.amarillonet.com. **Description:** Publishes morning and afternoon daily papers. The Sunday edition has a circulation of approximately 74,000.

AMERICAN AIRLINES PUBLISHING
14770 Trinity Boulevard, MD 1625, Fort Worth TX 76155. 817/967-1804. **Fax:** 817/967-1571. **Contact:** Laura Wilson, Office Administrator. **World Wide Web address:** http://www.americanway.com. **Description:** Publishes the in-flight magazine American Way.

AMERICAN BANK NOTE COMPANY
5307 East Mockingbird Lane, Suite 705, Dallas TX 75206. 214/823-2700. **Fax:** 214/821-9026. **Contact:** Human Resources. **Description:** A printer of counterfeit-resistant documents and one of the largest security printers in the world. American Bank Note creates secure documents of value for governments and corporations worldwide. Products include currencies; passports; stock and bond certificates; bank, corporate, government, and traveler's checks; food coupons; gift vouchers and certificates; driver's licenses; product authentication labels; and vital documents. **Corporate headquarters location:** New York NY. **Other U.S. locations:** Nationwide. **Operations at this facility include:** This location is a national sales office.

BANKERS DIGEST
9550 Forest Lane, Suite 125, Dallas TX 75243. 214/221-4544. **Contact:** Editor. **World Wide Web address:** http://www.bankers digest.com. **Description:** A trade magazine that provides Texas banking news. *Bankers Digest* has a circulation of 4,800.

CORSICANA DAILY SUN
P.O. Box 622, Corsicana TX 75151. 903/872-3931. **Contact:** Human Resources. **World Wide Web address:** http://www.corsicana

dailysun.com. **Description:** Publishes a daily newspaper with a circulation of 7,100 during the week and 8,100 on Sunday.

DALLAS BUSINESS JOURNAL

12801 North Central Expressway, Suite 800, Dallas TX 75231-2111. 214/696-5959. **Contact:** Personnel. **World Wide Web address:** http://www.bizjournals.com/dallas. **Description:** A weekly business periodical with a circulation of 18,000. **Parent company:** American City Business Journals Inc. (Charlotte NC) publishes 41 business journals in cities nationwide.

EL PASO TIMES INC.

P.O. Box 20, El Paso TX 79999. 915/546-6100. **Contact:** Human Resources. **World Wide Web address:** http://www.elpasotimes.com. **Description:** Writes, publishes, prints, and distributes a daily newspaper throughout Texas and New Mexico. The newspaper reaches 240,000 people daily and 250,000 on Sundays. The company also publishes and distributes the *El Paso Herald Post*.

ENNIS BUSINESS FORMS

1510 North Hampton, Suite 300, DeSoto TX 75115. 972/228-7801. **Contact:** Human Resources. **World Wide Web address:** http:// www.ennis.com. **Description:** Produces business forms, checks, and other printed forms. **Listed on:** New York Stock Exchange. **Stock exchange symbol:** EBF.

GREAT WESTERN DIRECTORIES

2400 Lakeview Drive, Suite 109, Amarillo TX 79109. 806/353-5155. **Contact:** Human Resources. **World Wide Web address:** http://www. worldpages.com. **Description:** A publisher of telephone directories. **NOTE:** Send resumes to: TransWestern Publishing Company, Human Resources, 8344 Claremont Mesa Boulevard, San Diego CA 92111. **Parent company:** Transwestern Publishing Company. **Corporate headquarters location:** Sandiego CA.

LEGAL DIRECTORIES PUBLISHING COMPANY, INC.

P.O. Box 189000, Dallas TX 75218-9000. 214/321-3238. **Contact:** Human Resources Department. **World Wide Web address:** http:// www.legaldirectories.com. **Description:** One of the nation's largest publishers of state legal directories.

LUBBOCK AVALANCHE-JOURNAL

P.O. Box 491, Lubbock TX 79408. 806/762-8844. **Contact:** Human Resources. **World Wide Web address:** http://www.lubbockonline. com. **Description:** A daily newspaper. The *Lubbock Avalanche-Journal* has a circulation of approximately 67,000 daily and 74,000 on Sundays.

McGRAW-HILL EDUCATIONAL & PROFESSIONAL PUBLISHING GROUP

220 East Danieldale Road, De Soto TX 75115. 972/224-1111. **Contact:** Human Resources Department. **World Wide Web address:** http://www.mcgrawhill.com. **Description:** McGraw-Hill is a provider of information and services through books, magazines, newsletters, software, CD-ROMs, online data, fax, and TV broadcasting services. The company operates four network-affiliated TV stations and also publishes *Business Week* magazine and books for college, medical, international, legal, and professional markets. McGraw-Hill also offers financial services including Standard & Poor's, commodity items, and international and logistics management products and services. **Operations at this facility include:** This location publishes text-books. **Listed on:** New York Stock Exchange. **Stock exchange symbol:** MHP.

MOTHERAL PRINTING COMPANY

510 South Main Street, Fort Worth TX 76104. 817/335-1481. **Contact:** Human Resources. **World Wide Web address:** http://www. motheral.com. **Description:** A commercial lithography and printing company. **Special programs:** Internships. **Corporate headquarters location:** This location. **Operations at this facility include:** Administration; Manufacturing; Sales.

PADGETT PRINTING CORPORATION

1313 North Industrial Boulevard, Dallas TX 75207. 214/742-4261. **Contact:** Human Resources. **World Wide Web address:** http://www. padgett.com. **Description:** A printing company. **Corporate headquarters location:** This location. **Operations at this facility include:** Administration; Manufacturing; Sales. **Listed on:** Privately held.

POLITICAL RESEARCH, INC.

Tegoland at Bent Tree, 16850 Dallas Parkway, Dallas TX 75248. 972/931-8827. **Contact:** Personnel. **World Wide Web address:** http://www.politicalresearch.com. **Description:** A publisher of reference services on current state, federal, and international governments. Primary customers include educational institutions, libraries, government offices, and businesses. **Corporate headquarters location:** This location. **Operations at this facility include:** Administration; Research and Development; Sales; Service.

QUEBECOR DALLAS
4800 Spring Valley Road, Dallas TX 75244. 972/233-3400. **Contact:** Human Resources. **World Wide Web address:** http://www.quebecor world.com. **Description:** A commercial printing company. Quebecor Dallas handles large print runs for commercial magazines including *Time* and *Sports Illustrated* for the regional market. The company also prints retail inserts and catalogs.

SHOPPER'S GUIDE
1209 West North Carrier Parkway, Suite 300, Grand Prairie TX 75050. 972/641-7690. **Contact:** Human Resources. **Description:** A weekly shopper's newspaper with a circulation of approximately 430,000.

STAR-TELEGRAM
400 West Seventh Street, Fort Worth TX 76102. 817/390-7459. **Fax:** 817/336-3739. **Contact:** Diana Oliveros, Employment Coordinator. **World Wide Web address:** http://www.star-telegram.com. **Description:** Publishes a daily newspaper. **NOTE:** Entry-level positions are offered. **Special programs:** Internships. **Parent company:** Knight Ridder. **Operations at this facility include:** Administration; Manufacturing; Sales.

TAYLOR PUBLISHING COMPANY
10365 Railroad Drive, El Paso TX 79924-1698. 915/857-4002. **Contact:** Human Resources. **World Wide Web address:** http://www. taylorpub.com. **Description:** A publisher of yearbooks and specialty books.

TAYLOR PUBLISHING COMPANY
1550 West Mockingbird Lane, Dallas TX 75235. 214/819-8458. **Fax:** 214/819-8141. **Contact:** Stacey Young, Employment Supervisor. **World Wide Web address:** http://www.taylorpub.com. **Description:** A publisher of yearbooks and specialty books. **Operations at this facility include:** Administration; Manufacturing; Research and Development; Service.

TAYLOR PUBLISHING COMPANY
NEWSPHOTO DIVISION
2027 Industrial Avenue, San Angelo TX 76904. 915/949-3776. **Contact:** Human Resources. **World Wide Web address:** http://www. taylorpub.com. **Description:** A publisher of yearbooks and specialty books.

TRAVELHOST
10701 North Stemmons Freeway, Dallas TX 75220-2419. 972/556-0541. **Fax:** 972/402-0721. **Contact:** Mr. Chung-Ping Chang, Controller. **World Wide Web address:** http://www.travelhost.com. **Description:** A travel, business, and entertainment magazine published weekly. Founded in 1967.

UMR COMMUNICATIONS
2400 Lone Star Drive, Dallas TX 75212. 214/630-6495. **Contact:** Human Resources. **World Wide Web address:** http://www.umr.org. **Description:** Publishes religious articles including the *United Methodist Reporter* and the *National Christian Reporter*. Founded in 1847.

VNU BUSINESS MEDIA
ADWEEK
3102 Maple Avenue, Suite 210, Dallas TX 75201. 214/871-9550. **Contact:** Human Resources. **World Wide Web address:** http://www. vnubusinessmedia.com **Description:** Publishes monthly trade magazines.

VERIZON INFORMATION SERVICES
P.O. Box 619810, DFW Airport TX 75261-9810. 972/453-7000. **Contact:** Human Resources. **World Wide Web address:** http://www. verizon.com. **Description:** This location is engaged in Yellow Pages publishing. Overall, Verizon Communications is a full-service communications services provider. Verizon offers residential local and long distance telephone services and Internet access; wireless service plans, cellular phones, and data services; a full-line of business services including Internet access, data services, and telecommunications equipment and services; and government network solutions including Internet access, data services, telecommunications equipment and services, and enhanced communications services. **NOTE:** Resumes must be submitted via the Website: http://www.verizon.com/careers. **Corporate**

headquarters location: New York NY. **Listed on:** New York Stock Exchange. **Stock exchange symbol:** VZ.

WACO TRIBUNE-HERALD
900 Franklin Avenue, Waco TX 76701. 254/757-5757. **Contact:** Human Resources. **World Wide Web address:** http://www.wacotrib. com. **Description:** Publishes a daily newspaper. **Parent company:** Cox Communication.

WILLIAMSON PRINTING CORPORATION
6700 Denton Drive, Dallas TX 75235. 214/904-2670. **Toll-free phone:** 800/843-5423. **Recorded jobline:** 214/904-2603. **Contact:** Human Resources Administrator. **E-mail address:** jobs@twpc.com. **World Wide Web address:** http://www.twpc.com. **Description:** A commercial printing company. **NOTE:** Entry-level positions and second and third shifts are offered. **Special programs:** Summer Jobs. **Corporate headquarters location:** This location. **Subsidiaries include:** Classic Color Corporation; Image Express; The Fulfillment Center. **Listed on:** Privately held.

REAL ESTATE

You can expect to find the following types of companies in this chapter:
Land Subdividers and Developers • Real Estate Agents, Managers,
and Operators • Real Estate Investment Trusts

ADLETA & POSTON, REALTORS

5956 Sherry Lane, Suite 100, Dallas TX 75225. 214/696-0900. **Fax:** 214/369-6996. **Contact:** Personnel. **World Wide Web address:** http://www.adletaposton.com. **Description:** A residential real estate brokerage specializing in the luxury housing and corporate relocation markets. **Positions advertised include:** Real Estate Agent; Receptionist; Secretary. **Special programs:** Internships. **Corporate headquarters location:** This location. **Operations at this facility include:** Administration; Sales. **Number of employees at this location:** 10.

COLDWELL BANKER

7447 North MacArthur Boulevard, Suite 100, Irving TX 75063. 972/659-1525. **Contact:** Personnel. **World Wide Web address:** http://www.coldwellbanker.com. **Description:** One of the largest residential real estate companies in the United States and Canada in terms of total home sales transactions. Coldwell Banker is also a leader in corporate relocation services. **NOTE:** This office hires agents only. **Corporate headquarters location:** Parsippany NJ. **Other U.S. locations:** Nationwide. **Parent company:** Cendant Corporation. **Listed on:** New York Stock Exchange. **Stock exchange symbol:** CD.

COLDWELL BANKER

2801 Gateway Drive, Suite 180, Irving TX 75063. 972/582-9200. **Contact:** Personnel. **World Wide Web address:** http://www.coldwellbanker.com. **Description:** One of the largest residential real estate companies in the United States and Canada in terms of total home sales transactions. Coldwell Banker is also a leader in corporate relocation services. **Corporate headquarters location:** Parsippany NJ. **Other U.S. locations:** Nationwide. **Parent company:** Cendant Corporation. **Listed on:** New York Stock Exchange. **Stock exchange symbol:** CD.

GRUBB & ELLIS

1000 Signature Place II, 14785 Preston Road, Suite 1000, Dallas TX 75240. 972/450-3300. **Contact:** Human Resources. **World Wide Web address:** http://www.grubb-ellis.com. **Description:** A real estate services firm dealing primarily with commercial properties including shopping centers, office buildings, and similar complexes. Founded in 1958. **Corporate headquarters location:** Northbrook IL.

KELLER WILLIAMS REALTORS
405 Mayfield Avenue, Garland TX 75041. 972/240-4416. **Contact:** Personnel. **World Wide Web address:** http://www.kw.com. **Description:** A realty company offering both residential and commercial properties.

LINCOLN PROPERTY COMPANY
500 North Akard Street, Suite 3300, Dallas TX 75201. 214/740-3300. **Contact:** Human Resources. **World Wide Web address:** http://www.lincolnproperty.com. **Description:** A property management company with commercial, residential, and industrial properties.

MACFARLAN REAL ESTATE
10100 North Central Expressway, Suite 200, Dallas TX 75231. 214/932-3100. **Fax:** 214/932-3199. **Contact:** Human Resources. **E-mail address:** careers@macfarlan.com. **World Wide Web address:** http://www.macfarlan.com. **Description:** A commercial real estate agency. **Corporate headquarters location:** This location.

PRUDENTIAL TEXAS PROPERTIES
3637 Highway 80, Mesquite TX 75150. 972/698-9700. **Contact:** Human Resources. **World Wide Web address:** http://www.prudentialtexas.com. **Description:** A local branch of the national realty company specializing in residential and commercial properties. **Positions advertised include:** Experienced Realtor. **Parent company:** Cendant.

TRAMMELL CROW COMPANY
3400 Trammell Crow Center, 2001 Ross Avenue, Dallas TX 75201-2997. 214/863-3000. **Contact:** Personnel. **World Wide Web address:** http://www.trammellcrow.com. **Description:** A national real estate development and brokerage agency. Founded in 1948. **Positions advertised include:** Accountant; Accounting Associate; Administrative Assistant; Director of Technical Services; Maintenance Technician; Payroll Analyst; Real Estate Manager; Security Shift Leader; Security Officer. **Special programs:** Internships. **Listed on:** New York Stock Exchange. **Stock exchange symbol:** TCC.

WYNNE/JACKSON, INC.
600 North Pearl Street, Suite 650, Lock Box 149, Dallas TX 75201. 214/880-8600. **Contact:** Frank Murphy, Vice President. **World Wide Web address:** http://www.wynnejackson.com. **Description:** A commercial real estate development and property management company. **Corporate headquarters location:** This location.

RETAIL

You can expect to find the following types of companies in this chapter:
Catalog Retailers • Department Stores; Specialty Stores•
Retail Bakeries • Supermarkets

BABBAGE'S ETC. LLC
2250 William D. Tate Avenue, Grapevine TX 76051. 817/424-2000.
Fax: 817/424-2002. **Contact:** Personnel. **World Wide Web address:**
http://www.gamestop.com. **Description:** A national retailer of
interactive games and accessories. Babbage's Etc. operates more than
475 stores in the United States and Puerto Rico under the names
Babbage's, Software Etc., Gamestop, SuperSoftware, and Planet X.
Corporate headquarters location: This location.

W.O. BANKSTON LINCOLN MERCURY
4747 LBJ Freeway, Dallas TX 75244. 972/233-1441. **Contact:**
Human Resources. **World Wide Web address:** http://www.bankston
lincoln.com. **Description:** A car dealer offering both new and used
vehicles.

BLOCKBUSTER ENTERTAINMENT GROUP
1201 Elm Street, Suite 2100, Dallas TX 75270. 214/854-3259. **Fax:**
214/854-3241. **Contact:** Tom Grissom, Personnel Director. **E-mail
address:** career@blockbuster.com. **World Wide Web address:** http://
www.blockbuster.com. **Description:** Operates a chain of video
rental and music retail stores. There are approximately 7,100
Blockbuster locations worldwide. **NOTE:** Entry-level positions are
offered. **Office hours:** Monday - Friday, 8:30 a.m. - 5:30 p.m.
Corporate headquarters location: This location. **Other U.S.
locations:** Nationwide. **International locations:** Worldwide. **Parent
company:** Viacom. **Listed on:** New York Stock Exchange. **Stock
exchange symbol:** BBI. **Number of employees worldwide:** 89,000.

THE BOMBAY COMPANY, INC.
550 Bailey Avenue, Suite 700, Fort Worth TX 76107-2111. 817/870-
1847. **Fax:** 817/348-7090. **Recorded jobline:** 817/339-3799.
Contact: Human Resources. **World Wide Web address:** http://www.
bombayco.com. **Description:** A specialty retailer of ready-to-
assemble home furnishings, prints, and accessories. Products are sold
through over 400 Bombay Company and Alex & Ivy Stores. **Special
programs:** Internships. **Corporate headquarters location:** This
location. **Other U.S. locations:** Nationwide. **International locations:**

Canada. **Operations at this facility include:** Administration; Sales. **Listed on:** New York Stock Exchange. **Stock exchange symbol:** BBA. **Number of employees nationwide:** Over 4,000.

BRIDGESTONE/FIRESTONE, INC.
9901 East Valley Ranch Parkway, Suite 3020, Irving TX 75063. 972/869-2303. **Contact:** Steve Kratohvil, Human Resources Manager. **World Wide Web address:** http://www.bridgestone-firestone.com. **Description:** A zone office of the tire and automotive services company. **Positions advertised include:** Automotive Mechanic; Retail Sales Worker. **Corporate headquarters location:** Rolling Meadows IL. **Operations at this facility include:** Administration; Service.

COMPUSA INC.
14951 North Dallas Parkway, Dallas TX 75254. 972/982-4000. **Contact:** Human Resources. **World Wide Web address:** http://www.compusa.com. **Description:** CompUSA Inc. operates over 218 high-volume computer superstores in 54 metropolitan areas throughout the United States. Each computer superstore offers more than 5,000 computer products including hardware, software, accessories, and related products, at discount prices to retail, business, government, and institutional customers. The computer superstores also offer full-service technical departments and classroom facilities. **Positions advertised include:** Bilingual Partner Support Representative; Customer Service Representative; General Manager; Income Tax Manager; Senior Tax Accountant; Copy Writer; Rebate Billing Coordinator; Commercial Sales Representative. **Corporate headquarters location:** This location. **Other U.S. locations:** Nationwide. **Parent company:** Grupo Sanborns. **Operations at this facility include:** This location houses administrative offices. **Listed on:** Privately held.

DUNLAP COMPANY
200 Bailey Avenue, Suite 100, Fort Worth TX 76107. 817/336-4985. **Contact:** Human Resources. **World Wide Web address:** http://www.dunlaps.com. **Description:** Operates a chain of department stores with over 50 locations. The stores operate under the following names: Dunlaps, McClurkans, M.M. Cohn, Heironimus, Stripling & Cox, Porteus, and The White House. Founded in 1892. **Corporate headquarters location:** This location. **Other U.S. locations:** Nationwide. **Operations at this facility include:** Administration. **Listed on:** Privately held. **President:** Edward Martin.

EVANS PONTIAC-GMC-BUICK
11438 LBJ Freeway, Dallas TX 75238. 214/328-8411. **Contact:** Human Resources. **World Wide Web address:** http://www. evanspontiacgmc.com. **Description:** A new and used car dealer.

F.F.P./NU-WAY OIL COMPANY, INC.
2801 Glenda Avenue, Fort Worth TX 76117. 817/838-4700. **Contact:** Controller. **World Wide Web address:** http://www. ffpmarketing.com. **Description:** Operates a chain of convenience stores that also offer drive-up gasoline pumps.

FIRST CASH, INC.
690 East Lamar Boulevard, Suite 400, Arlington TX 76011. 817/460-3947. **Contact:** Human Resources. **World Wide Web address:** http:// www.firstcash.com. **Description:** Acquires, establishes, and operates pawn stores that lend money on collateral of pledged personal property and retail previously owned merchandise acquired in forfeited transactions. First Cash also operates more than 25 check-cashing stores. **Corporate headquarters location:** This location. **Other U.S. locations:** CA; DC; IL; MD; MO; OK; SC. **International locations:** Mexico.

FOOD BASKET
1926 North Bryant, San Angelo TX 76903. 915/658-5602. **Contact:** Human Resources. **Description:** A grocery store chain with locations throughout Texas. **Corporate headquarters location:** This location.

FOXWORTH-GALBRAITH
P.O. Box 799002, 1711 Waterview Park, Dallas TX 75379-9002. 972/437-6100. **Contact:** Human Resources. **World Wide Web address:** http://www.foxgal.com. **Description:** A building materials retailer. **Listed on:** Privately held.

FRIENDLY CHEVROLET COMPANY, INC.
P.O. Box 7066, Dallas TX 75209. 214/920-1900. **Contact:** Hiring Manager. **World Wide Web address:** http://www.friendlychevy.com. **Description:** A dealership of both new and used automobiles.

JCPENNEY COMPANY, INC.
6002 Slide Road, P.O. Box 68611, Lubbock TX 79414. 806/792-6841. **Contact:** Human Resources. **World Wide Web address:** http:// www.jcpenney.net. **Description:** One location of the department store chain that sells apparel, home furnishings, and leisure lines.

Corporate headquarters location: Dallas TX. **Other U.S. locations:** Nationwide. **Listed on:** New York Stock Exchange. **Stock exchange symbol:** JCP. **Number of employees worldwide:** 267,000.

JCPENNEY COMPANY, INC.
P.O. Box 10001, Dallas TX 75301. 972/431-1000. **Contact:** Human Resources. **World Wide Web address:** http://www.jcpenney.net. **Description:** JCPenney Company is a national retail merchandise sales and service corporation with department stores nationwide. JCPenney sells apparel, home furnishings, and leisure lines in catalogs and 1,111 stores. **Positions advertised include:** Product Development Manager; Catalog/Internet Copywriter; Creative Director; Merchandising Project Specialist; Staff Auditor; Technical Support Manager; Assistant Buyer. **Corporate headquarters location:** This location. **Other U.S. locations:** Nationwide. **Operations at this facility include:** This location houses administrative offices. **Listed on:** New York Stock Exchange. **Stock exchange symbol:** JCP. **Number of employees worldwide:** 267,000.

KROGER'S
3612 North Beltline Road, Irving TX 75062. 972/252-7413. **Contact:** Human Resources. **World Wide Web address:** http://www.Kroger.. com. **Description:** A supermarket. **Parent company:** The Kroger Company (Cincinnati OH) is a major supermarket and convenience store operator and food processor. The company operates over 1,250 supermarkets, 789 convenience stores, and 398 jewelry stores. The Kroger Company also has 37 food processing plants. which supply over 4,000 private label products to its supermarkets. **Listed on:** New York Stock Exchange. **Stock exchange symbol:** KR.

LORD & TAYLOR
15350 Dallas Parkway, Dallas TX 75248. 972/387-0588. **Contact:** Human Resources. **World Wide Web address:** http://www.lordand taylor.com. **Description:** A full-line department store carrying clothing, accessories, home furnishings, and a wide range of other items. Founded in 1826. **Positions advertised include:** Sales Associate. **Corporate headquarters location:** New York NY. **Parent company:** The May Company. **Listed on:** New York Stock Exchange. **Stock exchange symbol:** MAY.

LORD & TAYLOR
450 Northpark Center, Dallas TX 75225. 214/691-6600. **Contact:** Human Resources Manager. **World Wide Web address:** http://www.

lordandtaylor.com. **Description:** A full-line department store carrying clothing, accessories, home furnishings, and a wide range of other items. Founded in 1826. **NOTE:** Part-time jobs are offered. **Positions advertised include:** Sales Representative. **Office hours:** Monday - Friday, 10:00 a.m. - 9:00 p.m. **Corporate headquarters location:** New York NY. **Parent company:** The May Department Stores Company. **Listed on:** New York Stock Exchange. **Stock exchange symbol:** MAY.

BRUCE LOWRIE CHEVROLET
711 SW Loop 820, Fort Worth TX 76134. 817/293-5811. **Contact:** Human Resources. **World Wide Web address:** http://www.bruce lowrie.com. **Description:** A new and used car dealership.

MASSEY CADILLAC
11675 LBJ Freeway, Garland TX 75047. 214/348-2211. **Contact:** Human Resources. **World Wide Web address:** http://www.massey cadillacdallas.com. **Description:** A new and used auto dealership. Massey Cadillac also offers maintenance and repair services.

MICHAEL'S STORES, INC.
P.O. Box 619566, Dallas TX 75261-9566. 972/409-1300. **Physical address:** 8000 Bent Branch Drive, Irving TX 75063. **Contact:** Human Resources. **World Wide Web address:** http://www.michaels.com. **Description:** A nationwide specialty retailer of art, crafts, and decorative items and supplies, offering over 40,000 items, from picture framing materials to seasonal and holiday merchandise. Michael's Stores operates 628 stores in 48 states, Canada, and Puerto Rico. **Corporate headquarters location:** This location. **Listed on:** New York Stock Exchange. **Stock exchange symbol:** MIK.

MINYARD FOOD STORES, INC.
P.O. Box 518, Coppell TX 75019. 972/393-8700. **Fax:** 972/304-3828. **Contact:** Human Resources. **World Wide Web address:** http://www.minyards.com. **Description:** A retail grocery chain with over 85 stores. Stores include Minyard Food Stores, Sack 'n Save, and Carnival Food Stores. **Corporate headquarters location:** This location. **Listed on:** Privately held.

THE NEIMAN MARCUS GROUP, INC.
1618 Main Street, Dallas TX 75201. 214/573-5688. **Contact:** Crystal Kettle, Manager of MDP Placement. **World Wide Web address:** http://www.neimanmarcus.com. **Description:** Operates two specialty

retailing businesses: Neiman Marcus and Bergdorf Goodman. Combined, these two chains offer men's and women's apparel, fashion accessories, jewelry, fine china, and moderately priced crystal and silver. **Corporate headquarters location:** This location. **Subsidiaries include:** NM Direct is a direct marketing company, which advertises primarily through the use of such specialty catalogs as Neiman Marcus and Horchow.

NICHOLS FORD
2401 East Interstate 20 at Campus Drive, Fort Worth TX 76119. 817/535-3673. **Contact:** Personnel. **World Wide Web address:** http://www.nicholsford.com. **Description:** A new and used car dealership.

PARK PLACE MOTORCARS
4023 Oak Lawn Avenue, Dallas TX 75219. 214/526-8701. **Toll-free phone:** 800/336-7073. **Fax:** 214/443-8270. **Contact:** Human Resources. **World Wide Web address:** http://www.parkplacetexas. com. **Description:** A new and pre-owned car dealership for Mercedes-Benz, Porsche, Lexus, and Audi automobiles. **NOTE:** Entry-level positions are offered. **Corporate headquarters location:** This location. **Other area locations:** Houston TX; Plano TX.

PIER 1 IMPORTS
P.O. Box 961020, Fort Worth TX 76161-0020. 817/878-8000. **Contact:** Staffing Manager. **World Wide Web address:** http://www. pier1.com. **Description:** Pier 1 Imports is engaged in the specialty retailing of handcrafted decorative home furnishings and accessories imported from approximately 50 countries around the world. **Positions advertised include:** Retail Sales Associate. **Corporate headquarters location:** This location. **Other U.S. locations:** Nationwide. **Operations at this facility include:** This location houses administrative offices. **Listed on:** New York Stock Exchange. **Stock exchange symbol:** PIR. **Number of employees worldwide:** 14,000.

RADIOSHACK
300 West Third Street, Suite 200, Fort Worth TX 76102. 817/415-3700. **Fax:** 817/415-3243. **Contact:** Employment Opportunities. **World Wide Web address:** http://www.radioshack.com. **Description:** Sells a wide variety of consumer electronic parts and equipment through more than 7,000 stores nationwide. **Corporate headquarters location:** This location. **Operations at this facility**

include: Administration; Advertising; Customer Service. **Listed on:** New York Stock Exchange. **Stock exchange symbol:** RSH.

RENT-A-CENTER

5700 Tennyson Parkway, 3rd Floor, Plano TX 75024. 972/801-1100. **Toll-free phone:** 800/275-2696. **Fax:** 972/943-0119. **Contact:** Staffing. **World Wide Web address:** http://www.rentacenter.com. **Description:** Rents furniture, appliances, stereos, and other furnishings and equipment. **Special programs:** Internships. **Corporate headquarters location:** This location. **Other U.S. locations:** Nationwide. **Listed on:** NASDAQ. **Stock exchange symbol:** RCII. **Number of employees nationwide:** 12,700.

SAKS FIFTH AVENUE

13550 North Dallas Parkway, Dallas TX 75240. 972/458-7000. **Contact:** Human Resources Manager. **World Wide Web address:** http://www.saksincorporated.com. **Description:** Saks Fifth Avenue is a 62-store chain emphasizing soft-goods products, primarily apparel for men, women, and children. **Parent company:** Saks Incorporated is a department store holding company that operates approximately 360 stores in 36 states. The company's stores include Saks Fifth Avenue, Parisian, Proffit's, Younker's, Herberger's, Carson Pirie Scott, Boston Store, Bergner's, and Off 5th, the company's outlet store. Saks Incorporated also operates two retail catalogs and several retail Internet sites. **Listed on:** New York Stock Exchange. **Stock exchange symbol:** SKS.

SHOWCASE CHEVROLET

5327 LBJ Freeway, Dallas TX 75240. 972/233-3500. **Contact:** Victor Mullino, Office Manager. **World Wide Web address:** http://www. showcasechev.com. **Description:** A new and used car dealership. **NOTE:** Salespeople should apply in person and be prepared to fill out an application.

SOUTHLAND CORPORATION

P.O. Box 711, Dallas TX 75221. 214/828-7011. **Fax:** 214/841-6688. **Contact:** Human Resources. **World Wide Web address:** http://www.7eleven.com. **Description:** Owns and operates 7-Eleven convenience stores. **Corporate headquarters location:** This location. **Listed on:** New York Stock Exchange. **Stock exchange symbol:** SE. **Number of employees nationwide:** 33,000.

SPORTS SUPPLY GROUP, INC.

P.O. Box 7726, 1901 Diplomat Drive, Farmers Branch TX 75234. 972/484-9484. **Contact:** Personnel. **World Wide Web address:** http://www.sportsupplygroup.com. **Description:** A catalog retailer of sporting goods and recreational products. **Corporate headquarters location:** This location.

STRIPLING & COX

6370 Camp Bowie Boulevard, Fort Worth TX 76116. 817/738-7361. **Contact:** Human Resources. **Description:** A department store offering men's and women's apparel and home furnishings.

TOM THUMB FOOD & PHARMACY

14303 Inwood Road, Dallas TX 75244. 972/661-9700. **Contact:** Recruitment Office. **E-mail address:** employment@tomthumb.com. **World Wide Web address:** http://www.tomthumb.com. **Description:** A supermarket. **Positions advertised include:** Management Trainee. **Note:** Resumes can be sent to the recruitment office located at 3663 Briar Park, Houston TX 77042. The fax number is 713/435-2499. **Special programs:** Internships. **Corporate headquarters location:** Houston TX. **Parent company:** Safeway. **Operations at this facility include:** Sales; Service. **Listed on:** New York Stock Exchange. **Stock exchange symbol:** SWY.

TOYOTA OF DALLAS INC.

2610 Forest Lane, Dallas TX 75234. 972/241-6655. **Contact:** Gary Brummett, Controller. **World Wide Web address:** http://www.toyota ofdallas.com. **Description:** Specializes in the retail sale of new and used Toyota cars. **Positions advertised include:** Sales Consultant; Business Development Consultant. **Corporate headquarters location:** This location.

TUESDAY MORNING CORPORATION

14621 Inwood Road, Addison TX 75001. 972/387-3562. **Contact:** Human Resources. **World Wide Web address:** http://www.tuesday morning.com. **Description:** Operates a chain of over 400 discount retail stores under the name Tuesday Morning Inc. The stores sell close-out gift and houseware merchandise at prices ranging from 50 percent to 80 percent below retail prices. **Positions advertised include:** Regional Real Estate Representative; Alarm Monitoring Operator; Store Manager; Assistant Store Manager. **NOTE:** The stores are open to the public eight times a year only for four- to eight-week sales events. **Corporate headquarters location:** This location. **Listed on:** NASDAQ. **Stock exchange symbol:** TUES.

WAL-MART STORES, INC.
3159 South Garland Road, Garland TX 75041. 972/278-8077. **Contact:** Human Resources. **World Wide Web address:** http://www. walmart.com. **Description:** One of the largest retail merchandise chains in the country, operating full-service discount department stores, combination grocery and discount stores, and warehouse stores requiring membership. **Corporate headquarters location:** Bentonville AR. **Other U.S. locations:** Nationwide.

ZALE CORPORATION
901 West Walnut Hill Lane, Mail Station 5B-12, Irving TX 75038. 972/580-4000. **Fax:** 972/580-5266. **Contact:** Manager of Corporate Staffing. **World Wide Web address:** http://www.zalecorp.com. **Description:** A specialty retail firm engaged in selling fine jewelry and related products. **NOTE:** Entry-level positions are offered. **Positions advertised include:** Senior Audit Accountant; Security Officer; Senior Planner; Senior Administrative Assistant; Detail Assistant; Senior Accountant; Distribution Center Clerk; Staff Accountant; Telecommunication Manager; Corporate Accounting/Finance Manager. **Corporate headquarters location:** This location. **Other U.S. locations:** Nationwide. **Listed on:** New York Stock Exchange. **Stock exchange symbol:** ZLC. **Number of employees worldwide:** 20,000.

STONE, CLAY, GLASS, AND CONCRETE PRODUCTS

You can expect to find the following types of companies in this chapter:
Cement, Tile, Sand, and Gravel • Crushed and Broken Stone •
Glass and Glass Products • Mineral Products

AMERICAN FLAT GLASS DISTRIBUTORS, INC. (AFGD)

1201 Highway 67 East, Alvarado TX 76009. 817/477-1144. **Toll-free phone:** 800/777-5171. **Fax:** 817/783-7123. **Contact:** Mr. Carl Frey, Branch Manager. **World Wide Web address:** http://www.afgd.com. **Description:** Specializes in architectural insulated glass units and custom tempering. AFGD manufactures a complete line of insulated glass units for commercial and residential applications. The product line includes clear, tint, and reflective glass; wire glass; and equipment for the handling, storage, and transportation of glass. There are 50 AFGD locations throughout North America. **Positions advertised include:** Inside Sales Representative. **Corporate headquarters location:** Atlanta GA. **Subsidiaries include:** AFGD Canada. **Parent company:** AFG Industries, Inc. **Operations at this facility include:** Manufacturing; Sales. **Listed on:** Privately held.

DAL-TILE INTERNATIONAL

P.O. Box 170130, Dallas TX 75217. 214/398-1411. **Contact:** Director of Human Resources. **World Wide Web address:** http://www.daltile.com. **Description:** Manufactures wall and floor tile. **Positions advertised include:** Staff Accountant. **Corporate headquarters location:** This location. **Parent company:** Mohawk Industries. **Operations at this facility include:** Administration; Manufacturing; Research and Development. **Listed on:** New York Stock Exchange. **Stock exchange symbol:** MHK.

ELK CORPORATION

202 Cedar Road, Ennis TX 75119. 972/875-9611. **Fax:** 972/872-2392. **Contact:** Human Resources. **World Wide Web address:** http://www.elkcorp.com. **Description:** Manufactures residential roofing products and fiberglass mats. Founded in 1955. **Corporate headquarters location:** Dallas TX. **Other U.S. locations:** Tuscaloosa AL; Shafter CA. **Parent company:** Elcor Corporation. **Operations at this facility include:** Administration; Manufacturing; Sales. **Listed on:** New York Stock Exchange. **Stock exchange symbol:** ELK.

GUARDIAN INDUSTRIES CORPORATION
3801 South Highway 287, Corsicana TX 75109. 903/872-4871. **Fax:** 903/874-8647. **Contact:** Employee Relations Manager. **World Wide Web address:** http://www.guardian.com. **Description:** Manufactures fabricated and float glass primarily for the construction and automotive industries. **Corporate headquarters location:** Auburn Hills MI. **Other U.S. locations:** Nationwide. **International locations:** Worldwide.

HANSON PIPE & PRODUCTS, INC.
P.O. Box 569470, Dallas TX 75356-9470. 972/262-1571. **Contact:** Personnel Manager. **World Wide Web address:** http://www.hanson concreteproducts.com. **Description:** Produces concrete pressure pipe and pipe fittings.

JOBE CONCRETE PRODUCTS INC.
One McKelligon Canyon Road, El Paso TX 79930. 915/565-4681. **Contact:** Joanne Qweedle, Personnel Administrative Assistant. **World Wide Web address:** http://www.jobeconcrete.com. **Description:** Manufactures concrete and related products. Jobe Concrete Products also provides landscaping services.

LONE STAR INDUSTRIES
1801 Lone Star Drive, Dallas TX 75212. 972/386-0400. **Contact:** Human Resources. **World Wide Web address:** http://www.lonsestar ind.com. **Description:** Manufactures and distributes cement, ready-mix concrete, and construction products.

MUR-TEX FIBERGLASS
P.O. Box 31240, Amarillo TX 79120. 806/373-7418. **Contact:** Human Resources. **World Wide Web address:** http://www.murtex. thomasregister.com. **Description:** Manufactures fiberglass tanks for industrial usage. **Corporate headquarters location:** This location.

OLDCASTLE GLASS GROUP
2805 Dallas Parkway, Suite 450, Plano TX 75093. 972/747-3800. **Fax:** 972/747-3838. **Contact:** Personnel. **World Wide Web address:** http://www.oldcastleglass.com. **Description:** A leading manufacturer of glass products. The company's product line includes laminated glass, insulating glass units, heat-treated glass, silk-screened and decorative glass, and structural glass wall systems. **Corporate headquarters location:** This location. **Parent company:** CRH plc.

OWENS-CORNING FIBERGLAS CORPORATION

P.O. Box 8000, Amarillo TX 79114-8000. 806/622-1582. **Physical address:** 1701 Hollywood Road, Amarillo TX 79114. **Contact:** Human Resources. **World Wide Web address:** http://www.owens corning.com. **Description:** Manufactures and sells thermal and acoustical insulation products including insulation for appliances, roofing shingles, roof insulation, and industrial asphalt. Other products include windows, glass fiber textile yarns, wet process chopped strands and specialty mats, and polyester resins. **Subsidiaries include:** Barbcorp, Inc.; Dansk-Svensk Glasfiber AS; Eric Co.; European Owens-Corning Fiberglas SA; IPM Inc.; Kitsons Insulations Products Ltd.; Owens-Corning AS; Owens-Corning Building Products; Owens-Corning FSC, Inc.; Owens-Corning Finance. **Listed on:** New York Stock Exchange. **Stock exchange symbol:** OWC.

TXI, INC.

1341 West Mockingbird Lane, Dallas TX 75247-6913. 972/647-6700. **Contact:** Human Resources. **E-mail address:** recruiter@txi.com. **World Wide Web address:** http://www.txi.com. **Description:** A leading supplier of cement and structural steel primarily to the construction industry. **Special programs:** Internships. **Corporate headquarters location:** This location. **Other U.S. locations:** LA. **Subsidiaries include:** Riverside Cement Company. **Listed on:** New York Stock Exchange. **Stock exchange symbol:** TXI.

TRANSPORTATION/TRAVEL

You can expect to find the following types of companies in this chapter:
Air, Railroad, and Water Transportation Services • Courier Services • Local and Interurban Passenger Transit • Ship Building and Repair • Transportation Equipment Travel Agencies • Trucking • Warehousing and Storage

ABILENE AERO INC.
2850 Airport Boulevard, Abilene TX 79602. 915/677-2601. **Fax:** 915/671-8018. **Contact:** Mr. Joe Crawford, General Manager. **World Wide Web address:** http://www.abileneaero.com. **Description:** Operates a small airport offering flight instruction, charter and pilot service, aircraft fueling, parts, and maintenance. Founded in 1968. **Corporate headquarters location:** This location. **Parent company:** Peerless Manufacturing (Dallas TX).

ALFORD REFRIGERATED WAREHOUSES
318 Cadiz Street, Dallas TX 75207. 214/426-5151. **Fax:** 214/426-0245. **Contact:** Human Resources. **Description:** A warehousing company engaged in the storage of frozen, cold, and dry food bought in grocery stores. **Number of employees at this location:** 182.

BALDWIN DISTRIBUTION SERVICES
7702 Broadway, Amarillo TX 79108. 806/383-7650. **Contact:** Human Resources. **World Wide Web address:** http://www.baldwin-dist.com. **Description:** Provides long-haul trucking services. Baldwin Distribution Services operates in 48 states, Canada, and Mexico. **Positions advertised include:** Truck Driver.

BOWDEN TRAVEL SERVICE
CLEBURNE TRAVEL
1643 West Henderson Suite A, Cleburne TX 76033. 817/641-3477. **Contact:** Human Resources. **World Wide Web address:** http://www.bowdentravel.com. **Description:** A travel agency. **Company slogan:** Let us take the ravel out of your travel. **Annual sales/revenues:** Less than $5 million.

BUDGET RENT A CAR CORPORATION
P.O. Box 111520, Carrollton TX 75011. 972/404-7600. **Physical address:** 3350 Boyington Drive, Carrollton TX 75006. **Contact:**

Human Resources. **World Wide Web address:** http://www.budget rentacar.com. **Description:** A car and truck rental service.

BURLINGTON NORTHERN AND SANTA FE RAILWAY COMPANY
2650 Lou Menk Drive, Fort Worth TX 76131. 817/333-2000. **Contact:** Human Resources. **World Wide Web address:** http://www. bnsf.com. **Description:** A railroad transportation company operating on 24,500 miles of track in 25 western states and 2 Canadian provinces. The company is one of the largest haulers of low-sulfur coal and grain in North America. **Positions advertised include:** Assistant Marketing Manager; Conductor Trainee; General Construction Supervisor; Management Trainee; Manager of Locomotive Utilization. **Corporate headquarters location:** This location. **Listed on:** New York Stock Exchange. **Stock exchange symbol:** BNI.

CENTRAL FREIGHT LINES, INC.
P.O. Box 540277, Dallas TX 75354-0277. 972/579-4111. **Contact:** Human Resources. **World Wide Web address:** http://www.central freight.com. **Description:** One of the largest regional motor carriers in the United States operating through 77 terminals. **Corporate headquarters location:** Waco TX. **Other U.S. locations:** Nationwide.

CITY MACHINE & WELDING, INC.
P.O. Box 51018, Amarillo TX 79159-1018. 806/358-7293. **Contact:** Human Resources. **World Wide Web address:** http://www.cm welding.com. **Description:** Manufactures transport trailers and performs welding services.

COMDATA CORPORATION
6000 Western Place, Suite 900, Fort Worth TX 76107. 817/731-8721. **Contact:** Human Resources. **E-mail address:** resumes@ comdata.com. **World Wide Web address:** http://www.comdata.com. **Description:** Provides transaction processing and information services to the transportation, gaming, and retail industries. Comdata links more than 20,000 telecommunication ports of entry, processing over 100 million transactions per year. Services for the transportation industry increase productivity and control for trucking companies and truck stops. Products encompass fuel purchase, cash advance, driver settlement, money transfer, load matching, route planning, legalization permitting, fuel tax reporting, and management reporting. Comdata's consumer services include money transfer for emergencies or leisure activities. The company helps gaming

organizations adapt to new technologies such as smart cards, linked progressive slot machines, and player tracking systems. Retail services include a check acceptance network to shorten customer checkout time and reduce losses from returned checks. **NOTE:** Send resumes to: Attention Human Resources, Comdata Corporation, 5301 Maryland Way, Brentwood TN 37027. **Parent company:** Ceridian Corporation.

DALLAS AREA RAPID TRANSIT (DART)
P.O. Box 660163, Dallas TX 75266-7240. 214/749-3259. **Fax:** 214/749-3636. **Recorded jobline:** 214/749-3690. **Contact:** Human Resources. **World Wide Web address:** http://www.dart.org. **Description:** A nonprofit, rapid transit system serving the Dallas metropolitan area. **Positions advertised include:** Senior Control Systems Programmer; Telecommunications Analyst; High Occupancy Vehicle Operator; Rail Operator; Maintenance Specialist; DART Police Officer; Passenger Amenities Mechanic. **Special programs:** Internships.

DALLAS-FORT WORTH INTERNATIONAL AIRPORT
P.O. Drawer 619428, DFW Airport TX 75261-9428. 972/574-6032. **Recorded jobline:** 972/574-8024. **Contact:** Human Resources. **World Wide Web address:** http://www.dfwairport.com. **Description:** An international airport with flights worldwide on 25 commercial airlines and several charter airlines.

DYNAMEX INC.
1870 Crown Drive, Dallas TX 75234. 214/561-7500. **Contact:** Human Resources. **World Wide Web address:** http://www. dynamex.com. **Description:** Offers customized warehousing and local outsourcing delivery services for companies with no trucks or delivery vehicles. Founded in 1985. **Listed on:** American Stock Exchange. **Stock exchange symbol:** DDN.

FFE TRANSPORTATION SERVICES, INC.
P.O. Box 655888, Dallas TX 75265-5888. 214/630-8090. **Contact:** Human Resources. **World Wide Web address:** http://www.ffeinc. com. **Description:** Provides trucking and transportation services nationwide.

FM INDUSTRIES, INC.
8600 Will Rogers Boulevard, Fort Worth TX 76140. 817/293-4220. **Contact:** Personnel Manager. **Description:** Produces hydraulic cushioning systems for railroad freight cars.

GREYHOUND LINES INC.
P.O. Box 660606, Dallas TX 75266-0606. 972/789-7000. **Contact:** Manager of Human Resources. **World Wide Web address:** http://www.greyhound.com. **Description:** One of the country's largest private transportation networks. Greyhound conducts regular route, package express, charter, and food service operations. The fleet consists of over 1,650 buses that travel to more than 2,600 destinations.

J.B. HUNT TRANSPORT SERVICES, INC.
5701 West Kiest Boulevard, Dallas TX 75236. 214/333-9768. **Contact:** Human Resources. **World Wide Web address:** http://www. jbhunt.com. **Description:** A major freight transportation company. **Corporate headquarters location:** Lowell AR. **Listed on:** NASDAQ. **Stock exchange symbol:** JBHT.

KITTY HAWK, INC.
1535 West 20th Street, P.O. Box 612787, DFW Airport TX 75261. 972/456-2498. **Contact:** Human Resources. **World Wide Web address:** http://www.kha.com. **Description:** Provides charter management and cargo services.

MARTINAIRE INC.
4745 Frank Luke Drive, Addison TX 75001. 972/349-5700. **Contact:** Human Resources. **World Wide Web address:** http://www.martin aire.com. **Description:** An air cargo carrier operating a fleet of 25 aircraft. **Positions advertised include:** Airframe & Powerplant Technician; Pilot.

MAYFLOWER TRANSIT, LLC
1735 West Crosby Road, Carrolton TX 75006. 972/466-1111. **Fax:** 972/233-3921. **Contact:** Human Resources. **World Wide Web address:** http://www.mayflower.com. **Description:** Offers a full range of moving and storage services to both commercial and individual customers. **Parent company:** Unigroup Inc.

SKY HELICOPTERS

2559 South Jupiter Road, Garland TX 75041-6011. 214/349-7000. **Contact:** Human Resources. **World Wide Web address:** http:// www.skyhelicopters.com. **Description:** Engaged in helicopter transportation for both public and private use.

SOUTHWEST AIRLINES COMPANY

P.O. Box 36644, Dallas TX 75235-1644. 214/792-4213. **Fax:** 214/ 792-7015. **Contact:** SWA People Department. **World Wide Web address:** http://www.southwest.com. **Description:** One of the only major short-haul, low-fare, high-frequency, point-to-point carriers in the United States. Southwest Airlines, a *Fortune* 500 company, flies to 58 cities in 30 states and offers over 2,500 flights daily. **Special programs:** Internships. **Corporate headquarters location:** This location. **Other U.S. locations:** Nationwide. **Listed on:** New York Stock Exchange. **Stock exchange symbol:** LUV. **Number of employees worldwide:** 34,000.

TURBO JET SPARES, INC.

2722 Burbank Street, Dallas TX 75235. 214/358-1777. **Contact:** Human Resources. **World Wide Web address:** http://www. turbojet.com. **Description:** Offers aircraft maintenance services.

UNITED PARCEL SERVICE (UPS)

P.O. Box 2047, Grapevine TX 76099-2047. 972/456-4928. **Recorded jobline:** 888/877-0924. **Contact:** Personnel. **World Wide Web address:** http://www.ups.com. **Description:** United Parcel Service is a parcel pickup and delivery service organization that provides service to all 50 states and to more than 185 countries and territories worldwide. The company delivers approximately 12 million packages daily. **NOTE:** The jobline lists mainly part-time position. **Positions advertised include:** Driver; Package Handler. **Operations at this facility include:** This location houses regional administrative offices.

VIRTUOSO

500 Main Street, Suite 400, Fort Worth TX 76102. 817/870-0300. **Fax:** 817/870-4645. **Contact:** Human Resources. **World Wide Web address:** http://www.virtuoso.com. **Description:** A travel consortium specializing in leisure travel.

UTILITIES: ELECTRIC/GAS/WATER

You can expect to find the following types of companies in this chapter:
Gas, Electric, and Fuel Companies; Other Energy-Producing Companies •
Public Utility Holding Companies • Water Utilities

AMERICAN ELECTRIC POWER (AEP)
P.O. Box 660164, Dallas TX 75266-0164. 214/777-1000. **Contact:** Human Resources. **World Wide Web address:** http://www.aep.com. **Description:** An electric utility company serving approximately 4.8 million customers in the United States and over 4 million customers outside the United States. **NOTE:** Send resumes to: American Electric Power, 1 Riverside Plaza, Columbus OH 43215. **Corporate headquarters location:** Columbus OH. **Other U.S. locations:** Nationwide. **Listed on:** New York Stock Exchange. **Stock exchange symbol:** AEP.

EL PASO ELECTRIC COMPANY
123 West Mills Avenue, El Paso TX 79901-1341. 915/543-5711. **Contact:** Human Resources. **World Wide Web address:** http://www.epelectric.com. **Description:** El Paso Electric generates and distributes electricity through an interconnected system to approximately 309,000 customers in El Paso and an area of the Rio Grande Valley in west Texas and southern New Mexico. The company's service area extends about 110 miles northwest from El Paso to the Caballo Dam in New Mexico and about 120 miles southeast from El Paso to Van Horn TX. Founded in 1901. **Listed on:** American Stock Exchange. **Stock exchange symbol:** EE.

EL PASO NATURAL GAS COMPANY
100 North Stanton, El Paso TX 79901. 915/496-2600. **Contact:** Human Resources. **World Wide Web address:** http://www.epenergy.com. **Description:** Owns and operates one of the nation's largest field and mainline natural gas transmission systems. The company has over 17,000 miles of pipeline connecting natural gas supply regions in New Mexico, Texas, Oklahoma, and Colorado to markets in California, Nevada, Arizona, New Mexico, Texas, and Mexico. **Positions advertised include:** Machinist. **Corporate headquarters location:** This location. **Listed on:** New York Stock Exchange. **Stock exchange symbol:** EP.

EL PASO WATER UTILITIES

P.O. Box 511, El Paso TX 79961. 915/594-5519. **Physical address:** 1154 Hawkins Boulevard, El Paso TX 79925. **Fax:** 915/594-5679. **Contact:** Fred Loweree, Human Resources Manager. **World Wide Web address:** http://www.epwu.org. **Description:** A nonprofit provider of water and wastewater services for the city of El Paso and the surrounding region. **NOTE:** Entry-level positions and second and third shifts are offered. **Special programs:** Co-ops.

TEXAS-NEW MEXICO POWER COMPANY

P.O. Box 2943, Fort Worth TX 76133. 817/731-0099. **Contact:** Human Resources Manager. **World Wide Web address:** http://www. tnpe.com. **Description:** A public utility engaged in the purchase, transmission, distribution, and sale of electrical power in Texas and New Mexico. **Corporate headquarters location:** This location. **Parent company:** TNP Enterprises Inc.

TEXAS UTILITIES COMPANIES

1601 Bryan Street, Dallas TX 75201-3411. 214/812-4600. **Fax:** 214/ 812-8419. **Recorded jobline:** 214/812-8633. **Contact:** Staffing and Placement Manager. **World Wide Web address:** http://www.txu. com. **Description:** A large, investor-owned, electric utility providing electric service to 2 million customers in north, central, and west Texas. **Positions advertised include:** Meter Reader Trainee; Protective Services Officer. **Special programs:** Internships. **Corporate headquarters location:** This location. **Subsidiaries include:** BRI; Chaco; TU Electric; TU Fuel Company; TU Mini; TU Services. **Parent company:** TXU Corporation. **Listed on:** New York Stock Exchange. **Stock exchange symbol:** TXU. **Number of employees nationwide:** 18,000.

XCEL ENERGY

P.O. Box 1261, Amarillo TX 79170-0001. 806/378-2121. **Contact:** Doris Brasille, Employee Services Manager. **World Wide Web address:** http://www.xcelenergy.com. **Description:** Provides electric service to the Amarillo area. **Corporate headquarters location:** Minneapolis MN. **Listed on:** New York Stock Exchange. **Stock exchange symbol:** XEL.

MISCELLANEOUS WHOLESALING

You can expect to find the following types of companies in this chapter:
Exporters and Importers • General Wholesale Distribution Companies

ABATIX CORPORATION
8201 Eastpoint Drive, Suite 500, Dallas TX 75227. 214/381-1146.
Fax: 214/381-9513. **Contact:** Human Resources. **E-mail address:**
hr@abatix.com. **World Wide Web address:** http://www.abatix.com.
Description: A supplier of industrial safety supplies, construction
tools, general safety products such as protective clothing and
eyewear, and clean-up equipment. Abatix Corporation has eight
distribution centers serving customers throughout the Southwest,
Midwest, and the Pacific Coast. **Corporate headquarters location:**
This location. **Other U.S. locations:** AZ; CA; CO; NV; WA. **Listed
on:** NASDAQ. **Stock exchange symbol:** ABIX.

ABATIX CORPORATION
1430 North Post Oak Road, Houston TX 77055. 713/956-2062. **Fax:**
214/381-9513. **Contact:** Human Resources. **E-mail address:** hr@
abatix.com. **World Wide Web address:** http://www.abatix.com.
Description: Provides the asbestos and lead abatement, hazardous
material remediation, and construction industries with a full-line of
durable and nondurable supplies. Products include industrial safety
supplies, construction tools, general safety products such as
protective clothing and eyewear, and clean-up equipment. Abatix
Environmental Corporation has eight distribution centers serving
customers throughout the Southwest, Midwest, and the Pacific Coast.
Corporate headquarters location: Dallas TX. **Other U.S. locations:**
AZ; CA; CO; NV; WA. **Listed on:** NASDAQ. **Stock exchange
symbol:** ABIX.

CELEBRITY, INC.
P.O. Box 6666, Tyler TX 75710. 903/561-3981. **Contact:** Human
Resources. **World Wide Web address:** http://www.celebrity-inc.com.
Description: A supplier of artificial flowers, foliage, flowering
bushes, and other decorative accessories to craft stores and other
specialty retailers and to wholesale florists throughout North America
and Europe. Celebrity imports over 7,000 home accent, decorative
accessory, and giftware items including artificial floral arrangements;
floor planters and trees; a wide range of decorative brass and textile
products; and a broad line of seasonal items such as Christmas trees,
wreaths, garlands and other ornamental products.

CLEMONS TRACTOR COMPANY
5000 Airport Freeway, Fort Worth TX 76117. 817/834-8131. **Contact:** General Manager. **Description:** A wholesale dealer of tractors, lawn mowers, and related equipment.

HALLIBURTON COMPANY
3600 Lincoln Plaza, Dallas TX 75201. 214/978-2600. **Fax:** 214/978-2611. **Contact:** Human Resources. **World Wide Web address:** http://www.halliburton.com. **Description:** A leading diversified energy services, engineering, construction, maintenance, and energy equipment company. **Positions advertised include:** Mechanical Engineer; Chemical Engineer. **Corporate headquarters location:** This location. **Other U.S. locations:** Nationwide. **Listed on:** New York Stock Exchange. **Stock exchange symbol:** HAL.

THE C.D. HARTNETT COMPANY
P.O. Box 1989, Weatherford TX 76086. 817/594-3813. **Contact:** Human Resources. **E-mail address:** resume@cd-hartnett.com. **World Wide Web address:** http://www.cd-hartnett.com. **Description:** Distributes groceries to convenience stores and food service companies. Products include produce, dairy items, frozen food, and candy. Founded in 1904.

HI-LINE
2121 Valley View Lane, Dallas TX 75234. 972/247-6200. **Contact:** Cindy Grieser, Human Resources Manager. **E-mail address:** employment@hi-line.com. **World Wide Web address:** http://www. hi-line.com. **Description:** A distributor of fasteners including nuts, bolts, screws, and rivets; terminals including solder splice connectors, mechanical lugs, and ferrules; cable lugs; battery terminals; insulating materials including shrink tubing, grommets, and specialty tape; wiring accessories; drill bits; and various other industrial products. Founded in 1959. **Positions advertised include:** Territory Sales Manager. **Corporate headquarters location:** This location. **Operations at this facility include:** Administration; Sales. **Number of employees at this location:** 160.

PASSAGE SUPPLY COMPANY
P.O. Box 971395, El Paso TX 79997-1395. 915/778-9377. **Fax:** 915/772-9602. **Contact:** Ron Passage, General Manager. **Description:** A heating and cooling systems distributor. **Corporate headquarters location:** This location.

INDEX OF PRIMARY EMPLOYERS

ACCOUNTING & MANAGEMENT CONSULTING

Cheshier and Fuller, L.L.P./52
Deloitte & Touche/52
Eckert, Ingrum, Tinkler, Oliphant, &
  Featherston, L.L.P./53
Ernst & Young LLP/53
Grant Thornton LLP/53
H&R Block/54
Mercer Management Consulting/54
PricewaterhouseCoopers/54

ADVERTISING, MARKETING, AND PUBLIC RELATIONS

Ackerman McQueen, Inc./55
Aegis Communications Group/55
Burk Advertising & Marketing,
  Inc./55
DDB Needham/55
Decision Analyst, Inc./56
The Dozier Company/56
Bernard Hodes Advertising/56
The M/A/R/C Group/56
Publicis USA/56
The Richards Group/56
J. Walter Thompson/57
Witherspoon Advertising & Public
  Relations/57

AEROSPACE

Associated Aircraft Supply Co.,
  Inc./58
Bell Helicopter Textron/58
Boeing-Irving/58
Foxtronics Inc./58
Gulfstream Aerospace
  Corporation/58
Heli-Dyne Systems, Inc./59
International Aviation Composites
  (IAC)/59
Lockheed Martin Tactical Aircraft
  Systems/59
Lockheed Martin Vought
  Systems/60
Luminator/60
Marathon Power Technologies
  Company/60

Pratt & Whitney/60
Precision Aviation/61
Skyline Industries, Inc./61
Unishippers Association/61

APPAREL, FASHION, AND TEXTILES

Border Apparel Inc./62
L.D. Brinkman/Hollytex/62
Brownwood Manufacturing
  Company/62
Haggar Clothing Company/62
HATCO/62
Justin Boot Company/63
Tony Lama Company/63
Lucchese Boot Company/63
Pillowtex Corporation/63
Pindler & Pindler Inc./63
Savane International
  Corporation/63
Stitches Inc./64
Tandy Brands Accessories/64
Walls Industries, Inc./64
Williamson-Dickie Manufacturing
  Company/64
Howard B. Wolf Inc./64

ARCHITECTURE/ CONSTRUCTION/ ENGINEERING (MISC.)

APAC Texas, Inc./65
Austin Commercial Inc./65
Buell Door Company/65
Cavalier Homes, Inc./65
Centex Construction Company,
  Inc./66
Elcor Corporation/66
FM Global/66
GAF Materials Corporation/66
General Aluminum Corporation/67
HDR, Inc./67
HNTB Corporation/67
D.R. Horton, Inc./67
Howe-Baker Engineers, Inc./68
Lauren Engineers & Constructors/68
Lennox International, Inc./68
Morgan/68
Morrison Supply Company/69
O'Hair Shutters/69
Overhead Door Corporation/69
Quality Cabinets/69
TD Industries, Inc./69

Huntsman Polymers
    Corporation/89
Industrial Molding Corporation/89
Jamak Fabrication, Inc./90
Jones Blair Company/90
Kelly-Springfield Tire Company/90
Lubrication Engineers Inc./90
Mohawk Laboratories/90
Occidental Chemical
    Corporation/91
Poly-America Inc./91
PolyOne Corporation/91
Regal International Inc./91
Ribelin Sales Inc./92
The Sherwin-Williams Company/92
StyroChem International/92
Texas Eastman/92
Texas Refinery Corporation/93
Toro Irrigation/93

COMMUNICATIONS: TELECOMMUNICATIONS/ BROADCASTING

Alcatel USA Inc./94
Andrew Corporation/94
A.H. Belo Corporation/The Dallas
    Morning News/94
Continental Electronics
    Corporation/95
Corning Cable Systems/95
Decibel Products Inc./95
Ericsson Inc./95
Fujitsu Network Communications
    (FNC)/96
General Cable Company/96
KFDA-TV/News Channel 10/97
KLBK-TV/97
KRLD/Texas State Networks/97
KVII-TV/97
KVIL-AM/FM 103.7/97
KXXV-TV/97
Lucent Technologies Inc./97
Marconi Communications/98
Motorola, Inc./98
NEC America Inc./98
Nokia Mobile Phones Inc./98
RF Monolithics, Inc./99
Susquehanna Radio Corp./99
Tellabs Texas Inc./99
Verizon Communications/99, 100
WorldCom/100
Xerox Corporation/101

COMPUTERS (MISC.)

Analysts International Corporation
    (AiC)/102
Avnet, Inc./102
BancTec, Inc./102
Calyx Software/103
Compaq Computer
    Corporation/103
CompuCom Systems, Inc./103
Computer Associates International,
    Inc./103
Computer Horizons
    Corporation/104
Computer Sciences Corporation
    (CSC)/104, 105
Corel, Inc./105
DNS-Solutions/105
EDS (Electronic Data Systems
    Corporation)/106
ExecuTrain of Texas/106
Farsight Computer/106
Fujitsu Consulting/106
Hewlett-Packard Company/106
IBM Corporation/107
I.T. Partners, Inc./107
I2 Technologies/107
Interphase Corporation/108
InterVoice-Brite, Inc./108
Itac Systems, Inc./108
Kaneb Services, Inc./108
Linx Data Terminals, Inc./109
Merlin Software Services, Inc./109
Mesquite Software, Inc./109
Micro Computer Systems, Inc./109
NCR Corporation/110
Network Associates, Inc./110
OpenConnect Systems, Inc./110
Per-Se Technologies, Inc./111
RVSI Acuity CiMatrix/111
Raytheon Systems Company/111
Siemens Business Services, Inc./112
Software Spectrum Inc./112
SourceSuite LLC/112
StorNet/112
S2 Systems, Inc./113
Tandy Wire and Cable
    Company/113
ThinkSpark/113
United States Data Corporation
    (USDATA)/113

EDUCATIONAL SERVICES

Abilene Christian University/115
Amarillo College/115

ELECTRONIC/INDUSTRIAL ELECTRICAL EQUIPMENT AND COMPONENTS

ENVIRONMENTAL & WASTE MANAGEMENT SERVICES

FABRICATED METAL PRODUCTS AND PRIMARY METALS

FINANCIAL SERVICES (MISC.)

FOOD AND BEVERAGES/ AGRICULTURE

GOVERNMENT

HEALTH CARE: SERVICES, EQUIPMENT, AND PRODUCTS (MISC.)

HOTELS AND RESTAURANTS

INSURANCE

Chubb Group of Insurance
  Companies/181
Crum & Forster Insurance/182
GeneralCologne Re/182
INSpire Insurance Solutions/182
Lawyers Title Insurance
  Corporation/182
National Foundation Life Insurance
  Company/182
State Farm Insurance/
Travelers Property Casualty
  Company/183
United Insurance Companies
  Inc./183
Wausau Insurance Companies/183

LEGAL SERVICES

Ackels & Ackels LLP/184
John Atwood Law Office/184
Baker Botts LLP/184
Baron & Budd, P.C./184
Cantey & Hanger, LLP/184
Davis & Munck/184
Fred Misko, Jr., P.C./185
Thompson & Knight LLP/185
Webb, Stokes & Sparks, L.L.P./185
Winstead Sechrest & Minick
  P.C./185
Offices of Norman A. Zable,
  P.C./185

MANUFACTURING: MISCELLANEOUS CONSUMER

APW Wyott Food Service
  Equipment/186
Atlas Match Corporation/186
Dart Container Corporation/186
Design Source/186
Fossil, Inc./186
Hasbro, Inc./187
Helen of Troy Ltd./187
Jostens, Inc./187
Jumpking Inc./188
Kohler Company/18
Lasting Products/188
Mary Kay, Inc./188
Nash Manufacturing, Inc./189
National Banner Company/189
Pro-Line Corporation/189
Rubbermaid, Inc./189
Samsill Corporation/189

Skeeter Products Inc./190
Sweetheart Cup Company, Inc./190
Temtex Industries Inc./190
Texas Recreation Corporation/190

MANUFACTURING: MISCELLANEOUS INDUSTRIAL

Abco Industries Inc./191
Booth, Inc./191
The Brinkmann Corporation/191
Conveyors, Inc./191
Ferguson Manufacturing and
  Equipment/191
Flowserve Corporation/192
Forney Corporation/192
Hart & Cooley/192
Hobart Corporation/192
Ingersoll-Rand Company/192
John Deere Company/193
Johnson Controls, Inc./193
Madix Inc./193
Martin Sprocket & Gear Inc./193
Mykrolis Corporation/194
NCH Corporation/194
National Oilwell/194
Noble Construction Equipment,
  Inc./195
Parker Hannifin
  Corporation/Stratoflex
  Aerospace/Military Connectors
  Division/195
Perry Equipment Corporation/195
Steelcase Inc./195
3M/196
The Trane Company/196
Traulsen & Company, Inc./197
Tyler Pipe Industries, Inc./197
Vecta/197
Virginia KMP Corporation/197

MINING/GAS/PETROLEUM/ ENERGY RELATED

Aeriform Corporation/198
Amerada Hess Corporation/198
Atmos Energy Corporation/198
BP Amoco PLC/198
Computalog/Wireline Products,
  Inc./199
ENSCO International Inc./199
ExxonMobil Corporation/199
Gas Equipment Company/199

PAPER AND WOOD PRODUCTS

PRINTING AND PUBLISHING

REAL ESTATE

RETAIL

STONE, CLAY, GLASS, AND CONCRETE PRODUCTS

TRANSPORTATION/TRAVEL

UTILITIES: ELECTRIC/GAS/WATER

MISC. WHOLESALING

Your Job Hunt
Your Feedback

Comments, questions, or suggestions? We want to hear from you!
Please complete this questionnaire and mail it to:

The JobBank Staff
Adams Media Corporation
57 Littlefield Street
Avon, MA 02322

or send us an e-mail at **jobbank@adamsmedia.com**

Did this book provide helpful advice and valuable information which you used in your job search? What did you like about it?

How could we improve this book to help you in your job search? Is there a specific company we left out or an industry you'd like to see more of in a future edition? No suggestion is too small or too large.

Would you recommend this book to a friend beginning a job hunt?

Name: _____

Occupation: _____

Which JobBank did you use? _____

Mailing address: _____

E-mail address: _____

Daytime phone: _____

 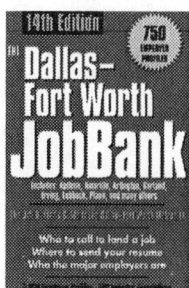 
  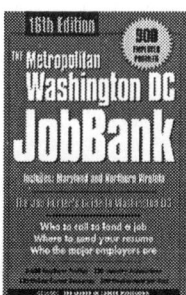

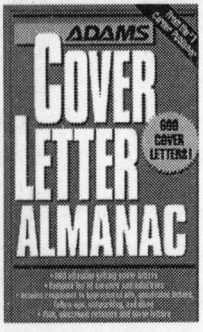
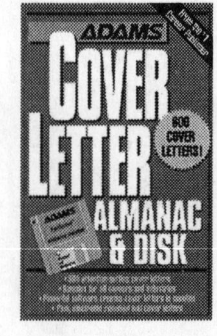

Adams Job Interview Almanac

The *Adams Job Interview Almanac* includes answers and discussions for over 1,800 interview questions. There are 100 complete job interviews for all fields, industries, and career levels. Also included is valuable information on handling stressful interviews, strategies for second and third interviews, and negotiating job offers to get what you want. 5½" x 8½", 840 pages, paperback, $12.95. ISBN: 1-55850-612-8.

Adams Job Interview Almanac & CD-ROM

Beat the competition with the *Adams Job Interview Almanac and CD-ROM*! The CD-ROM features more than 300 video and 200 audio clips to guide you through an interview. Decide how many questions you want to answer and go one-on-one with one of the world's top experts on job interviewing. Stuck for an answer? Expert advice is just a click away. 5½" x 8½", 840 pages, Adams Job Interview Pro software included (one CD-ROM), trade paperback, $19.95. ISBN: 1-55850-709-4.

Adams Jobs Almanac, 8th Edition

Updated annually, the *Adams Jobs Almanac* includes names and addresses of over 7,000 U.S. employers; information on which positions each company commonly fills; industry forecasts; geographical cross-references; employment prospects in all 50 states; and advice on preparing resumes and cover letters and standing out at interviews. Trade paperback, $16.95, 5½" x 8½", 952 pages. ISBN: 1-58062-443-X.

Available wherever books are sold.

For more information, or to order, call 1-800-872-5627
or visit *www.adamsmedia.com*
Adams Media
57 Littlefield Street
Avon, MA 02322. U.S.A.

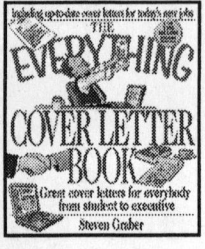